THE JEFFREY EPSTEIN CASE
TRAFFICKING

CONCHITA SARNOFF

Post Hill
PRESS

A POST HILL PRESS BOOK
ISBN: 978-1-64293-531-8
ISBN (eBook): 978-1-64293-532-5

TrafficKing:
The Jeffrey Epstein Case
© 2020 by Conchita Sarnoff
All Rights Reserved

Cover photo by Gregory P. Mango/Polaris

Post Hill Press
New York • Nashville
posthillpress.com

Published in the United States of America

"Rape Trees" or "Rape Bushes" mark the spot where sexual assaults and gang rapes occur along the United States and Mexico border. The child's undergarments are thrown on the branches as markers to intimidate the victims and convey to Border Patrol and Immigration and Customs Enforcement (ICE) officials that traffickers have successfully committed a sexual crime within the U.S. border. Rape Trees instill fear in the victims and deter potential witnesses from coming forward to the police.

Table of Contents

Acknowledgments

Many people made this book possible. This book is dedicated to each and every one of you. Thank you. If your name is not mentioned, you know why.

To my publisher, Victor Ostrovsky, the only man who had the courage to publish this manuscript. Thank you for your encouragement, guidance, patience and generosity of spirit. To my wonderful editors who shall remain nameless, thank you for the many hours you invested in this project. Your remarkable patience and encouragement allowed me to move forward in the darkness. To my friends who read the manuscript in its various incarnations, thank you for your time and guidance.

I wish to express my deepest gratitude to the many lawyers, law enforcement officials, journalists, friends and colleagues who in the course of six years stood by me every step of the way. Three insightful and extraordinary agents worked diligently to see this project to fruition although they were held back. Andrew Stuart, principal at the Andrew Stuart agency in NY who represented me in 2010 and 2011. Four years later, Alex Hoyt and Alfred Regnery represented me in 2015 and January 2016. Thank you for your time, guidance, trust, and the many generous hours invested in this project.

To Renee and Carlos Morrison their friendship, grace, and generosity will be forever in my heart. Sally Fitz Morrison, thank you for believing in me, this story and providing shelter during the cold days. I cherish your friendship. To Lisa and Rick Moreno, true friends are hard to find and impossible to forget. Fausto Sanchez, my earth Angel. Thank you for your loving kindness. Jorge Castaneda, Mexico's former Foreign Minister, thank you for your friendship and taking care of me in Mexico during the investigation. Larry Leibowitz, an extraordinary friend and man. I am blessed to have you as my friend. Thank you for your support and guidance. Three extraordinary and steadfast friends guided me to the finish line: Sergio Balsinde, Richard Kramer, and William von Raab, thank you for your faith and nuggets of wisdom and guidance. Vivien Weisman, thank you for friendship when it was most needed. William Stadiem, an extraordinary author, loving friend and dedicated son, thank you for your many pearls of wisdom. Two extraordinary men taught me the reality of modern day politics: my late father, Pedro Suarez, former Minister of Public Works, Havana, Cuba (1948) and Jose Maria Aznar, former Prime Minister of Spain (1996-2004). Thank you Jose Maria for taking me on an exhilarating journey into your world and showing me what political power can achieve when the goal is to improve the human condition.

My everlasting gratitude and respect goes to the survivors and thousands of unsung heroes, abolitionists, police officers, district attorneys, law enforcement agents, NGO leaders and opinion leaders fighting at the frontlines. Your courage, faith, tenacity, hard work and generosity have laid the groundwork for my book, the foundation and provided the strength to carry on. To the countless others who shall remain nameless, thank you for your incredible behind the scenes work, tenacity and faith. The time will come when the truth shall be revealed.

Disclaimer

This book reflects my opinion about the challenges facing the U.S. government and the Department of Justice while prosecuting high profile human trafficking cases. In 2006, when I began investigating the issue of modern day slavery, specifically child sex trafficking, the business was fast becoming a global industry. In 2014, Time magazine reported, "Inside the Scarily Lucrative Business Model of Human Trafficking," and assessed the business of human trafficking at over $100 million dollars.

Several reasons might help explain the increasing figures and unending surge: greater demand; greater accessibility to child pornography online; increased distribution routes; the risk/reward ratio of child prostitution; and the limited enforcement of Trafficking Victims Protection Act (TVPA) in some states.

The Trafficking Victims Protection Act (TVPA) is a federal law that helps to protect victims and prosecute human traffickers. TVPA was passed, in 2000, under President Bill Clinton, reauthorized under President George W. Bush, and reauthorized once again under President Obama.

Anti-child pornography laws and the challenges facing law enforcement while prosecuting pedophiles remain in the early stages of enforcement. In 2009, as a result of my extensive fieldwork and research, I began to write this book. Most of the information included in this book was discovered between 2008 and 2016. After my first Epstein report was published in The Daily Beast in 2010, the story went viral.

Given the recent figures, 20.9 million, reported by the International Labour Organization (ILO), representing the number of trafficked victims worldwide, this book aims to help support The Abolitionist Movement and promote the universal message that human trafficking must stop now. Federal laws that prosecute traffickers must be enforced in every state. The Trafficking Victims Protection Act is an important federal law that needs enforcement in every state.

When I started this journey the most effective way to help rescue survivors was to provide long term "safe houses" for victims. That fact remains true today. With this goal in mind, I established a foundation with a group of talented and like-minded community leaders. It took approximately two years to identify the board members. By mid October 2013 we joined forces and created the Alliance to Rescue Victims of Trafficking (www.atrvt.org), a bipartisan organization in Washington D.C. Our mission is to help stop child sex trafficking and our dream is for ATRVT to live on long after we are gone so that we may continue to help survivors.

The information contained in this book was partly derived from my own observations and conversations taken from official records, court documents, testimonies, written communication, interviews, e-mails, and media reports. The facts and certain anecdotes were taken directly from court files, depositions, police records and hundreds of hours of interviews and conversations conducted over a considerable period of time with countless collaborators, Wall Street insiders, government officials, law enforcement agents, prosecutors, private investigators, lawyers, numerous victims, a victim's mother, accountants, journalists, banking officials, NGOs, Jeffrey Epstein, Ghislaine Maxwell, Alan Dershowitz, a number of their attorneys, and hundreds of media reports.

TrafficKing describes my experience while investigating modern day slavery between 2006-2016. The views and opinions reflect my attitudes relating to those incidents. Some names, identifying details, and events have been changed to protect survivors and the innocent. For fear of retribution, including death, most underage survivors prefer to remain anonymous. Victims also fear going to the police and other law enforcement officials because they fear they will become homeless and possibly violently abused once their case is tried in Court, if it ever reaches Court. This is particularly true in cases involving foreign-born underage victims forced into prostitution and trafficked across borders. Many cases in the U.S. and abroad involve children forced to have sex with men in positions of power and influence. If and when the survivors manage to escape and tell their story, their primary concern is always homelessness and retribution.

Jeffrey E. Epstein, a Wall Street hedge fund manager is a convicted pedophile and level-3 registered sex offender. He served 13 months out of an 18 months sentence in a Palm Beach county jail. As part of the sentence he served an additional 18 months under community control or 'house arrest' in his Palm Beach estate. As of 2016, there are three related civil cases pending, two in Florida and one in New York.

Since the first police report was filed, in 2005, fragments of the Epstein case have been widely publicized in a variety of media outlets in the United States: Financial Times, Wall Street Journal, New York Times, Washington Post, Washington Times, Boston Globe, Chicago Tribune, Palm Beach Daily News, Palm Beach Post, Reuters, Associated Press, The Miami Herald, Newsweek, Reuters, AP, The Daily Beast, Politico.com, Drudge Report, The Daily Caller, Mail on Sunday, Mother Jones, Huffington Post, New York Magazine, and others.

Almost every national television network, a slew of online news services and many radio stations have reported snippets of the Epstein case including: ABC, CBS, FOX and NBC, Telemundo and Univision. Cable networks, CNN and MSNBC also aired the bits of the story.

Since 2010, when my story was fist published in The Daily Beast, the foreign press began to follow it attentively. Some of the most widely read and largest circulating journals and magazines in Europe included: *ABC España (Spain)*, *El Pais (Spain)*, *Corriere della Serra (Italy)*, la Repubblica (Italy), Paris Match (France), *Le Figaro (France)*, *Tribune de Geneve (Switzerland)*, *Suddeutsche Zeitung Germany)*, *Die Welt* (Germany), *Bild* (Germany), The Guardian (England), The Telegraph (England), The Observer (England), The London Times, Tatler (England), and others. The Epstein case traveled several continents and reached audiences as far as: Asia, Australia, Canada, India and Russia.

Then between July 20, 2010 and March 25, 2011, my agent, Andrew Stuart, approached a handful approximately fifteen publishers who rejected the English language manuscript for fear of libel. In England, the book was probably rejected because of the obvious relationship between HRH Prince Andrew, Duke of York Fifth in Line to the Throne and the level-3 sex offender, Jeffrey Epstein.

It is no secret that publishing houses with interests in businesses regulated by the Federal government tend to be gun shy. Some of the responses conveyed to my agents including, Andrew Stuart, principal at the Stuart Agency in New York and years later, Alex Hoyt and Alfred Regnery, a former Justice Department official and head of the Office of Juvenile Justice and Delinquency Prevention, who together represented me in 2015 and 2016, revealed that publishers were afraid to print my book for fear of:

1. Libel

2. Legal action by Jeffrey Epstein

3. Legal action by Alan Dershowitz

4. Legal action by Epstein's lawyers
5. Legal action by Epstein's associates implicated in the case
6. Legal action by the investors funding the publishing house

In January 2014, after five years "editing" my original manuscript, Random House Mexico killed the book deal that was signed in 2009. I was not surprised. In fact a former CEO of Random House U.S. and former in-law mentioned that might happen. On November 5, 2014, Richard Johnson published a story about my book deal on page six of The New York Post: "Author Faces Off Clinton." His story revealed how Random House Mexico killed the book deal, in 2014, because of the alleged inference to former President Clinton and his association with Jeffrey Epstein.

Ironically, on December 1, 2015, Johnson published a follow up story in The New York Post printed on page twenty-five. This time, "Epstein (sex scandal) Book Clears Clinton," implied something quite different than the previous article. The New York Post story revealed that a former U.S. president apparently "cleared" a book deal negotiated between renowned author James Patterson and former NYPD officer, John Connelly, detailing the same criminal case I reported in The Daily Beast, in 2010.

The implication seemed extraordinary. Johnson's story apparently suggested that someone, in this case America's number one author, James Patterson and his co-author, John Connelly, had perhaps approached former president Clinton concerning the Epstein criminal case and received the former president's blessings to publish a book about the Epstein case. Why?

Three questions popped out. Why did America's number one fiction author appeal to former President Clinton to write a book about the Epstein criminal case? Why did the author feel the need to clear the former president? What happened to the First Amendment and freedom of expression?

Johnson's article also revealed that former NYPD police officer, John Connelly, who approached me several times while I was writing The Daily Beast report, would co-author the book with James Patterson, Mr. Epstein's neighbor in Palm Beach. Little Brown & Co. will publish their book in the fall of 2016, right before the November presidential elections. Perhaps, given the timing of the book's publication the story will focus on exonerating the former president of any wrongdoing?

For readers wondering why I'm promoting Connelly and Patterson's upcoming book, there are two reasons. First, I believe the more authors expose the alleged sexual abuse crimes perpetrated against the victims, the better; Secondly, Tina Brown's Tweet deserves a mention:

> *"Conchita Sarnoff broke and owned the Epstein story on the Beast in 2010. No one knows more on this story."*

Unexpectedly, in December 2015, two months after Dershowitz was deposed, my former agents, Alex Hoyt and Al Regnery returned with a proposition. The pitch process in New York began for a third and final time. Six publishers expressed an interest in my book. This time their focus was different. Most publishers wanted a manuscript about the Epstein-Clinton relationship. Given the political climate and the upcoming presidential elections their request should not have surprised me. After several conversations my story was rejected a third time.

To be clear, my interest in pursuing this story has never been to write a political book about anyone much less the Clinton's. There are plenty of books written about the political couple both pro and con. Most importantly, the reason for investigating this case was never to discredit former President Clinton, his wife, Secretary of

State Hillary Clinton or the Clinton administration. In fact, it was under President Clinton's administration The Trafficking Victims Protection Act was passed as legislation in 2000.

The investigation and consequently this book, was based on the need to expose the truth, the whole truth and nothing but the truth about what is happening in the United States in the field of human trafficking. It was also important to uncover the reasons why the Epstein case remains noteworthy eleven years after his Non Prosecution Agreement. Unlike many other predators who committed similar sex crimes against minors, Mr. Epstein was not charged under the federal Trafficking Victims Protection Act (TVPA).

In the fight to stop human trafficking it remains relevant and of primary importance to reveal the egregious sex crimes committed, by a handful of alleged procurers never charged with any crimes. Why was a very rich predator, with a high level of political influence, who implicated a number of politicians, British Royalty, opinion leaders, victims and possible procurers allowed to get off easy? Was his "sweetheart deal" a factor of his wealth and generous donations to his political party? Why did all the alleged procurers get off without being charged? How did that negotiation take place and why? Why did the opposing political party apparently agree to go along with the predator's attorneys' final request for a Non Prosecution Agreement? Why did Mr. Epstein not serve the minimum mandatory sentence demanded of most convicted level-3 registered sex offenders given the number of crimes he allegedly committed and the number of victims who testified?

These and other reasons are the basis for this book. The facts exposed focus on the alleged predator and his alleged procurers. What follows might seem like a fictional account of a man and "his team of alleged predators," who had the resources to hire the most talented lawyers to influence the system. Perhaps because of his political relationships the case became a globally recognized story about the power of money and the power of persuasion and how both can undermine justice? It is a story about a billionaire sex offender who knows how to leverage his assets in order to corrupt a system that should be incorruptible.

In the Epstein case, perhaps party politics and campaign donations played a role in the non-prosecution agreement? Perhaps his generosity was targeted at this---protecting the man who allegedly molested dozens if not hundreds of underage girls over a period of several years. The mere association of a powerful leader entangled in such a sordid story, should have caused the media to demand an investigation, much like the investigation during the Watergate and Lewinsky scandals. Perhaps, it should have propelled the former leader to come forward and communicate his version?

Political leaders are symbols of authority and leadership. Citizens and voters expect their leaders to be trustworthy, respected and above reproach. In the United States, political leaders are handed their power by citizen voters thereby assuming great and noble obligations and duties. The primary obligation of any political leader is to their constituents and those they lead. The second obligation is to defend their country.

The former president Clinton is tangential to this case as one publisher pointed out, however, records demonstrate there was undoubtedly a relationship between the two men for a couple of years while Mr. Epstein was allegedly trafficking underage girls for sex and the former president was jetting about on his friend's plane. The degree of friendship between the two will remain a mystery until one or both men decide to address the issue.

Despite their friendship, my goal was never to prevent the Clinton's from reaching The White House; stir up sex scandals for political purposes; or focus on the Clinton-Epstein-Dershowitz relationship.

On the contrary, the motivation behind this story was to understand the reasons why the system failed the victims; why the Department of Justice, given the evidence, chose not to prosecute Epstein under the federal law Trafficking Victims Protection Act (TVPA), enacted in Florida, in 2000; And why the Department of Justice chose to identify the underage victims as "prostitutes" in the Non Prosecution Agreement rather than what they really were: child victims of sex trafficking.

The inspiration for this book came from elsewhere: the need to shed light on a dark issue and steps needed to stop child sex trafficking in the United States. Human trafficking destroys millions of young lives every day the world over. No one in the United States or abroad should ignore this issue.

Unlike some predators, the global networks that traffick children for sex are unbiased. In the United States alone, according to a 2012 Congressional Report, there were more than 300,000 children trafficked that year. These children represent every creed and ethnicity although most are born into lower socio economic families.

In addition to a lack of housing, short and long term, one of the greatest problems confronting survivors is the limited and outdated data available. Without the ability to measure the problem, the government cannot begin to make changes to stop human trafficking. In many states, local law enforcement officials are not educated about the issue or even made aware about how human traffickers recruit their victims. In 2016, only a handful of law enforcement officials at the Department of Justice are aware of the urgency to enforce the Trafficking Victims Protection Act (TVPA) in all human trafficking cases of this magnitude.

Proceeds

Five percent of the proceeds from the sale of this book will go to Alliance To Rescue Victims of Trafficking, a Washington D.C. foundation that raises awareness of human trafficking and expects to open a safe house to rescue and rehabilitate trafficked survivors.
http://www.atrvt.org

Dedication

I dedicate this book to the countless children who died as victims of sex trafficking and to the million more that survived but remain silent and in darkness.

To the memory of my father whose love and generosity inspire me still and to my inimitable mother who teaches me everyday how to persevere and find strength in pain.

To Deborah Sigmund who changed the direction of my life and became a good friend in this journey; and to my esteemed colleague and friend, Andres Oppenheimer, for generously paving the way forward so that I could write this book. Thank you.

To Cristina and Nicholas. Thank you for your love and unyielding loyalty.

Facts

- 2.2 million children (a person under the age of 18) are sold into the sex trade every year. That means over 4 children per minute.

- Average age of entry into the sex trade in America is 12–14 years old according to Shared Hope International, reported in, May 2009.

- 63% of survivors included in the 2013 report, wearethorn.org, revealed they were sold via the Internet at some point during their trafficking situation.

- The United States has a federal law that can be enforced in every state: Trafficking Victims Protection Reauthorization Act (TVPA).

- There are almost 21 million victims of human trafficking worldwide.

- 75% of underage sex trafficking victims said they had been advertised or sold online according to the Report on the Use of Technology to Recruit, Groom and Sell Domestic Minor Sex Trafficking Victims published, in 2015.

More Facts

- I am a mother, first and foremost. I am also a victim's advocate. This story is about survivors and the need to enforce the Trafficking Victims Protection Act (TVPA) in every state.

- Like the survivors portrayed in this story, I too feel victimized by a system that filters the truth when it deems expedient.

- Living this experience has been gut wrenching and at times agonizing.

Cast of Characters

Attorneys

R. Alex Acosta, former U.S. Attorney for the Southern District of Florida, Department of Justice and prosecutor in the Epstein case. Currently Dean of Florida international University School of Law since 2009.

Roy Black, civil and criminal trial attorney known for high profile civil litigation and criminal defense cases. Represented Jeffrey Epstein during criminal investigation. Partner, Black, Srebnick, Kornspan & Stumpf, Miami, Florida.

David Boies, litigator N.Y. firm Boies, Schiller & Flexner. Represents Virginia Louise Roberts Giuffre in defamation case against Ghislaine Maxwell. Represented Vice President Al Gore in *Gore vs. Bush* case, 2000.

Paul Cassell, former Federal District Judge from 2002-2007. Appointed by president George W. Bush now Special Council with Hatch James & Dodge in Salt Lake City. Also a Professor of Law at University of Utah Law School and proponent of Victims Rights. Represents several victims in Jeffrey Epstein-related cases.

Robert (Bob) Critton, Personal Injury Lawyer, West Palm Beach, Florida and Partner at Critton, Lutier, & Coleman and Epstein's attorney during criminal investigation.

Alan Dershowitz, former Harvard University law professor Emeritus, jurist, author, political commentator and scholar on U.S. constitutional law. Friend of Jeffrey Epstein's and implicated in Epstein case. Involved in civil litigation, defamation case against attorneys Brad Edwards and former federal Judge Paul Cassell. Retired, Miami Beach, Florida.

Brad Edwards, former Trial Attorney at Broward County State Attorneys Office. Senior partner: Farmer, Jaffe, Weissing, and Edwards, Ft. Lauderdale, Florida. Represented and continues to represent several victims in Epstein related cases.

Alice S. Fisher, Assistant Attorney General for Criminal Division in 2007, during Epstein's Non-Prosecution Agreement (NPA). Partner: Latham & Watkins LLP, Washington D.C.

Jack Goldberg, Criminal Defense Lawyer. Represented several victims. Senior Partner: Atterbury, Goldberger & Weiss, Palm Beach, Florida.

Alberto Gonzalez, Attorney General of the United States February 3, 2005- September 17, 2007.

Robert Josefsberg, Partner Podhurst Orseck PA, Miami, Florida, white collar, criminal defense and commercial litigation attorney. Represented a number of victims in civil cases during Epstein criminal case including Virginia Louise Roberts.

Peter D. Keisler, Partner Sidley Austin, in Washington D.C. Former Acting Attorney General September 18, 2007- November 9, 2007.

Spencer Kuvin, Partner Craig Goldenfarb, West Palm Beach, Florida. Trial attorney. Represented several victims during civil litigation in Epstein case.

Gerald Lefcourt, Partner: Gerald B. Lefcourt Firm, New York. Leading trial attorney. Represented Jeffrey Epstein during criminal investigation and negotiated non-prosecution agreement (NPA).

Jay Lefkowitz, Senior Partner Kirkland Ellis, New York. Former General Counsel at Office Of Management and Budget (OMB) during President George W. Bush administration. Represented Epstein during NPA negotiations, in 2007. Together with Kenneth Starr negotiated Non-Prosecution Agreement.

Kenneth A. Marra, Federal Judge. Nominated by President George W. Bush to U.S. District Court for Southern District of

Florida January 23, 2002. Presided over Epstein criminal case and continues to oversee several related cases.

Sigrid McCawley, Complex Litigation Attorney at Boies Schiller & Flexner, Fort Lauderdale, Florida. Represents Virginia Louise Roberts in New York defamation case. *Virginia L Robert Giuffre vs. Ghislaine Maxwell.*

Laura Menninger, Criminal Defense Attorney and Litigator, Haddon Morgan Foreman, Denver, Colorado. Represents Ghislaine Maxwell in defamation case in New York, *Virginia L. Roberts Giuffre vs. Ghislaine Maxwell.*

Jeffrey Pagliuca, Haddon Morgan Foreman, Denver, Colorado. Criminal Defense Attorney represents Ghislaine Maxwell in defamation case in New York: *Virginia Louise Roberts Giuffre vs. Ghislaine Maxwell.*

Bruce Reinhart, former Assistant U.S. Attorney. Represented Government at commencement of Epstein criminal case. Left the Government then represented Epstein. In private practice: Bruce E. Reinhart attorney at law. West Palm Beach, Florida.

Jack Scarola, Partner, Searcy Denney Scarola, Barnhart & Shipley PA. Represented Brad Edwards in case against Jeffrey Epstein and represented Edwards and former Federal Judge Paul Cassell in defamation case against Alan Dershowitz.

Ken W. Starr, former Federal Court of Appeals Judge, 39th Solicitor General under George H. Bush. Independent Counsel during President Bill Clinton's Impeachment Proceedings. Former President Pepperdine University Law School, Malibu, California. Currently the President and Chancellor Baylor University. Negotiated Non Prosecution Agreement together with Jay Lefkowitz and represented Jeffrey Epstein.

Thomas Scott, Partner Cole Scott Kissane, PA. Miami, Florida. Former US Attorney for Southern District of Florida, former Circuit Judge for Eleventh Judicial Circuit for Dade County.

Represented Alan Dershowitz in defamation lawsuit filed by attorneys Edwards and Cassell.

Ann Marie Villafaña, Prosecutor. Assistant U.S. Attorney Department of Justice, United States Attorneys Office, Southern District of Florida. Worked with R. Alex Acosta's prosecution team on Epstein's criminal case.

FBI Agents

FBI Special Agent Nesbitt Kuyrkendall
FBI Special Agent Jason Richards
FBI Special Agent Jonathan I. Solomon. Retired. Special Agent in Charge (SAC) 2006-2009 Miami, Florida. Headed Epstein's federal investigation.

Alleged principal procurers paid by Jeffrey Epstein. Never arrested, never charged.

Jean Luc Brunel
Lesley Groff
Sarah Kellen
Nadia Marcinkova
Ghislaine Maxwell
Adriana Ross Muscinska
Haley Robson

Predator and Registered Sex Offender Level-3

Jeffrey E. Epstein

Principal victims

Virginia Louise Roberts Giuffre identified as Jane Doe #102 in the criminal case and Jane Doe #3 in the civil case.
Jane Doe #1 a.k.a. Rosemary

Jane Doe #1 & Jane Doe #2, plaintiffs in CVRA case filed against the United States Government, in 2008.

Johanna Sjoberg

Jane Doe's: Names given to all the female victims, identified in the criminal investigation, that later sued Epstein in civil court. Their identities were undisclosed to protect their privacy and for security reasons.

Friends of Epstein Mentioned and Implicated in Epstein Case

HRH Prince Andrew Fifth in Line to The British Throne, third son of HRH Queen Elizabeth II and Prince Philip.

Allegedly had sexual relations with underage victim, Virginia Louise Roberts, a.k.a. Jane Doe #102.

Bill Clinton: former President of the United States (1992-2000). Impeached by the House of Representatives on two charges, one of perjury and one of Obstruction of Justice on December 19, 1998.

In a landmark U.S. Supreme Court case the judges ordered that a sitting president of the United States had no immunity from civil law litigation against him or her, for acts done before taking office and unrelated to the office. In 1997, President Clinton was issued a 5-year suspension of his law license in the State of Arkansas, *Clinton v. Jones 520, and U.S. 681.*

A close friend of Ghislaine Maxwell and via the Clinton Global Initiative a recipient of Maxwell's Terra Mar Project donation.

Recipient of Epstein's many generous donations.

David Copperfield, magician, entertainer, friend and Epstein houseguest.

Alan Dershowitz, former Harvard Law School professor, friend of Epstein's and his attorney during the criminal investigation also implicated in Epstein case.

Governor Bill Richardson, 30th Governor of New Mexico (2003-2011). U.S. Secretary of Energy during Clinton Administration (August 1998-January 2001) and friend of Epstein's and recipient of his donations.

Leslie Wexner, CEO and founder L brands formerly The Limited Brands Corporation. Original owner of several assets and properties later gifted or sold to Epstein. Close friend, former business associate and client of Jeffrey Epstein. Wexner foundation. Personal estimated net worth: six billion dollars.

Chronology

1976

Jeffrey E. Epstein becomes an Options Trader at Bear Stearns. Ace Greenberg and Jimmy Cayne hired Epstein after resigning from the elite Upper East Side Manhattan Dalton School where he taught mathematics and piano.

1981

Approximately two months after he is made partner, Epstein is fired from Bear Stearns for securities law violations in other words, insider trading.

1982

Epstein opens for business as J. Epstein Trust Co. New York. His clients and sources of funding remain unknown. Epstein allegedly worked for Steven Hoffenberg founder of Towers Financial Corporation.

1984

Wexner establishes The Wexner Foundation to strengthen the field of Jewish leadership.

1986

Leslie Wexner, CEO and founder of The Limited (L Brands) invests $1 billion with Epstein's new Manhattan-based investment company.

J. Epstein Trust Co. According to insiders Wexner develops a close relationship with Epstein.

1989-1993

Kenneth Starr is named Solicitor General under George H.W. Bush.

1989

Leslie Wexner purchases the Birch Wathen School, a 21,000 sq. feet property built for Herbert N. Strauss, an heir to Macy's fortune. Located at 9 East 71 Street New York the house boasts a heated sidewalk. Wexner paid $13.2 million for the property and invests millions of dollars in renovation according to the New York Times. Epstein reveals to the New York Times, "Les never spent more than two months there." In 1996, Epstein became its new owner.

1990

Forbes magazine estimates Epstein net worth is unknown, in part because his wealth is concealed in a financial entity in the United States Virgin Islands (USVI), a tax shelter where he owns a private island and his primary residence. The only public source of income is derived from his association with his friend, Leslie Wexner. According to Epstein, he receives management fees for advising and investing Mr. Wexner's capital. He receives a commission as most financial advisors on Wall Street.

1990s

Epstein creates two foundations both domiciled in the U.S. Virgin Islands. Since he began his business in the early eighties and throughout the nineties, Epstein acquired properties around the world. Some of his properties originally belonged to the estate of Leslie Wexner. Those properties include: the Manhattan triplex on East 71, the Zorro Ranch in Stanley, New Mexico, a USVI island, the Avenue Foch Paris apartment, the London flat, Palm Beach estate, 727 private jet, helicopter, yacht, etc.

1991

July, publishing magnate and former member of Britain's parliament, Robert Maxwell dies leaving scandal in his wake. The Maxwell family is now bankrupt. Two sons, Ian and Brian Maxwell are charged with malfeasance.

1992

Maxwell's youngest daughter, Ghislaine Maxwell, moves to New York City where she meets Jeffrey Epstein. Epstein and Maxwell begin a relationship. He purchases a townhouse for her on 65th Street off Park Avenue.

1992

Arkansas Governor, William J. Clinton is elected 42nd President of the United States. He is in Office for two terms.

1993

January 23, Leslie Wexner (56) marries Abigail S. Koppel (31), Barnard graduate magna cum laude, associate at Davis Polk & Wardell and friends with Epstein.

1994

Starr joins Kirkland Ellis law firm. Kirkland Ellis is largest private law firm in the U.S. Starr is criticized for conflicts of interest stemming from his position as independent counsel and ongoing association with Kirkland Ellis since firm was representing clients in litigation with the government. On one occasion, Starr spoke with lawyers for Paula Jones, who was at the time was suing

President Clinton over an alleged sexual assault charge. Starr maintained that a sitting U.S. president was not immune to a civil suit.

1994-1995

R. Alex Acosta, federal prosecutor during the Jeffrey Epstein criminal case, a Harvard University Law graduate, serves as a law clerk to Judge Samuel Alito for the US Court of Appeals for the Third Circuit.

1995

R. Alex Acosta hired by Kirkland Ellis befriends Kenneth Starr. Acosta specializes in employment and labor issues and teaches at George Mason University Law School.

2000

Jeffrey Epstein opens a U.S. Virgin Island office and creates a third foundation, Jeffrey Epstein VI Foundation.

2000

Famed lawyer and Clinton supporter, David Boies, represents former Vice President Al Gore in the legal fight over the *Bush versus Gore* 2000 election.

2001

January 20, President Clinton's second term expires. He leaves The Oval Office for the last time.

2001-2003

Clinton takes 17 trips on board Epstein's private jet. Clinton is accompanied on Epstein's jet with his secret service details, friends, at times Doug Band, plus unidentified females. The pilot manifesto and pilot logs are incomplete and redacted.

Other passengers identified on the jet include Alan Dershowitz, Larry Summers, Vernon Jordan, Jean Luc Brunel, Kevin Spacy, Ghislaine Maxwell, Virginia Louise Roberts, several unnamed females, unidentified males and others.

2002

Newly licensed pilot Ghislaine Maxwell pilots Epstein's black hawk helicopter and flies Clinton out of the U.S. Virgin Islands during his visit. According to Virginia Louis Roberts, an underage victim, two underage girls are reported to be visiting Epstein's island while Clinton is a guest. Maxwell, Roberts and Epstein are in residence during same visit.

2002-2003

Jeffrey Epstein donates $4 million to start the Clinton Global Initiative, according to a source.

2003

Jay Lefkowitz leaves the Bush White House to join Kirkland Ellis. Lefkowitz is made senior partner.

2005

The Clinton Foundation opens as public charity. By 2013, contributions have grown to $144 million.

2005

March 14, Palm Beach Police begin investigation into sex crimes allegedly carried out by Epstein. Dozens of underage girls come forward individually.

2005

Epstein is charged with sex abuse of minors. Over 100 underage girls testify against him.

2005

Virginia Louise Roberts identified on court documents as Jane Doe #102, identifies Bill Clinton, Prince Andrew, Alan Dershowitz and others amongst Epstein's close friends. Roberts' implicates them as material witnesses. Roberts' accuses Maxwell and Epstein of sexual abuse.

2005-2007

Law enforcement investigates Epstein's human trafficking case. The Palm Beach Police investigation led to a Grand Jury and a two-year federal investigation.

2007

Between September and October a Non-Prosecution Agreement is negotiated. The original federal indictment included potential money laundering charges.

2007

October 25-27, Prosecutor's federal order charging Epstein is dismissed. Former Bush Administration Mid East Envoy Jay Lefkowitz and former Solicitor General Kenneth Starr renegotiate the Order and a new deal with the Department of Justice in Washington D.C. is struck effectively side stepping federal prosecutor's R. Alex Acosta's order.

Hillary Clinton receives a $25,000 donation from Epstein after his indictment. She does not return donation.

2008

Jeffrey Epstein begins his 18-month prison sentence.

2008-2009

Underage victims begin to file dozens of civil suits against Epstein.

2009

July, R. Alex Acosta becomes the second Dean at Florida International Law School.

2010

September, Ghislaine Maxwell is subpoenaed at Clinton Global Initiative in reference to Epstein case and her relationship with several public figures including former President Clinton. She leaves country and escapes to London.

2010

July, Alan Dershowitz speaks to Sarnoff on the record for the first and last time. Bill Clinton does not return call.

2010

New York: Epstein registered as a Level-3 sex offender.

2010

Chelsea Clinton marries hedge fund investor, Mark Mezvinsky at fabled Vincent and Brooke Astor estate in Rhinebeck, New York. Ghislaine Maxwell is photographed in the U.S. attending Clinton wedding.

2010

December, HRH Prince Andrew's former wife, the Duchess of York, Sarah Ferguson receives 15,000 pounds sterling ($24,000) from Jeffrey E. Epstein, following his arrest to pay off her debts. Sarah Ferguson admits details of loan to news media.

2012

One of three of Epstein's foundations, allegedly the foundation employed to transfer money to Clinton, becomes inactive.

2014

December 31, New Year's Eve, Josh Gerstein reporter at politico.com, exposes victim's sexual abuse claim against Professor Alan Dershowitz.

2015

January, The Duchess of York, admits she had not repaid Epstein's loan when asked about the status of the loan by the Daily Mail.

2015

January, Brad Edwards and former Federal Judge Paul Cassell file a complaint against Alan Dershowitz for defamation.

2015

January, Alan Dershowitz countersues lawyers Edwards & Cassell.

2015

The FBI investigation into Hillary Clinton's use of private email as Secretary of State has expanded to look at whether the possible "intersection" of Clinton Foundation work and State Department business may have violated public corruption laws, according to three unnamed intelligence cited by Fox News.

2015

FBI agents investigate the possible intersection of Clinton Foundation donations, the dispensation of State Department contracts and whether regular processes were followed," one source said. This new investigative track is in addition to the focus on classified material found on Clinton's personal server.

2015

The federal prosecutor, R. Alex Acosta, and other assistant U.S. Attorney's Office officials, plus FBI agents who worked on Epstein's criminal case, are issued subpoenas. They are to be deposed on matters pertaining to the Epstein case. The case is ongoing.

2015

October 15-16, Epstein lawyer and one-time friend, Alan Dershowitz, takes deposition and identifies Bill Clinton's association with Epstein and his presence on the private Caribbean island.

2015

September 21, David Boies agrees to represent one victim, Virginia Louis Roberts, a.k.a. Jane Doe #102 in a New York State defamation case against Ghislaine Maxwell. The case is pending. Maxwell is alleged to be a principal procurer in the Epstein case and pivotal to the triangular relationship between Clinton and Epstein.

2015

Boies Schiller act as a go between Dershowitz and Edwards and Cassell in defamation case. Boies sought an Emergency Order in December 2015 to seal Dershowitz's affidavit, which the court granted.

2015-2016

It remains unclear which of the two lines of inquiry, (the email server or the public corruption), was opened first by the FBI and whether eventually they will be combined and presented before a special grand jury. One intelligence source said the public corruption angle dates back to at least April 2015. The FBI's official website lists "public corruption as the FBI's top criminal priority."

2015-2016

The development follows press reports over the past year about the potential overlap of State Department and Clinton Foundation work, and questions over whether donors benefited from their contacts inside the Obama administration.

2016

January, Fox News is told that about 100 special agents assigned to the investigations were asked to sign non-disclosure agreements, with as many as 50 additional agents on "temporary duty assignment." The request to sign such agreements could reflect that agents are handling highly classified material in the emails, or serve as a reminder not to leak about the case.

2016

January, inside the FBI pressure is growing to pursue the case.

One intelligence source told Fox News that, "FBI agents would be "screaming" if a prosecution is not pursued because 'many previous public corruption cases have been made and successfully prosecuted with much less evidence than what is emerging in this investigation.'"

2016

January, ongoing Epstein related cases and possible tie in with Clinton scandals. Two open Epstein cases in Florida and one in New York. One case allegedly implicates former President Clinton given his association with Epstein, Maxwell, and Virginia Louise Roberts.

2016

January 13, Sarnoff speaks with New York Supreme Court County Judge, Ruth Pickholz -- the presiding Judge during Epstein's Sex Offender Registration case in New York. Judge reveals she refused to agree with the prosecutor's recommendation and assigned Epstein highest offender status, level 3. Epstein appeals Judge's decision. Pickholz's ruling affirmed.

2016

January, Epstein remains a level-3 sex-offender in New York. Pickholz mentioned how "surprised" she was that Manhattan DA's Office "requested a downward registration to lowest level, level 1," after requesting the highest level of registration for a United States, 24 year old, soldier who was accused of having consensual sex with a 17 year old girl, in a recent case. In the soldier's case, District Attorney's Office requested the highest sexual offender registration permissible, level 3.

2016

April 8, Alan Dershowitz, Brad Edwards, former Federal Judge Paul Cassell settle defamation lawsuit.

2016

April 10, According to The American Lawyer, Edwards and Cassell agree to waive confidentiality. Dershowitz agrees to waive it provided Edwards, Cassell and David Boies agree to unseal Virginia Louise Giuffre's deposition and Boies Schiller agree to release Dershowitz's affidavit relating to David Boies.

2016

April 14, former Epstein victim, Virginia Louise Roberts, continues litigation in New York, *Virginia Roberts Giuffre vs. Ghislaine Maxwell.*

April 14, Jane Doe #1 & Jane Doe #2, former Epstein victims, continue litigation in Florida, *Jane Doe #1 & Jane Doe #2 vs. United States Government.*

April 14, The American Lawyer reported: In January Boies Schiller also sought sanctions against Dershowitz for violating terms of the order. Sanction Hearing is scheduled for May 2016.

2016

May

David Boies claims in Motion that Dershowitz repeatedly tried to expose false information from confidential settlement discussions on the record.

Boies refuses to release the documents that are the condition of Dershowitz's waiver. Both sides seem to be withholding something they don't want revealed.

May 5, Maxwell's townhouse is sold for $15 million dollars to real estate investors Frederick and Kim Rudd.

Links

http://pagesix.com/2014/11/05/
author-faces-off-against-bill-clinton/

http://pagesix.com/2015/12/01/
epstein-sex-scandal-book-clears-bill-clinton/

http://www.thedailybeast.com/articles/2010/07/20/jeffrey-ep-
stein-billionaire-pedophile-goes-free.html

http://www.dailymail.co.uk/news/article-2897086/
Cash-strapped-Fergie-took-15-000-paedophile-billionaire-centre-
claims-Prince-Andrew-slept-age-sex-slave.html

http://www.politico.com/blogs/under-the-radar/2014/12/
woman-who-sued-convicted-billionaire-over-sex-abuse-levels-
claims-at-his-friends-200495

http://www.dailymail.co.uk/news/article-2897086/
Cash-strapped-Fergie-took-15-000-paedophile-billionaire-centre-
claims-Prince-Andrew-slept-age-sex-slave.html

http://www.americanlawyer.com/the-careerist/
id=1202754581393/Dershowitz-Settles-Sex-Case-But-Is-He-Vin-
dicated?mcode=1202616610377&curindex=3

http://www.americanlawyer.com/the-careerist/
id=1202754666961/Did-Dershowitz-Pay-Big-Bucks-to-Settle-
Sex-Case-?mcode=1202616610377&curindex=2

http://time.com/105360/
inside-the-scarily-lucrative-business-model-of-human-trafficking/

http://www.americanlawyer.com/the-careerist/
id=1202755043865/Whats-Everyone-Hiding-in-the-Dershow-
itz-Case?mcode=1202616610377&curindex=1

http://www.americanlawyer.com/id=1202755043865/
Whats-Everyone-Hiding-in-the-Dershowitz-Case#ixzz46JNvBKaI

https://twitter.com/tinabrownlm/status/551577276333428736

http://www.nyu.edu/clubs/act/EventsPage/SCTNow.pdf

http://www.congress.gov/bill/113th-congress/house-bill/898

http://www.weforum.org/agenda/2015/02/
how-data-can-help-fight-human-trafficking

http://therealdeal.com/2016/05/05/
investor-frederick-rudd-buys-ghislaine-maxwellsues-townhouse

CHAPTER ONE

GATHERING OF THE VULTURES

"You cannot change what you do not measure."
New York City, February 2005

Minutes before the slick, 52 year-old Jeffrey E. Epstein, boarded his private plane in Teterboro, New Jersey, he rang Sarah Kellen, an attractive, blond-haired, 27 year-old woman. Kellen, a college graduate and Epstein's personal assistant was born May 25, 1979. She worked at his Palm Beach estate on 358 El Brillo Way.

Her boss, a rich Wall Street hedge-fund manager was twenty-six years her senior. Born in Coney Island, New York, on January 20, 1953, Epstein was raised in Brooklyn in a middle class family. He graduated from Lafayette High School. Early on he learned to play classical piano. Epstein was also gifted at mathematics.

Soon after his high school graduation, Epstein attended Cooper Union from 1969-1971 but did not receive a degree. Later, he enrolled at the Courant Institute at New York University and again the young Epstein left without a degree.

Irrespective of his formal education, Epstein was good with numbers and found work teaching calculus and piano at the Dalton School in Manhattan. Dalton a private, co-educational day school, on the Upper East Side between Park and Madison Avenues at 96th Street, is considered one of the top schools in the City. His tenure there was short lived.

Thanks to the after school tutorial sessions his life took a sharp turn, more about how later. By the mid nineteen eighties and throughout the nineties, in a relatively short period of time, Epstein went from working as a high school teacher and tutor to a jet setting financial advisor to Leslie H. Wexner. Wexner, founder and CEO of The Limited, recently re-named L Brands, became a longtime client and close friend. According to a recently filed complaint in New York on May 27, 2016, Epstein also worked with Towers Financial Corporation prior to his association with Leslie Wexner.

The six-foot tall, salt and pepper-haired Epstein, made so much money, after he left Dalton, although no one is still quite certain how he made his money between the late seventies and nineties, that to this day he continues, 'Living the Life of Riley.'

Splitting his time between several homes while satisfying his predilection for very young girls, he can still be spotted, in 2016, by the *paparazzi* that follow him on the streets of New York, in the company of beautiful young girls of ages unknown. As luck would have it, Epstein who owns homes in New York, Palm Beach, London, Paris, Little St. James, a private island in the U.S. Virgin Islands and a 10,000 acres Zorro Ranch near Stanley, New Mexico, purchased some of the properties from his friend, Leslie Wexner.

Back to that fateful day before Epstein's private jet landed in Palm Beach. Epstein asked Sarah Kellen to have, "Everyone ready and waiting." According to court files, "Everyone," referred to underage girls who provided him with "sexually charged massages, three times a day."[1]

Under Kellen's vigilant supervision, *El Brillo,* Epstein's Palm Beach estate, immediately sprang into action in preparation for his arrival. After they hung up the phone, Kellen rang Haley Robson.

Haley Robson, a 17-year-old girl at the time she met Epstein was his dutiful subordinate. Prior to Robson's "employment" with Epstein, she was presumably a victim who almost instantly according to her police confession became a principal procurer. In 2005, during her interrogation, Robson told the police in The Probable Cause Affidavit that whenever, "Epstein told Sarah he was traveling to Palm Beach, Sarah, would contact Robson to arrange girls for Epstein because... Jeff likes to have his fun with the girls."[2]

Robson was introduced to Epstein at his Palm Beach house. She was there to give him a massage and earn a couple hundred dollars. Robson also told the police that besides giving him the massage, Epstein attempted to molest her. When she rejected his sexual advances, Epstein artfully changed course and convinced the teenager to procure for him "young girls."

Epstein paid Robson two hundred dollars that day and promised to pay her two hundred more for every underage female she recruited to "work" for him. In the affidavit filed by the Palm Beach Police, "work" was a euphemism for "giving Epstein (sexually explicit) massages."[3]

Robson was the daughter of a retired Florida policeman. Born April 9, 1986 in rural Loxahatchee, Florida, the teenager had finished high school and enrolled at the Palm Beach Community College when she first met Epstein, in or around 2004.

Robson and Epstein met through a mutual friend, Molly, a young woman approximately Haley Robson's age. Based on Robson's testimony filed with the Palm Beach Police Department, Molly, family name unknown, might also have been one of Epstein's victim's. By the time Robson was brought in for questioning at the Palm Beach Police Department, she identified Molly as the person who introduced her to Epstein and approached her to work for him. Apparently, they were lounging around at the

Canopy Beach Resort in nearby Riviera Beach, Florida when Molly made the proposition.

The Police files stated that Molly, "Asked Robson if she wanted to make money." When Robson asked her what sort of work was involved, Molly told her friend that she would have to "provide a massage to a man and should make about two hundred dollars." Robson agreed.[4]

That same day, Molly, Robson, and a friend named Tony, family name also unknown, drove to Epstein's house. Molly introduced them in Epstein's kitchen. Robson also met Epstein's assistant, Sarah Kellen. Unbeknownst to Robson at that time, Epstein's kitchen was apparently the usual meeting place for Epstein's first-time victims. There, the girls would meet Kellen, Epstein, some of his staff and at times other procurers.

That day, after Epstein approved, Kellen led Robson upstairs to his master bedroom. She laid out the massage table and organized the massage oils. Before leaving the room, Kellen told Robson, "Jeff will be here in a minute."[5]

Robson and many other victims described their first meeting with Epstein in much the same way and in great detail. A procurer always drove the girls to his house, probably because they were not old enough to drive a car or have a valid driver's license.

Either Kellen or Robson would apparently be in charge of taking the girls to Epstein's bedroom or bathroom suite. The two women would also prepare the massage table. The procurers, or at times his house manager, would then pay the girls in cash after they finished the "massage." Hundreds of pages of testimony illustrated almost identical testimonies.

Almost all the victims identified a grand staircase wall that led to the second floor. In one deposition Robson said the walls "were lined with black and white poster-sized framed photographs of naked young girls and boys." Some photos, according to a victim first identified as Jane Doe #102, later known as Virginia Louise Roberts, were images of girls he had sexually abused.[6]

On the day Robson met him, "Epstein entered the bedroom wearing only a towel," as he apparently always did during the sessions. "He removed the towel and lay nude on the massage table" then he "laid on his stomach and chose a massage-oil for her to rub on him."[7]

During the massage, Robson said, "He tried to touch me and I stopped him." The police asked Robson to describe how he tried to touch her. Robson claimed that Epstein grabbed her buttocks. That made her feel very uncomfortable, so she told Epstein, "I'll massage you but I don't want to be touched." While she performed the massage, she was naked. At the end of the massage, "Epstein paid Robson two hundred dollars."[8]

That was the first and last "massage" Robson gave Epstein according to her police statement. Robson explained this type of arrangement was not good for her. On the "Arrest Report," Robson described her "occupation" as "student." Robson said Epstein tried to make light of the situation and told her he understood that she felt uncomfortable but promised to continue to pay her if she brought him other girls. "The younger the better," he told Robson. On one occasion, Robson revealed she tried to bring a 23-year-old female and Epstein responded, "She was too old."[9]

It seems that Epstein's unexpected financial offer pushed Robson in the opposite direction turning her, perhaps unwittingly, into an accomplice. Over time, she allegedly became a key procurer, who according to court files and police reports, identified, sourced and transported dozens of underage girls to Epstein's house to apparently perform sexual favors for Epstein. Robson made two hundred dollars in cash for every girl she procured. After Robson told her story and admitted to participating in a number of likely crimes, "Sergeant Frick of the Palm Beach Police Department entered the room and explained that based on her own statements, she had implicated herself by bringing underage girls to Epstein's house. Robson then provided the cellular telephone numbers and addresses for the girls she had mentioned previously…"[10]

Robson explained that, "Once her parents discovered she had been visiting Epstein, she stopped." In a 2006 report, Robson said that, "Sara still tried to call the house and leaves messages."[11] During her confession, Robson described how she lured another victim, a.k.a. Rosemary, to Epstein's house. On that fateful day, Robson called several underage girls from a list she had created over time. Epstein had apparently approved the list. None of the girls on her list who were all teenagers seemed to be available that day. All the girls lived on the other side of the bridge, in West Palm Beach, in less privileged neighborhoods.

In order to make money, Robson felt obligated to find girls outside her list. Thanks to her supposed 'boss,' Ghislaine Maxwell, an alleged procurer and Epstein's former girlfriend cum-Girl-Friday, Robson developed a somewhat fail-proof system of identifying the perfect candidates for their boss.

Maxwell, now in her fifties, is the daughter of the late, Elisabeth "Betty" Maxwell (*nee* Meynard) and Robert Maxwell. In 1991, father Maxwell, a former British Member of Parliament (MP) and media tycoon, was either killed or committed suicide. The circumstances of his death remain a mystery. Media reports maintain that he disappeared while sailing in the Canary Islands on his yacht, *The Lady Ghislaine*, christened in honor of his youngest daughter, Ghislaine.

A few media reports attributed the elder Maxwell's death to the Mossad while others maintained he was besieged by debt and consequently ended his life. During my investigation, a former Mossad agent, who wishes to remain anonymous, suggested the Mossad killed Maxwell. Whatever the truth is, Maxwell died a tragic death given the many blessings bestowed upon him throughout his colorful life.

Unlike her father, Ghislaine is known as a "fixer." She has to this day an impressive list of friends from around the globe including presidents, heads of state and a bouquet of British aristocrats. For years she was known as the go-between former President Clinton and Jeffrey Epstein.

On July 31, 2010 Maxwell was among the few guests to attend Chelsea Clinton's wedding at the former Astor estate in Rhinebeck, New York. This auspicious event followed an embarrassing incident for Maxwell.

Only a few months earlier, while attending the Clinton Global Initiative in New York City, at the end of an Indian summer, in September 2009, a process server walked through the packed lobby of the Sheraton Hotel on Eighth Avenue close to the theater district and served Ghislaine Maxwell papers for a deposition.

As the server approached Maxwell, she was huddled in a small group talking to other guests unaware of what was about to take place. The man called out her name and I suppose with so many people surrounding her, Maxwell was unsuspecting. She confirmed her identity and he served her notice. The deposition was in relation to Epstein's sexual abuse case. The server left at once. Maxwell must have been shocked. Ironically, photographs of Maxwell taken by a private investigator who accompanied the process server showed Maxwell receiving notice while standing beneath a human trafficking banner. Human trafficking was the Conference's theme at the 2009 Clinton Global Initiative.

Maxwell never appeared at the deposition claiming, the day prior to her testimony she had to immediately return to England to care for her dying mother. At the time of that trip, some reports revealed the elder Mrs. Maxwell was not gravely ill. Not long after the deposition was scheduled, Maxwell was spotted again in New

York. As a British subject there was nothing the attorneys could do to force her to take the deposition.

It was Maxwell, according to Haley Robson, who apparently instructed her and several victims, including Virginia Louise Roberts (known as Jane Doe #102 in the criminal case), how to procure young girls for Epstein. Court files indicate that Maxwell familiarized most of 'Epstein's girls' with his likes, dislikes, and the type of adolescent victims he desired. Britain's *Daily Mail* published several stories about a number of survivors who came forward and exposed how Maxwell instructed the girls on the ways to best to service Epstein.

Among the many recruits that Maxwell introduced to Epstein to "work" at the Palm Beach house, was a young Johanna Sjoberg. The attorney, Brad Edwards, an arduous former lead trial attorney from Broward County said that unlike most other girls, Sjoberg was twenty and a college student when they met. The "all-American brunette," grew up in "a church going family," according to her story, and entered Epstein's household in 2001 as an occasional 'housekeeper.' Sjoberg candidly described her meeting with Maxwell and the "strange proposition" that followed.[12]

The young woman was studying psychology at Atlantic College in Palm Beach expecting to become a family therapist when Maxwell approached her. Apparently, sometime around midday Maxwell spotted Sjoberg sitting on a campus bench near one of the parking areas. Maxwell walked toward the girl and introduced herself. They began a conversation. Not long into the conversation she offered Sjoberg part-time work, "Twenty an hour to answer the phones and serve occasional drinks at Epstein's Palm Beach home." Sjoberg admitted she, "Thought it was a great opportunity! It seemed pretty easy. I felt as if I had fallen into a pot of gold. All my friends were jealous of me for getting such a great job."[13]

On January 27, 2010 Brad Edwards said that according to Sjoberg's testimony, "Epstein paid for her college and living expenses, etc." Soon after, Maxwell made another type of proposition: "Do you want to make $100 rubbing feet?" Sjoberg replied, "I would love to do that."[14]

It was then Epstein befriended Sjoberg. Within a short period of time, he invited the young woman to his New York triplex to meet HRH Prince Andrew. According to Sjoberg's affidavit, "It was Easter 2001, when I first met Prince Andrew." Maxwell and another victim, Virginia Louise Roberts were there, in addition to a couple of other underage girls unnamed in the deposition."[15]

Sjoberg described how, "Ghislaine came down from the second floor with a present for Prince Andrew—a latex puppet of him from Spitting Image." They all had their picture taken together. Sjoberg said, "Virginia and another girl sat on a chair," and, "Virginia had the puppet on her lap. Andrew sat on another chair, while I sat on his lap…"[16]

"He put his hand on my breast. Ghislaine put the puppet's hand on Virginia's breast, and then, Andrew put his hand on mine… Ghislaine made a lot of sexual jokes…She had a very dirty sense of humor." Eventually, Sjoberg was lured to perform sexual services for Epstein. She claims she refused. Sjoberg also kept quiet for many years.[17]

Unlike Roberts, Sjoberg was an adult. As an adult she could not have accused Epstein of sexual abuse with a minor although she might have been able to bring charges of sexual harassment against him since she claimed, "I felt preyed upon all the same."[18]

According to Sjoberg, the other victim who stayed at his house, Virginia Louise Roberts, was supposedly in New York as part of Epstein's entourage. The girl was fifteen years old at the time. In 2005, Roberts' spoke to the FBI during the investigation. Years later, in 2011, Roberts spoke out once again, only the second time she went public and sold her story to a popular London tabloid, Mail On Sunday. Roberts' alleged that for many years, after she "escaped" from his "clutches" and moved to Australia for fear of Epstein's wrath, more about the young Roberts' later.

One of dozens of depositions taken during the civil investigation stated that Epstein disliked African-American girls, whatever their age and beauty. According to the Statement of Facts, Case # 09-80656, filed May 1, 2009 in the Southern District Court of Florida, the attorney wrote, "To the Plaintiff's knowledge, the only females specifically excluded from Defendant's sexual escapades were African Americans."[19]

Apparently, Epstein wanted 'his girls' to be very young, pretty and fair skinned. I suspect he also preferred underage girls who came from disadvantaged families in case they decided to go public and report him to the police. In one of the depositions, Brad Edwards identified the initials of a number of victims he represented. The girls identified in Edwards' case went by the initials: "S.G.; A.D.; V.A.; N.R.; J.S.; V.Z.; J.A.; F.E.; M.L.; M.D.; D.D., and D.N. All the girls were between the ages of 13 and 17 when Epstein allegedly abused them." Every girl testified independently. So far, Edwards has invested more than eleven years defending several victims possibly sexually abused by Epstein and in the process has argued forcefully on behalf of Crime Victim's Rights Act and children's rights.[20]

CHAPTER TWO

SODOM AND GOMORRAH

Epstein's criminal investigation formally began March 15, 2005. It ended February 2006. During that period, the Palm Beach Police Department conducted a sexual battery investigation of Jeffrey Epstein, Sarah Kellen, Haley Robson and Ghislaine Maxwell.

After a one-year police investigation, the Palm Beach Police Department decided the defendants should be charged with sexual battery felonies. Epstein was charged with "unlawful Sexual Activity with a Minor (4) counts and Lewd and Lascivious Molestation. Robson was charged with Lewd and Lascivious Act on a child under 16 years of age (1) count and Kellen was charged with Principal in the 1st Unlawful Sexual Activity with a Minor (4) counts and Principal in the 1st Lewd and Lascivious Molestation (1) count."[21]

Irrespective of the victim's sworn statements the only alleged procurer not charged was Ghislaine Maxwell. Why? Dozens of sworn statements were taken from five victims and seventeen witnesses. All the witnesses gave testimonies relating to criminal sexual activities that occurred at Epstein's Palm Beach residence. Epstein's pilots, Larry Visoski and David Rogers, two former house managers, Juan Alessi and Alfredo Rodriguez, and the entire Palm Beach staff were interrogated.

Several more victims beside those identified in the police reports were brought in for questioning. The sworn statements revealed that Epstein usually paid the victims directly or via his staff, to provide him with special 'massages.' At the beginning of the investigation, in order to determine the range of crimes perpetrated by Epstein and the number of adolescents recruited, the Palm Beach Police together with the Sanitation Bureau of the Town of Palm Beach hid trash pulls outside his house to retrieve the trash.

Telephone messages and other information that was discarded inside the bins by Epstein and the staff helped police learn much more about their comings and goings. A few important messages were found from one particular victim, Jane Doe #102 or Virginia Louise Roberts whose deposition was filed on May 1, 2009. Her case, *Jane Doe #102 v. Jeffrey Epstein,* best illustrates the scope of crimes committed by Epstein and his entourage of procurers. Her story, described in later chapters, is revealing.

As for Haley Robson, on February 6, 2005, the alleged procurer made the fatal mistake of calling "Rosemary." Known as "Jane Doe 1" in the original criminal investigation, she was the first victim to come forward. Rosemary was also Robson's neighbor and a family friend. According to the Police Report, the day Rosemary met Epstein her academic life was fragile.[22]

The fourteen-year old American girl of Cuban extraction was very pretty. Fair-skinned, soft-spoken and demure, Rosemary had large brown eyes and long brown silky hair. She wore reading glasses and was attending a school for kids with special needs when she met Epstein. Although her parents had divorced, the family lived in Royal Palm Beach about twenty minutes north of Palm Beach. Rosemary had a twin sister who did not meet Epstein. Rosemary lived mostly at school during the week and would spend most weekends with her father and stepmother. Her twin lived with the mother.

Early during Rosemary's childhood, her father had gone through a series of jobs including several construction projects that had not worked out. According to Rosemary's mother, he exposed his family to financial hardship. Perhaps the father's lack of steady employment threatened the marriage and his ability to meet his parental responsibilities? Her parents eventually divorced and each remarried. Living in this family environment must have been very difficult for young Rosemary. No doubt creating a breeding ground for trouble- the kind of trouble- adolescents find difficult to get out of.

During the investigation her father told the police that the first time his daughter met Epstein was on Sunday, February 6, 2005. According to the deposition, her father was unaware of his daughter's whereabouts that day and thought she was being driven to a nearby shopping mall by Haley Robson. Instead, Rosemary--"was driven to Epstein's house by Robson and a Hispanic female in a pick up truck in order to provide a massage for him." It turned out the Hispanic looking female was in fact Adriana Ross of Eastern European descent.[23]

By the time the girls arrived at Epstein's gate, Epstein's houseman, Alfredo Rodriguez, let them through, according to the police report. Rodriguez worked for Epstein from November 2004 until May 2005. During the interrogation, Rosemary told the Palm Beach Police she had, "Met the house chef in the kitchen." Minutes later the girl was introduced to Sarah Kellen and Epstein. After a brief introduction, perhaps five minutes or so, Epstein nodded and left the kitchen. Kellen led the girl upstairs and into the master bedroom.[24]

Once inside the bedroom, Kellen prepared the massage table located inside his large bathroom suite. Rosemary said the bathroom was so large it contained a couch. Epstein entered the room wearing only a towel. He dropped it exposing himself completely. Before he lay on the table Epstein told Rosemary to take off her clothes. Nervous and frightened Rosemary did as she was told. "It was hard," she said, "to be believable in his eyes." She took off her clothes, save for the undergarments, and began to give Epstein a massage. Apparently, she was so short that she could not stand up tall enough to reach his back.[25]

Although Rosemary never acknowledged this during our taped interview, the police report stated Epstein used a purple vibrator to massage her vagina. According to the Notice to Appear/Arrest Report, there was no penetration. The vibrator was evidently used on top of her undergarments. While driving to Epstein's house, Robson had instructed Rosemary to say she was eighteen if anyone asked. Rosemary said that while she was "massaging" Epstein she pretended to be eighteen; acting and talking like what she thought an eighteen-year-old girl would be. She had to constantly remind herself not to act so fidgety.

Yet at fourteen, like most teenage girls her age, Rosemary was not very mature and did not know how to behave in situations that were inappropriate for her age. Several times during the interview she repeated how strange she felt to be in the company of such an "old man" and know what to do to make him believe she was 18. The videotaped interview I produced and later posted in The Daily Beast on January 25, 2015 revealed that, "Epstein must have known I was younger than 18 because I had no boobs and was little and very skinny, like a shrimp."[26]

At some point during the "massage, "Epstein grabbed her buttocks and pulled her close to him." Rosemary confessed that Epstein made her feel uncomfortable, but was too nervous to say anything. At the end of the massage, she was paid three hundred dollars rather than the usual two hundred, "Because, he said, I watched him masturbate." Rosemary claimed she never returned to Epstein's house.[27]

The girl confirmed that after the investigation began, Epstein's representatives constantly harassed her. A man followed her from school several times. She does not remember his name. Another man, perhaps, she does not remember his name, rang her many times at home almost everyday to ask if she was going to testify. The man on the phone offered her monetary compensation to prevent her from testifying. She said they made her life miserable almost unbearable.

I believe Rosemary was telling the truth because, in 2009, a similar situation happened to me. One morning a friend rang. I did not know my friend was also friendly with Epstein so when prompted I spoke candidly about my research and the book during our conversation. I had no reason to suspect otherwise. During our conversation our friend made an offer. Would I continue to write this book if I were given five million dollars? I challenged my friend. My friend repeated the offer and said that five million dollars would be "a life changer." That assumption was correct. Five million dollars would have been a "life changer," only it would have changed my life in the wrong direction.

That same year, 2009, I found Rosemary's mother, a kind soft-spoken Southern woman. Mrs. Doe had moved out of Florida shortly after the scandal broke and was living further north. For security reasons and fear of what Epstein might do to her family, she does not wish to be identified. By the time we met, Mrs. Doe was remarried and working a full time job. She was trying to go about her life and forget Epstein ever existed. It was challenging. Over the course of two years we had many conversations and eventually struck up a friendship.

At one point, she acknowledged how agonizing her life too had become during the criminal investigation. She was angry at the system but more upset at her ex husband for forcing their young daughter into a life-altering situation. Mrs. Doe revealed that her daughter never wanted to move forward with the investigation. In fact, it was Rosemary's father who initially insisted their daughter talk to the police. The father had found out about his daughter's meeting with Epstein through his second wife, Rosemary's stepmother.

Apparently, Rosemary was talking on the telephone with a friend sharing secrets about the encounter with Epstein. Perhaps mistakenly, the friend's mother picked up the line. She eavesdropped on their conversation. According to Rosemary, the mother immediately rang Rosemary's stepmother and explained what she had overheard. The following day Rosemary's friend, who apparently was not such a good friend after all, started to spread rumors at school. She revealed Rosemary's secret with several students.

As in most schools, gossip spreads quickly. At some point there was a physical altercation between Rosemary and another female student and both were brought into the Principal's office. It was then the story erupted and took the inevitable turn. Two hundred dollars were found in Rosemary's handbag. Rosemary finally confessed and her parents were called in. Rosemary admitted she had been paid $200 to give "an old man" a massage. The man, she said, lived in Palm Beach.

At the time of the investigation, her father, a thirty something year old Cuban-American, was not financially secure. For many years he had been unable to provide for the girls and was struggling. Perhaps he was searching for retribution or conceivably, he wanted to right a wrong. Whatever the reason, he decided to go to the police. After their first visit to the police department he hired a lawyer to represent Rosemary. Soon after the case began, unhappy with their choice of legal representation the family decided to change lawyers. They met Brad Edwards. Edwards, currently a partner at Farmer, Jaffe, Weissing, & Edwards PL, agreed to represent Rosemary.

Under a 1997 Florida State law, it is a felony for an adult to practice massage without a massage therapist license. It is also against the law for anyone under the age of 18 and without a high school diploma or graduate equivalency diploma (GED) to provide paid for massage therapy. A minimum of 500 hours and a board approved massage course must be completed and certified to practice massage therapy.

Throughout the investigation, Rosemary was an emotional wreck. The police report revealed that on October 4, 2005 Kellen left Rosemary a voice message asking her to call. Kellen wanted to know about Rosemary's conversations with the police. Kellen left her cell number. It seemed odd Kellen was aware of Rosemary's visit to the police unless of course someone on the inside had snitched. So far, no one has exposed the informant.

When we first spoke, Rosemary hardly said a word. It was difficult for her to trust and open up to me no matter how much I tried. It was difficult for me to get through to her. I suppose it was tough for the young girl to trust anyone after what she had gone through during the criminal investigation. I am certain she did not want to relive her worst nightmare. At times when we spoke, Rosemary would talk for five minutes then make up some excuse and quickly hang up. This happened many times over the course of a year before the entire story finally surfaced.

Thanks to the relationship I developed with Rosemary's mother, the girl finally agreed to meet and give me an on camera interview. She was approximately 20 years old, nervous and timid when we met in person. We agreed to meet mid morning in Palm Beach at a well-known open-air shopping mall on Worth Avenue. I wanted her to feel safe and at ease so I brought along a female friend and well-known television anchor who stayed with us throughout the interview. The interview went very well. Rosemary was receptive and informative. Segments of that interview are available on The Daily Beast January 25, 2015 story, "Before Randy Andy's Accuser, A Jane Doe #1."

Rosemary has come a long way since our first telephone conversation. She remains a tender, sweet and soft-spoken young lady with perhaps a perceptible wariness of men and people in general. Now a college graduate, she found work that she enjoys. Recently, she became engaged to a wonderful young man. How lucky she was to make a U turn. Outwardly, she seems happy although admits she is still ashamed and does not like to talk about the incident. Mrs. Doe explained her daughter still bristles at the mention of Epstein's name.

The last time we spoke, in 2015, Rosemary told me she wanted to put the entire incident behind and move forward with her life. She is quickly moving in the right direction. Rosemary and her twin sister are very close and both have a wonderful relationship with their mother, now a proud grandmother thanks to Rosemary's twin sister. She prefers not to talk about the relationship with her father. I have no doubt that as Rosemary matures she will evolve into an even stronger and more caring woman. She is one of the lucky few to have emotionally survived. When I met her mother I knew why, the girls have an extraordinary role model.

As for Rosemary's procurer, Haley Robson, she is no longer involved in any criminal or civil investigation thanks to the attorneys who negotiated Epstein's deal. Interestingly, the Complaint and Demand for Jury Trial filed May 1, 2009 in *Jane Doe #102 vs. Jeffrey Epstein*, said, "On the day of Epstein's arrest, police found two hidden cameras and photographs of underage girls on a computer in Defendant's home." No charges were filed against Robson irrespective of the accusers. Robson, like the other alleged procurer remains free. According to an online social media application, in 2006 Robson was spotted living in Orlando, Florida.[28]

During Robson's investigation, she went to the police station voluntarily after Sergeant Frick and Officer Recarey drove to her home for questioning. Immediately following the interrogation at the police station she was driven home. During the drive a tape recorder inside the police car was turned on to record conversations. Some time during the drive, Robson made a strange remark revealing her arrangement with Epstein. "I'm like a Heidi Fleiss," Robson told the police, 'referring to the Hollywood madam and television personality who ran an infamous prostitution ring in Los Angeles, California.'[29]

The other alleged pimps who worked directly for Epstein and were also identified in police reports and depositions included: Leslie Groff, Nadia Marcinkova, Ghislaine Maxwell, and Adriana Ross Muscinska, a Polish girl living in Miami.[30]

During Ross-Muscinska's deposition, following in her former boss's footsteps, Ross, who Rosemary had first identified as a young Hispanic looking woman and friend of Haley Robson's, cited the Fifth Amendment throughout the entire testimony. No doubt to protect herself from self-incrimination. Many times she brazenly responded, "I refuse to answer."[31]

It seems that for several years, Robson was at the epicenter of Epstein's life although she told the police that her relationship with Epstein did not start out that way. As a matter of fact, the first time they met Epstein told her, "I was too old for him." Robson was 17 years old.[32]

It remains unclear for what length of time Robson procured underage girls for Epstein, although there was a period of at least two years during which Epstein paid her for every girl she procured for him according to legal filings. As their relationship grew, court documents confirmed, Epstein came to rely on Robson's services more than any other procurer with the possible exception of Maxwell and Kellen.

In spite of the many sworn testimonies, the Palm Beach Police Department had a difficult time convincing the federal government to investigate the case. All charges were eventually dropped although Robson's information along with several others alleged procurers and victims were ultimately submitted to the Grand Jury.[33]

In 2009, I reached out to Robson several times. She did not return my calls. Unable to convey Robson's version of the story there are details that will remain a mystery. Epstein's attorneys, who are also not talking for now, are mindful of Robson's long list of secrets and suspected crimes. Perhaps, after publication of this book, victims who have not come forward will find the courage to do so.

If police reports are accurate, Kellen, Robson, Ross, Groff, Marcinkova and Maxwell apparently committed unjustifiable sex crimes against countless underage girls. Yet, in spite of what seems to be overwhelming evidence, the United States Attorney's Office was unable to convict these women for the suspected crimes. A number of criminal attorneys following the case suggested that, "Hardball tactics and 'chits' leveraged by Epstein's attorneys during the negotiations with the Justice Department, insulated the procurers from criminal prosecution."

CHAPTER THREE

PRINCIPAL PROCURERS

The five foot eight, hazel-eyed, Sarah Lynnelle Kellen also became a suspect. An attractive brunette, Kellen was young, calculating and driven. Kellen and Robson worked closely together. At first, when Kellen was brought in for questioning she told the police a number of misleading facts including her home address.

Kellen resided in South Florida yet gave the police Epstein's New York business address as her own. In fact, the address written on the police report, The Villard House at 457 Madison Avenue in New York City is an office building. It was never Kellen or Epstein's home address.

The Villard House is one of the most prestigious and smallest of commercial properties in New York City. It adjoins the New York Palace Hotel. The two-story architectural gem constructed in 1884 and designed by McKim, Mead & White sits between 51st and 50th Street smack in midtown Manhattan. As the former parish house to St. Patrick's Cathedral it remains a popular tourist destination. Back in the late eighties and early nineties, Epstein leased an office space on the second floor. Epstein's offices have since closed.

Kellen's sworn statement and inaccurate details should have drawn immediate concern with the police, Grand Jury and the

Federal Bureau of Investigation. Yet the Palm Beach Police was the only agency that raised its eyebrows. If Kellen could have so easily lied about her home address to the police during questioning, other more important facts could just as easily have been fabricated. To this day nothing about Kellen appears genuine.

In 2010, after my Daily Beast stories posted, Epstein's principal assistant changed her name from Sarah Kellen to Sarah Kensington. Adopting her mother's maiden name in an obvious attempt to hide from her past and ongoing friendship with Epstein might have made it easier to continue her social life. In 2009, I rang Kellen several times. She too did not return my calls.

Sworn taped statements were taken from five victims and seventeen witnesses regarding massages and unlawful sexual activity that took place at Epstein's Palm Beach residence. Some facts were discovered in police reports—primarily, Kellen's role as principal procurer, her close relationship with Epstein and Maxwell, and the multiple introductions of underage girls she provided Epstein. Exhibit C, document #1603-3 filed on 4/8/11 titled the *Undisputed Statement of Facts in the Epstein vs. Edwards Case pages 1 and 2* stated the, "Defendant, Epstein, has a sexual preference for young girls… He repeatedly assaulted more than 40 young girls on numerous occasions between 2002-2005 in his mansion in Palm Beach, Florida."[34]

During the visits, when the girls were introduced to Sarah Kellen in the kitchen she apparently recorded their telephone numbers and names. Most meetings between the underage victims and Epstein first took place in the presence of Sarah Kellen and or Haley Robson.[35]

Once inside his bedroom, "Epstein would rub his fingers on their vaginas and on occasion introduce a massager/vibrator or rub the victim's vaginas as they gave him 'the massage.' On three known separate occasions, according to the report, Epstein had intercourse and inserted his penis and fingers inside the victim's vaginas."[36]

"At the end of each massage the victims were paid between two hundred and one thousand dollars." Several depositions revealed the assaults included vaginal penetration. Epstein abused dozens if not hundreds of girls over a period of several years.[37]

During a sworn taped interview recorded in Sarah Kellen's Probable Cause Affidavit the Arresting Officer, Joe Recarey, explained that when he executed the search warrant at Epstein's home he, "located various phone message books. First names of girls, dates and telephone numbers were on the copy of the messages." Officer Recarey recognized some of the names and numbers of the girls since they had been interviewed at the station. "The messages included the time of day they called and Kellen's signature at the bottom of the messages."[38]

Several victims confirmed the interior of Epstein's bedroom. One victim said, "Upon entering his room there was a large bathroom to the right and a hot pink and green sofa in the room. There was a door on each side of the sofa. While describing the bedroom, a number of girls mentioned a mural of a naked woman in the room, as well as several photographs of naked women on a shelf." Two years later, during Epstein's deposition he was questioned about all the allegations. Epstein pled the Fifth Amendment from beginning to end.[39]

In addition to paying a multitude of women and young girls to procure for him, supposedly Epstein also befriended a different type of procurer. The co founder and eighty five percent stakeholder of a modeling agency, MC2, was a Frenchman known as Jean Luc Brunel. For many years, Brunel apparently provided a dozen or more young and underage models for Epstein. A story posted in the Daily Mail on January 18, 2016, suggested that Brunel continues his association with Epstein even after Epstein was incarcerated. Apparently, Brunel has been providing young models to please his friend for many years.[40]

A case in point is the story of a girl, allegedly a model, "Svetlana Pozhidaeva who was spotted leaving the Epstein house in Manhattan while eating a whole avocado. The brown-haired, blue eyed girl-who goes by 'Lana'— and is represented by MC2 Model Management in New York and Elite Model Management in Milan."[41]

It seems strange, as the Complaint revealed, that the 71 year-old Frenchman who sued Epstein as recently as January 2015, for unspecified damages, would then allow his young employee, a foreign model under contract, visit and associate with the defendant only one year after the lawsuit was filed. If Brunel believes, as he claimed in the complaint that Epstein ruined his business and reputation, why would he allow his young model, 'Lana,' to visit Epstein's home?[42]

When asked, 'Lana' claimed she was not underage and has a college degree. Her social media app says she obtained a 'politics degree' in Moscow before moving to the U.S. Beside 'Lana,' other young women of unnamed ages have been photographed outside his Manhattan triplex following his registration as a sexual offender. When asked by the Daily Mail about their relationship with Epstein, none of the young women photographed were willing to talk to the reporters.[43]

On March 8, 2016, Richard Johnson published a story in The New York Post about Epstein and the model, 'Lana.' According to his source, a woman living inside Epstein's Manhattan triplex confirmed that Epstein still had girls of unidentified ages brought from Russia. The Russian girls, revealed Johnson's source, were living with Epstein in New York and traveling together on his private jet to his island home. When I communicated with Johnson via e-mail, he said that with the exception of Svetlana, the informant did not know if other girls associated with Epstein worked for MC2.

Perhaps for fear of retribution the girls and the MC2 and Epstein employees are not talking. Epstein apparently has contacts in Moscow who make the introduction to the girls and, "When the Russian girls arrive in the city, they already have Jeffrey's phone number," the New York Post reported.[44] Photographs and multiple media reports illustrated that some girls who continue to visit Epstein are American born girls while others come from Russia.

Given the usually stringent requirements enforced by the probation enforcement guidelines especially registered level 3 sex offenders in the State of New York, it is surprising no one has filed a complaint. It seems odd in light of the frequent media stories that have emerged about Epstein and pending cases, that Manhattan's District Attorney has not opened an investigation.

As for Jean Luc Brunel, his history with Epstein dates back to the late eighties. Brunel whose reputation precedes him, moved to the United States from France supposedly because he and his brother, who jointly owned a modeling agency in Paris, were fighting over the business. A Brunel insider explained the agent had unresolved legal issues with his brother and was forced to leave the country. When Brunel exiled to New York he met Epstein. Soon, they became close friends.

Maritza Vazquez a former accountant at MC2 and associate of Brunel's revealed in a 2010 interview that Epstein agreed to fund Brunel's MC2 agency by providing a generous 'loan' of one million dollars. Not long after she discovered the extent of the Epstein-Brunel association, Vazquez was fired from MC2 and charged with embezzling company funds. Vazquez has a criminal record.[45]

After the Daily Beast published my story, Brunel and Epstein vehemently denied it. All the same, the accountant's information was correct and became part of Brunel's legal filing in his 2015 complaint against investor and alleged friend, Jeffrey Epstein. With Brunel and MC2 as the presumed 'partners-in-crime,' Epstein was seemingly able to create a well-structured trafficking network that sourced, transferred and distributed young women from all over the world, some assumingly underage, into out of the United States without suspicion.

The business model of identifying, sourcing, transporting and distributing underage victims under false pretexts is used extensively by the Russian and Ukrainian trafficking cartels that smuggle children to the United States for the purposes of sex trafficking. Research shows that human trafficking cartels sometimes set up modeling, au pair and domestic staffing agencies in their countries as the perfect alibi.

These so called modeling agencies lure girls under false pretenses in foreign countries, apply for U.S. visas using legitimate reasons for travel and then purchase airfare and supply the girls with all the necessary documents to enter and 'work' in the U.S. Once inside the U.S. however, their documents, visas and other official documentation are taken away. Some cartels force the girls to work as "prostitutes." Once the girls are in the U.S. many agencies force the girls to work as prostitutes in order repay them for the cost of transportation and documentation to the U.S. By observing the ever-stringent U.S. Immigration laws, agencies remain under the radar.

Much like the Russian and Ukrainian human trafficking cartels, the Epstein-Brunel association apparently found a way to identify, source and transport underage girls legally by allegedly employing some of the girls under false pretenses as models hired to work for MC2. One such girl corroborated the testimony given by a number of victims in their depositions, that Epstein had promised her and other underage girls modeling jobs at MC2 and Victoria's Secret.

It is also true however that some girls brought to the U.S. by MC2 are in fact working models with legitimate contracts that have never met Mr. Epstein. In light of this information a better question might be: what percentage of the girls brought into the U.S. actually earn a living as MC2 models?

Over the years, it seems Epstein relied on Brunel's friendship and modeling business to source underage girls for sex. Evidently, thanks to his one million dollar capital investment in MC2, the predator was introduced to a slew of underage and pretty young girls, according to Maritza Vazquez and Sergio Cordero, a former Brunel associate and another source I interviewed in Miami, Florida. Sergio Cordero claims he met Epstein and worked with Brunel and MC2 for more than ten years.

Brunel's lawsuit against Epstein disclosed that one-year after opening his agency Brunel "received a letter of credit from Epstein at 5% interest." The case, *Brunel vs. Epstein*, filed as No 14-21348CA-01 in the Dade County Eleventh Judicial Circuit Court, accused Epstein of accountability for MC2's losses and Brunel's current financial distress.

Brunel explained in paragraph nine of the complaint that he, "lost multiple contacts and business in the modeling business as a direct result of Epstein's illegal actions." In paragraph 22 of the complaint, Brunel's attorney claimed that his client "lost potentially ten million dollars in profits to his $1 million loan."[46]

Documents filed during the lawsuit uncovered that, "MC2 employees told attorney Brad Edwards, at the time was representing several victims, that Epstein's Manhattan condominium at 301 East 66th Street was housing some young models." The complaint revealed, "MC2 brought underage girls from all over the world, promising them modeling contracts. Epstein and Brunel would obtain a visa for the girls and would charge the underage girls rent."[47]

Brunel admitted he, "Evaded depositions by Brad Edwards on behalf of several of Epstein's victims and that his "Evasion was due to Epstein's instructions." In paragraph 33, Brunel said Epstein insisted he "leave Palm Beach in anticipation of a deposition linked to Epstein's criminal case."[48]

Other relevant charges in the *Brunel vs. Epstein* case exposed how Brunel "was forced to commit illegal acts by traveling away from the sight of the deposition and during the time period of the deposition." Epstein's instructions prevented Brunel from clearing his name and clarify the relationship with Epstein in order to clear his name from any wrongdoing. Brunel claimed, "Epstein attempted to subvert justice and contributed to the destruction of my business, MC2."[49]

Two former underage survivors who don't wish to be identified came forward in 2009 and 2010. The girls corroborated the information revealed in the Brunel Complaint and took it a step further. They claimed Epstein lured a number of victims by baiting them with potential modeling contracts if they "massaged" him. The girls mentioned MC2 and Victoria's Secret as the dangling carrots. Victoria's Secret is a lingerie chain owned by Epstein's close friend Leslie Wexner.

Jérôme Bonnouvrier, a Brunel acquaintance told the press that, "Jean-Luc is considered a danger." According to Bonnouvrier, Brunel "Knows exactly what girls in trouble are looking for. He's always been on the edge of the system. The late John Casablanca, a renowned model agent, gets with girls the healthy way. Girls would be with him if he were the butcher. They're with Jean-Luc because he's the boss. Jean-Luc likes drugs and silent rape. It excites him."[50]

"I really despise Jean-Luc as a human being for the way he's cheapened the business," said the celebrated Casablanca, who died in 2013. "There is no justice. This is a guy who should be behind bars. There was a little group, Jean-Luc, Patrick Gilles, and Varsano…They were very well known in Paris for roaming the clubs. They would invite girls and put drugs in their drinks. Everybody knew they were creeps."[51]

Vazquez and two survivors, who asked to remain nameless, acknowledged that MC2 provided legal passage and all the necessary visa requirements to transport the girls into the United States, including all appropriate documentation that would allow the girls to earn a salary and work as models independent of their age. Apparently, Epstein not one to forfeit a good deal, provided some of the aspiring young models, under contract with MC2, with accommodations and transportation.

The apartment complex in question is on the Upper East Side, on Second Avenue and East 66th Street in Manhattan, and managed by his younger brother, Mark Epstein. Presumably, the building continues to provide a few accommodations for several foreign-born models that work for MC2. MC2 has offices in Tel Aviv, Miami and a satellite office in New York.

Although sex trafficking is a crime against humanity it is disguised in many forms. The business of luring, coercing, and transporting underage girls for sex can be executed in many ways and is punishable in the United States by State and Federal Courts.

In most cases, the United States government aggressively prosecutes trafficking networks, large and small, no matter what size, as well as local operators that work with international cartels. These operations mostly engage in a "combination of deception, fraud, coercion, rape, threats, physical violence, isolation, intimidation, psychological manipulation, to compel their victims to engage in prostitution." Under state and federal laws including the currently reauthorized Trafficking Victims Protection Act (TVPA), human trafficking operators once arrested are usually prosecuted stringently.

CHAPTER FOUR

SO MANY VICTIMS

On November 21, 2005, the Palm Beach Police Department interviewed Jose Alessi, Epstein's former houseman. Alessi worked for Epstein between 1993 and 2004. Like the houseman who followed, Alfredo Rodriguez, Alessi was fired in 2004 for allegedly stealing. Alessi's responsibilities included a number of chores such as: preparing the house for Epstein's arrival, driving his guests, driving staff, and overseeing the maintenance of the house. Unlike most of Epstein's chefs, house staff and personal assistants, Alessi never traveled with Epstein on his private plane. During the police interrogation, Alessi told the police that his boss usually, "received three massages per day," when he was in residence.[52]

"Each masseuse that visited the house," Alessi said, "was different." Toward the end of his employment he revealed Epstein's, "masseuses were getting younger and younger. Some appeared to be sixteen or seventeen years of age at most." The massages were given in Epstein's bedroom and bathroom and many times Alessi set up the table.[53]

After Alessi's dismissal, Officer Recarey interviewed his successor, Alfredo Rodriguez, on January 4, 2006. The new houseman lasted a very short period at his new employ and like his predecessor was let go for apparently the same reason: stealing. During his sworn video taped statement, Rodriguez said he worked for Epstein for approximately six months from November 2004 through May 2005. Rodriguez's responsibilities consisted of running errands, cooking on occasions, chauffer duties and acting as a full time butler. Rodriguez told the police he was, "Expected to make the girls comfortable until either Sarah Kellen or Epstein met them."[54]

One of their duties included meeting the girls upon their arrival and escorting them to the kitchen. There, the staff would offer the girls something to drink although never alcoholic since Epstein did not allow it and does not drink alcoholic beverages. Rodriguez acknowledged he "knew the girls were still in high school." After every massage Rodriguez, "often cleaned Epstein's bedroom. Rodriguez discovered hand held massagers, vibrators and sex toys scattered on the floor," and then revealed, "the girls always needed rides to and from the house."[55]

During the investigation, the police issued subpoenas for several cell numbers and home lines. Records from several victims and witnesses including Sarah Kellen's telephone numbers were investigated. Records showed that many telephone calls were made between Kellen and the victims and were "consistent with the dates and times the victims stated they were contacted." Records also, "showed Kellen called Robson during the exact times and dates when the victims advised the incidents occurred." Kellen coordinated the encounters with several victims and nine initials were entered during the same time frame the girls indicated they occurred."[56]

The Probable Cause Affidavit corroborated much of the information conveyed by the victims. For example, "Sarah Kellen coordinated and aided in the recruitment of minors to "work" for Epstein. She also allegedly secured their appointments for the purposes of lewd and lascivious acts and arranged the bedroom for the minors to perform sexual activities with Epstein."[57]

Of the two-dozen or more victims allowed to testify, not all their stories were included mainly because the majority shared similar accounts of abuse. A few cases stood out. The most troubling incidents became the basis for this book. The level of abuse and recurring criminal activity was heinous. Document #1603-3, referred to as Exhibit C, filed on April 8, 2011, identified dozens of victims. According to the court file, "Epstein repeatedly sexually assaulted more than forty (40) young girls on numerous occasions between 2002 and 2005 in his mansion in West Palm Beach, Florida."[58]

The same document revealed, "Epstein has a sexual preference for young children." In addition, Jeffrey Epstein's deposition taken March 17, 2010 made known that "Epstein invoked his Fifth Amendment right to remain silent rather than make an incriminating admission when questioned about his participation in the sexual abuse of minors.[59] "Epstein abused many of the girls dozens if not hundreds of times," the deposition stated. When asked, "How many times did he engage in oral sex with females under the age of 18," Epstein again, "invoked the Fifth Amendment."[60]

Another Deposition dated September 24, 2009 and continued on March 11, 2010, identified a minor girl as 'Jane Doe.' Doe "was sexually abused at least 17 times by Epstein." Doe stated there was, "vaginal penetration by Epstein with his finger and vaginal penetration by Epstein with a massager."[61]

On the same day that Jane Doe gave her statement, September 24, 2009, another victim, L.M., revealed in her deposition, "the way in which Epstein abused her beginning when [she] was 13 years old." According to L.M., "Epstein touched her vagina with his fingers and vibrator." She "was personally molested by Epstein more than 50 times and was paid $200 per underage girl she introduced to Epstein. L.M. said, "She brought him more than seventy (70) underage girls." At one point, L.M. told Epstein she, "did not want to bring him any more girls and he insisted she continue to bring him underage girls."[62]

Another victim identified as E.W. was deposed May 6, 2010. E.W. explained that, "beginning at age 14, Epstein paid me to touch my vagina. He inserted his fingers and used a vibrator. He also paid me $200 for each other underage female I brought him to molest." E.W. indicated she brought him between twenty (20) to thirty (30) underage females."[63]

Jane Doe #4, also a minor, declared in her deposition she was, "fifteen years old when she was first taken to meet Epstein." According to Doe #4, Epstein, "fingered her, used a vibrator, grabbed my nipples, smelled my butt, jerked off in front of me, and licked my clit, several times."[64] In light of the number of testimonies, Brad Edwards concluded that, "Epstein was able to access a large number of underage girls through a pyramid scheme in which he paid underage victims $200-$300 cash for every underage victim brought to him.[65]

The Palm Beach Police Incident Report gave a solid description of Epstein's sex scheme. "Among other things," the Incident Report detailed a number of sexual abuse crimes allegedly perpetrated by Epstein on his victims. For example, "S.G. a 14 year old girl at the time of the incident was brought to Epstein's home, she was taken upstairs by a woman she believed to be Epstein's assistant. The woman started to fix up the room, putting covers on the massage table and organizing lotions on the table."[66]

The 'assistant' then left the room and told S.G. that Epstein would be up in a second. "Epstein walked over to S.G. and told her to take her clothes off in a stern voice. S.G. explained she did not know what to do, as she was alone with him. S.G. took off her shirt, leaving her bra on."[67]

"Epstein came in covered only by a towel wrapped around his waist. He told her to take everything off. S.G. removed her pants leaving on her panties. Epstein instructed S.G to give him a massage. As S.G gave Epstein a massage, Epstein turned around and masturbated. S.G. was so disgusted she could not speak. Epstein told her she, 'had a really hot body.' S.G. admitted she saw Epstein's member and stated she thought Epstein was on steroids…"[68]

Only Epstein knows the exact number of underage girls he sexually molested over the years. However, the attorneys, including Edwards and former federal Judge Paul Cassell, believe there were substantially more than forty, (40) female victims. "Given the number of girls who confessed and testified they had introduced Epstein to other underage girls in order to make their two hundred dollar ($200) commission, the total number of victims identified on the police report could be a conservative estimate."[69]

A Complaint filed on April 14, 2010 stated, "There is overwhelming proof that the number of underage girls molested by Epstein through his scheme was in the hundreds." During his depositions taken to assess the accuracy of the claims, Epstein "Invoked the Fifth Amendment on questions about his daily abuse and molestation of children."[70]

Edwards and most of the attorneys representing the victims believed, "Epstein and his attorneys knew of the seriousness of the criminal investigation against him and corresponded constantly with the United States Attorney's Office in an attempt to avoid the filing of numerous federal felony offenses. In retrospect, it seems their efforts were successful."[71]

In spite of the level of exploitation and abuse, the cases failed to answer a number of important questions. One in particular troubled me: How did this middle class boy from Brooklyn, a true rags to riches 'boy wonder' and savvy Wall Street investor, grow to be such a menacing pedophile and registered sex offender?

Perhaps some day if a different victim comes forward and the Courts administer an independent and objective psychological examination, a more accurate evaluation of Epstein's profile will reveal the truth.

CHAPTER FIVE

VIRGINIA LOUISE ROBERTS: THE PROPOSITION

Since 2011, so many stories surfaced about Virginia Louise Roberts Giuffre, in newspapers, online and television, that the alleged victim deserves at least an entire chapter dedicated to her relationship with Epstein.

Years after the criminal case was closed, on April 7, 2011 South Florida attorneys, Jack Scarola and Brad Edwards, interviewed the alleged victim, Virginia Louise Roberts, on the telephone. At the time of their conversation, Roberts, now in her thirties, was living with her husband and three children in Australia. Roberts', one of more than two-dozen victims who testified against Epstein, had been sexually abused before she met Epstein. Her home life, not unlike Rosemary's, the first victim to come forward, was tough. Identified as Jane Doe #102 in the criminal case filed in 2005, Roberts' agreed to talk with attorneys Edwards and Scarola, only after she settled with Epstein and sold her story to The Mail on Sunday.

Although her attorney, Robert Josefsberg, spoke with me several times while Epstein was still serving time under house arrest, he did not disclose details of his client's settlement agreement. Several other attorneys working the Epstein case mentioned Epstein had agreed to settle with the victims by paying each victim approximately $150,000. I had no way other than through conversations with attorneys and victims to confirm this information. Most victims who agreed to speak with me would not say how much they received in restitution since they were directed by their attorneys not to disclose the information. When I spoke with Rosemary's mother she mentioned that her daughter received only a fraction of that amount.

I suppose, Virginia too was unsatisfied with the amount she received and so decided at some point to sell her story to the highest bidder. The Mail on Sunday originally published Virginia Louise's story on February 26, 2011. It was later redacted and an edited version was reprinted on March 5, 2011.

This chapter includes a transcription of the telephone conversation between Virginia, Scarola and Edwards, filed in the Fifteenth Judicial Circuit in Palm Beach County on behalf of Brad Edwards. In this incredible twisted tale and case within a case, the victims' attorney, Edwards, became the defendant in a separate case filed by Epstein. Talk about "switching the witch!" In the *Jeffrey Epstein vs. Scott Rothstein, Bradley Edwards and LM* (an underage victim), Epstein filed a civil suit against Edwards, his former boss, Rothstein and another victims L.M. implicating them of wrongdoing.

The *Epstein vs. Rothstein, Edwards and LM* case, although for the most part inconsequential to the ongoing civil cases, was filed in 2009. In Epstein's complaint, he attempted to derail Edwards' efforts by falsely accusing the lawyer of conspiring with his former boss, Scott Rothstein, to swindle Rothstein's clients out of millions of dollars in "settlement" funds.

Epstein falsely claimed that Edwards' and Rothstein had notified potential investors of having reached a large settlement with Epstein that they could eventually share in the profits, "for as much as $200 million." When I spoke with Edwards about this case, he explained Epstein's accusations.[72]

Several other journalists were investigating the Rothstein Edwards' case so there was a lot of information to pool from during the investigation. After most of the facts were established, I concluded Edwards was never involved in the Rothstein scheme and left the firm before Rothstein was indicted as Edwards had mentioned.

The Florida judge also quickly ascertained that very same conclusion and perhaps saw right through Epstein's charade. He swiftly dismissed the *Epstein vs. Edwards* case since there was no evidence whatsoever that Edwards committed any criminal and unethical activities. Scott Rothstein on the other hand, was sentenced to prison and continues to serve a 50-year sentence for cheating his clients out of $1.2 billion.

Jack Scarola, while attempting to find out more information on behalf of his client, conducted a telephone interview of Virginia Louise Roberts. The conversation that follows took place between Virginia and Jack Scarola. Edwards was present during the entire conversation but did not ask any questions.

> Virginia:
>
> I walked away from it all… it hadn't really ended… Jeffrey sent me to Thailand where I met my husband and escaped to Australia, never to return back to the States. Six months prior to that, he came up with a proposition that I thought was really disgustingly sick. And it really showed me for the first time in four years, I had been with him, that nothing was going to change and that I was always just going to be used by him.
>
> He offered me a mansion and some of his money every month. I forget what he called it, a monthly income, in order to bear his child.

The proposition was to have a child with him but to sign my child over to him. Basically the child would be his and Ghislaine's and I would be looking after it as long as nothing happened between Jeffrey and me. So, I was kind of freaked out by all of that.

I was 19 (by then) and he likes females a lot younger, so I pushed Jeffrey to get me some more training since I was getting older and no longer of much interest to him. He sent me to Thailand in September 2002, where I was supposed to meet a girl and bring her back for him, but I never met up with her. Instead, I got a short course in Thai massage. Sending me there was his way of shutting me up about my training... so I went.

One day one of my friends from school invited me to watch a *Muay Thai* fight, which is a form of kickboxing. I went and saw this guy who was a really good fighter... and looked really hot. I asked my friend, who knew him, to introduce me. We fell in love immediately. Three days later Rob proposed and seven days later I was married in a Buddhist temple.

I called Jeffrey and told him I'm never coming back, I'm married I've fallen in love. I thought he'd wish the best for me. He was rude and said, "Have a good life," and hung up the phone. That was the last time I talked to him- ever- until all this started again.

In the summer of 1998, before her fifteenth birthday, Virginia Louise Roberts was working as a bathroom attendant at Donald

Trump's *Mar-A-Lago* Club in Palm Beach, Florida. Following Mr. Epstein's arrest, Mr. Trump publically admitted that Epstein's membership to Mar-A-Lago had been revoked after his arrest.

Born August 9, 1983, Roberts was earning $9 an hour the day she met Ghislaine Maxwell and Epstein. Her father, Sky William Roberts, a maintenance manager at Mr. Trump's property helped his daughter secure the job. The fourteen-year old Roberts' was working only part time when Maxwell made the proposition. The telephone interview was later filed as a court document to "Supplement the Proffer made in support of Edward's Motion for Leave to Amend to Assert Punitive Damages," in relation to the ongoing Jeffrey *Epstein vs. Bradley Edwards* Palm Beach, Florida case.

> While reading a book about anatomy, Ghislaine Maxwell, met me at the spa, not having an education or anything behind me, I thought this was a great opportunity to work for her...to make some extra money and learn about massage. So, I went to Jeffrey's mansion about five or six that afternoon.

> My dad drove me there. My dad worked at Mar-A-Lago with me and he met Ghislaine (the same afternoon) and she seemed (to him) like such a nice and proper English lady, and I mean, you know... She just seemed really nice and like someone who would like to help me out. So, my dad dropped me off and I had no problem getting home that night. One of her drivers would take me back after my trial.

> She led me upstairs into Jeffrey's bedroom past Jeffrey's massage room that has a steam room,

shower and massage table. There is actually an extra room that has- that nobody knows about- a kind of secret room and it's got a whole bunch of pictures of pornographic literature and sex toys and I can just imagine what happened in there.

The room wasn't concealed. It was more like a door that you would normally go into, like some kind of special opening you open and then a little door, so it looks like it's a little closet so-to- speak, but when you walk in, it's obviously a lot bigger than just a closet. It wasn't too big, but it was bigger, you know. It wasn't a gigantic room it was just like a small room, which probably could fit some shoes in there. It had racks of shoes, boxes, some sweatshirts neatly folded and from the ceiling to floor covered in pornographic pictures of the girls that he had met.

By the time Victoria met Epstein, "he was lying naked on top of the massage table. And for a recently turned 15 year old girl seeing a man on the table like that was weird, but having to learn about anatomy and massage, I thought this would be part of the massage program, so I said to myself ok, this is fine."

He instructed me how to touch his body, how to massage him and for the first hour, it was actually a real massage, maybe not an hour, maybe like 40 minutes or something like that; and then he turned over on the other side and exposed himself fully. Ghislaine who had stayed in the room told me to

undress and began to take off my shirt and skirt-
that is- my white Mar-A-Lago uniform. Suddenly,
she took off her shirt and got undressed.

I was there with just my undies on, and she was
completely bare, and she made some kind of flakey
remark about my underwear because it wasn't my
normal sexy-girl underwear, I think it had red hearts
on it or something like that; just your normal, you
know, real cute underwear. Anyway, during all of
this time I'm kind of like wondering what's going
on, how do I act, what do I say? I was so afraid.

Not afraid or fearful for my life but unsure of how
all this started and wanting to obtain a profession,
I was so afraid about upsetting and disappointing
them, I don't know, it was a weird situation... and
I was expected to lick his nipples and give him
oral sex while he fondled me and then at the end
I was told by Ghislaine to get on top and straddle
Jeffrey sexually.

When we were done, we all went and had a shower
in the bathroom and Jeffrey told me to wash him
up and down, you know with a bar of soap and
make sure he was all cleaned up. And then he took
me downstairs to meet two of his guards and told
John to bring me home. John Alessi was the butler
at the time.

Virginia admitted during their telephone conversation she had
been sexually abused as a child by a close family friend.

I was on the streets at 13 years old. I was picked up by a 67 year old man named Ron Eppinger, who did exactly what Jeffrey did to me- abuse and violate my youth- and I was with him for six months.

After Ron, the victim had a boyfriend "who was like a school friend from young days but we just kept in contact with each other and we were on and off constantly, and that was Tony Figueroa. There was another younger guy near my age, Michael, I can't remember his name, but yea, there, I mean, there wasn't like a string of men or anything like that. But there was Ron."

Like I told you, he was the first guy expecting me to do so-called disgusting affairs. Jeffrey actually knows Ron; it was quite weird when I told Jeffrey the Ron story, Jeffrey had actually met him.

From floor to ceiling there must have been one hundred, even more, pornographic photographs, even more in boxes. Some of them were A4 photographs, like the large size, some of naked women posing in positions, sexy positions. Others were of girls with bikinis on. But they were all of women and all had a sexual nature... There were lots of naked photographs... Some photographs had frames, some of them were out of frames, but they were all of women and all sexual in nature.

Ghislaine took several nude photographs of me for Jeffrey... and since he wasn't shy, that wasn't the only place in his house that he kept the photos. He liked photos all over his house. If you looked in his den or on his desk or in the hall table, a giant hall table in his house, there were at least a hundred photos of girls in frames. Not all of them were naked. A lot of the ones that were around his house were pictures of celebrities and politicians he has known.

Sometimes, Jeffrey could have 7 girls in one day, and he would only see those girls once if he got bored. I heard he's gotten a lot sloppier since I left… But, when I knew him, there was just such an influx of girls coming in and out, so I did not recognize a lot of them. They were all definitely beautiful they were all ranging in age, some of them young- but all beautiful.

I knew from my first visit they were pleased with me and after that encounter was finished, the sexual encounter, he went and told me I did well and I have a lot of potential to becoming a massage therapist. He asked me if I could return tomorrow, you know, and do the same thing and get paid two hundred dollars an hour.

Jeffrey insisted that I come after work and over the next few days the relationship grew more, and within a couple of weeks, not even a couple of weeks, maybe one week I had quit Mar-A-Lago and was working for Jeffrey full time.

While her father was still "a maintenance supervisor managing the tennis courts and air conditioners and things like that," Virginia was making two hundred dollars an hour giving Epstein happy ending massages.

> "I came out in public," Virginia said, "because after seeing Epstein and Prince Andrew together again in a picture published in December 2010 in the New York Post, I am angry about how they, (Epstein and Prince Andrew), are still up to their old ways together and that they're still hanging out; however I didn't contact the media including the Mail on Sunday and didn't bring the story out.

> According to the transcript Virginia said she was out, "To help the bigger picture. You know, I think all of us can make a big difference in a lot of other people's lives and I think that this has gone on long enough and it's a big slap in my face that he can get away with hurting me so bad let alone so many other girls and laugh about it."

> I guess I talked to you guys because I want to see the right thing happen, not just to him, but I want people in the world to understand this is not the way of life, you know, it's not acceptable to go out and procure young girls and make them think that, this is the way you should be living.

> That's all. Yeah, I guess my reason for doing this is to help the bigger picture, you know, I'm a big believer in karma and I believe that good things will come back to you, so I guess that's why I'm doing this.

During her first conversation with Edwards and Scarola, Virginia said:

> Nobody has made me feel like I've been bribed or bought or had to say anything. I've told you everything that I know not things somebody told me. If anything, Brad's been extra careful not to tell me anything and let me do all the talking, so it's quite opposite I think.

> You know I was just a locker room attendant and sometimes I did babysitting for the rich and famous so, I wasn't anything big. I worked in a spa. That's why I was studying anatomy, because I was really, really interested in becoming a massage therapist and at the locker room, I didn't do much. I mean I was making tea for a living, I would, you know, make sure the toilet paper had a little triangle in it after everybody went to the toilet or wipe down the water from the basin, you know, it was a very easy-peasy job.

> During the entire hour of what I call the legitimate massage, it was a cat and mouse game trying to get information from me in order to find out who I am, if I was a willing participant in these kind of things and how would I react if they were about to take the next step.

> They got information off me, they got my age, they got my, a little bit of history so they knew I was, you know, not very stable at home, and they knew

that I was actually interested in making my life better by studying so what they were offering me was a chance to become a legitimate masseuse but it was the getting trained…

They would have people show me how to work the body called massage therapists and buy me books on it and you know, keep me interested. Every time I was with Jeffrey, literally it was about massages, I don't mean just going in and having sex with him. I mean giving him a massage. Because it would always start out with a massage and then it would lead into sometimes other things.

By the time the fifteen year old was Epstein's full time employee or masseuse, Virginia began to travel with Epstein.

When he was in Palm Beach, I stayed at my apartment, and he would call me once or twice a day sometimes to do things with him. Sometimes, we'd go out shopping, sometimes, we'd go out and watch a movie. You know, simple things like that, go to an expo or a fair, whatever it was.

But when we were in other cities, I lived with him full time. Even in the middle of the night, I could get a ring on my phone and he would tell me to come in his room, you know, so it was literally full time. After I quit Mar-A-Lago, Jeffrey offered to get me an apartment in Palm Beach, somewhere on Royal Palm Beach Boulevard, and it was a nice apartment. He furnished it for me, it was absolutely beautiful, but yeah, that was the only time I would spend time away from him really.

The FBI asked me the same question about where I lived and I've been trying to rack my brain… to find out… I didn't get to spend as much time there since I was only there about an entire week out of every month probably because the majority of the time I was with Jeffrey.

Because of her age, Virginia could not drive without a license and would be driven to and from her apartment. The apartment Epstein rented for her was close to her family since Virginia said she, "wanted to be close enough to everybody else so that when I was in town, I could just go see them quickly."

There were times we would fly back from some city maybe too late at night for me to really want to go back home, so you know, it's like midnight or one in the morning and I would just stay in the yellow room, or one of the guest rooms in his house in Palm Beach. But the majority of the time, I would definitely want to get back to my own apartment.

There were no set hours. It wasn't like logging, and you know, hitting the shift button, nothing like that. The way I would get paid would be if I was in Palm Beach, I would get $200 an hour to massage Jeffrey or some of his friends and then go home. If I were traveling with him, it would be per massage, so I would be getting paid per day.

So I wouldn't be getting paid on an hourly rate. He wouldn't say ok, today you're going to work for me from seven in the morning until eight at night. It was never like that. I was on call all the time... I was paid from the time the massage started.

Sometimes we'd go there and I would wait for a while or talk with Ghislaine and Jeffrey about something or we'd meet somewhere and talk about something. A lot of times, I'd meet him upstairs in his room when he was ready for me. But then there were a lot of times where it didn't start right away, so he couldn't really pay me from the time I got there. I was paid from the time I massaged him until the time the massage was over."

According to Virginia's testimony she "was asked to do the same things that I did to Jeffrey to a few of his fellow colleagues."

Those were my duties. Jeffrey looked at it this way. I was going to be a professional massage therapist and maybe I needed some clientele, so he had me perform erotic massages on a few people.

The first massage started in Palm Beach County about six to nine months after she first met Jeffrey. He would always pay for her services. "I would get paid the next time I saw Jeffrey, so if I was invited to the Breakers Hotel to give a massage to one of his buddies, I would give the massage, I would go home, and the next day when I saw Jeffrey, he would pay me for what I did. So, it was paid always

by him, it was set up by him, so he always knew
what to pay me. I did get tips and things like that,
if you call it that, you know, like a hundred dollar
tip or something from a few of them.

In so many ways, Jeffrey really, really, had to train
me, and that was why Ghislaine said that she and
Jeffrey enjoyed me so much because they never
really had to speak much to tell me what they
wanted me to do. You know, I wasn't waiting for
their directions.

Jeffrey would tell me to go give an erotic massage
to (his) friends, he wouldn't give me many details,
but he would say "treat them like you treat me." So
I would do what he wanted without having him
say anything.

I complied with what he wanted because it was
somewhat of a... I mean... I don't know how
to say it, it was just very mindboggling how I let
him have so much control or power over me basically. The massages would be routine... with my
so-called new clients, and in their own words they
would ask me to provide them with sexual pleasure
after the massage.

I always reported back to Jeffrey about what
happened after I provided massages to his friends
and I knew that his friends were reporting back
to him as well because there were times where
he would instigate a conversation by saying,

'You know, so and so had a great time, you did wonderful, and he gave me a call and told me how it went.' Jeffrey would have a laugh with me a few times about some of their different mannerisms, I guess you would say, like some of them, one guy had a foot fetish and that was really weird and I mentioned it to Jeffrey and we had a laugh over it.

Virginia told Scarola she provided massages for perhaps "about eight guys," beside Epstein, that Jeffrey always paid for. Roberts' described the massages as "services" according to the telephone transcription. When asked by Scarola to identify the eight men Virginia grew scared and refused.

No, not at this stage, I just—some of these people are really influential and powerful and I don't want to start another shit-storm with a few of them. I'll tell you there were some erotic massages given to… I'm just afraid to say it to you. I'm really scared of where this is going to go.

Detecting Virginia's distress, Scarola quickly changed the subject and questioned the girl about her travels with Epstein.

I started traveling immediately. Not internationally until I think about, gosh, I can't remember, I think it was a year later, that we started doing international travel maybe like 9 months to a year—somewhere in the summer of 1999. But like I said, we started doing domestic traveling immediately, so my first destination with him was New York then Santa Fe, the Caribbean and California.

I would take trips with him occasionally. Sometimes we would travel to St. Louis or New Orleans or Santa Cruz. We were traveling just about everywhere I think in Jeffrey's private jet. Unless I was being sent somewhere by myself for a client, then I would travel on what do you call a public jet, whatever it is. "Commercial flight" interrupted Scarola, 'Yes,' Virginia said, 'Just a normal flight, an e-ticket.' "Like the rest of us common folk," Scarola said.

But when I was with Jeffrey, the majority of the time would be on the black jet. If one of his colleagues would be at the Caribbean or Santa Fe or even New York home, or wherever, he would call me up when I was not with him and ask me to get on the next plane to so and so and go meet so and so, and that's when I would use e-tickets. His assistant would organize the trip for me and give me the details and I would just walk up and they'd let me right through.

"On those occasions how much time would you spend with one of Jeffrey's friends when you were sent to a location that you would have to travel to," Scarola asked.

Only a couple of days, only two days, that's it. I would be paid in cash upon my return back with Jeffrey. So, whenever I was back with Jeffrey, he would count up how many days I've had, sometimes give me even more than what I deserved, not deserved, but what I earned and give me a little extra. I would do to them the same thing I would do to Jeffrey.

Again, it would start out as a massage, which would start with them being naked, and give him a legitimate massage to begin. I'd start with his feet, go up to his calves, up his legs, buttocks, back, his neck, his head, his arms, yada yada… and then it would be time to flip over, and some of the men would want me to massage the front side of them and they would instigate it so I would have to begin having sex with them or foreplay, whatever you want to call it.

"So routinely," Scarola said, "These massages involved sexual activity. Is that accurate?"

"Yes," replied Virginia. According to the pilot manifesto, pilot logs and several depositions, the passengers on the plane when Virginia traveled consisted of "Larry the pilot, a short, small old guy, I don't know his name, but he was the copilot, and then he changed and there was another guy brought in."

Generally, there was always Jeffrey, sometimes Ghislaine, sometimes Emmy Taylor, sometimes a whole bunch of other girls, sometimes famous people, sometimes politicians or just about anybody could fly on his plane. There was never any set routine. It was an influx of people on Jeffrey's airplane. There was Naomi Campbell, Heidi Klum, and Bill Clinton. There was Al Gore, a whole bunch of models. There was also Matt Groening, producer of The Simpsons cartoons, Jack Cousteau's granddaughter a lot of interior designers, architects, and politicians.

What went on the airplane was a lot of the same thing that went down on the ground. A lot of times, it would just be me and Jeffrey, or me and Jeffrey and Ghislaine, or me and Jeffrey and some other girl, sometimes Emmy, Sarah, and Nadia Bjorlin.

Nadia Bjorlin, now an opera singer is married and has a son. She is also a television actress on 'Days Of Our Lives.' According to the Daily Mail report, published March 7, 2011 Bjorlin's mother, Fary Bjorlin, said her husband an esteemed classical conductor, Ulf Bjorlin, died when Nadia was 13, a year before her daughter met Maxwell and Epstein. The couple might have thought the "mourning schoolgirl must have appeared an easy target." At the time the young teenager was studying at the Interlochen Music Center in Michigan. "My daughter was a baby. She was a skinny little girl, not mature for her age. She was 13, but everyone thought she was nine or ten."

Back to Virginia's testimony:

There would be sexual conduct, there would be foreplay, and there was a bed, so we could basically reenact exactly what was happening in the house. It would start off with massaging or we would start off with foreplay, sometimes it would lead to, you know orgies.

There was a constant influx of girls coming in and going out. And we were all very young. On occasion, there were some older girls, and I don't mean older as in like in there 30s. I mean like 28, 29, just very rarely; the majority of the girls that Jeffrey actually met or had on his plane or in his house were under age.

Jeffrey would send me personally or with other girls to clubs or shops to pick up other girls anywhere, I mean we were constantly on the lookout for other girls that might satisfy, Jeffrey.

Our instructions were clear: young, pretty, a fun personality. They couldn't be black. If the girls were any other race other than white, they had to be exotically beautiful. That was about it.

They both gave us instructions and it wasn't just me, Jeffrey asked most girls to bring a friend to make extra money. They would use us young girls so that way it probably looked a lot safer to a girl that we were procuring younger girls that were already doing it. That was the way Jeffrey did it. Jeffrey and Ghislaine both taught me how to, depending on the circumstances, depending on the girl, how to procure a girl.

You could offer them a job as a massage therapist or you could tell them you have a really rich friend with great contacts in the acting world or modeling world and he loves pretty girls, you should come back and meet him, make some money… We had a whole bunch of ways to be able to procure girls.

There could have been a hundred girls, there could be more, honestly. I'm not sure how many girls, really. I wish I did know. Like I said there were so many over the course of 4 years, between 1998-2002, with Jeffrey... I would say definitely more than one hundred.

Epstein's gifts didn't stop at tipping Virginia. He loved to dress her as well.

He wasn't out to dress me like a porn star or anything. He would always dress me very classy, but we'd just go shopping all the time together... It was nice, classy outfits I was wearing like Gucci, Dolce Gabbana, Chanel, and things like that.

He was buying me a lot of very, very nice clothing. It was provocative. I mean I was wearing miniskirts and tight short shorts and little shirts that showed my belly and my cleavage and everything, but they were expensive clothes. There was, also role playing-lots of it.

Jeffrey loved the latex outfits Ghislaine had for us girls. He had bondage outfits, he had all different kind of outfits, but his favorite was the schoolgirl. Ghislaine would dress me up to surprise Jeffrey or Jeffrey would ask me to get dressed up. This would include wearing a tiny little skirt with nothing underneath, a white collared shirt that you would be wearing to school with a tie, tied up in a bow, my hair in pigtails, stockings up to my knees and

I would go in there and act like a kid and we'd do role playing sex.

Apparently, Epstein boasted to Virginia all the time and to some friends about the ages of the girls with whom he had sex.

The worst story I heard directly from his own mouth was about these pretty 12 year-old girls he had flown in, transported to Palm Beach by somebody else, for his birthday. It was a surprise birthday gift from one of his friends. They were from France. I did see them. I did meet them. Jeffrey bragged after he met them they were 12 years old and flown over from France because they are really poor over there, and their parents needed the money or whatever. That was the worst. He was constantly bragging about the girls' ages or where he got them from or about their past and how terrible their past was and good he is making it for them.

Scarola circled back to question Virginia about what took place on Epstein's jet.

The crew was told to knock if they had to come out of the cockpit and told to come out as little as possible. So they were not hanging out watching everything. But it doesn't take an idiot to put two and two together to say well there's a whole bunch of half-dressed teenagers on board with this old man who is constantly being massaged by them and he wants me to keep the door shut for what reason? I mean, only they could figure that out, but yeah, they knew.

He would laugh about it. I never really knew what to take seriously, because he was such a funny character at times. Yeah, lots of people owed him favors from what he told me. He's got everybody in his pocket, and he would laugh about how he helps people for the sole purpose- in the end- to owe him something. That's why I believe he does so many favors in the first place.

Scarola: Do you have any recollection of Jeffrey Epstein's specifically telling you that Bill Clinton owes me favors?

Virginia: Yes, I do. I remember asking Jeffrey what's Bill Clinton doing here… he laughed and said, 'Well he owes me a favor.' He never told me what favors they were. I never knew… He told me a long time ago that everyone owes him favors. They're all in each other's pockets…

Scarola: Virginia, when you asked Epstein why is Bill Clinton here, where was here?

Virginia: On the island, besides living in Palm Beach, Epstein owns a private island, Little St. John's in the U.S. Virgin Islands (USVI).

Scarola: When you were present with Jeffrey Epstein and Bill Clinton on the island, who else was there?"

Virginia: Ghislaine, Emmy (Taylor), and there were two young girls that I could identify. I never really knew them well anyways. It was just 2 girls from New York.

Scarola: And were all of you staying at Jeffrey's house on the island including Bill Clinton?

Virginia: That's correct. Jeffrey's house has about 4 or 5 different villas on his island separate from the main house and we all stayed in the villas.

Scarola: Were sexual orgies a regular occurrence on the island at Jeffrey's house?"

Virginia: "Yes."

A 2015 online advertisement posted one of the villas at a daily rental of $2,317 per night. That particular villa contains 5 bedrooms and 2 bathrooms. There is a 7 night minimum stay.

Scarola: If we were to take sworn testimony from the people I am going to name, and if those people were to tell the truth about what they knew, do you believe that any of the following people would have relevant information about Jeffrey's taking advantage of underage girls?

Virginia: Yes.

Scarola: So, I'll just name a name, and you tell me 'yes' if they told the truth, I think they have relevant information or 'no', I don't think they would, or 'I don't know whether they would or not.' Ok? You understand?

Virgnia: Yes.

Scarola: Ok, Les Wexner?

Roberts: I think he has relevant information, but I don't think he will tell you the truth.

Scarola: What about Alan Dershowitz?

Roberts: Yes

Scarola: David Copperfield?

Roberts: Don't know.

Scarola: What about Tommy Matola?

Roberts: Don't know.

Scarola: Prince Andrew?

Roberts: Yes, he would know a lot of the truth. Again, I don't know how much he would be able to help you, but seeing he's in a lot of trouble himself these days, I think he might, so I think he may be valuable.

Scarola: Ok Virginia, I think that's all I have for you…

As I told you in the beginning of this conversation, we've been recording it, and hopefully, we've got a clear enough recording so that we've taken down everything accurately and when it's transcribed, it will be clear and accurate, but what I would like to do is transcribe it, sent it to you, have you take a look at it, and if there's anything that we got wrong in the statement, you can write back and you can make changes in the transcript so that it is accurate. Is that fair? Virginia responded, "No worries. That is fair. No problem."

Brad and Scarola said goodbye to Virginia and thanked her for her time.

Tagnotes

On January 2, 2015, The Guardian, a British daily, contacted Buckingham Palace for comment. According to the report: "Buckingham Palace declined to comment on the allegations contained in the court document. A palace spokesperson said the royal household would, 'Never comment on an ongoing legal matter.'"

Buckingham Palace issued the following statement: "This relates to the long-running and ongoing civil proceedings in the United States to which the Duke of York is not a party. As such we would not comment in detail. However, for the avoidance of doubt, any suggestion of impropriety with underage minors is categorically untrue."

Virginia's telephone testimony substantiated many of the facts previously included in her earlier testimonies given under the alias Jane Doe No. 102. Her earlier Complaint described in detail how Maxwell apparently recruited underage girls turning the victims of sex trafficking into both procurers.

CHAPTER SIX

IN HER OWN WORDS: VIRGINIA MAKES A U TURN

On December 23, 2014, Virginia Roberts Giuffre incorporated a non-profit foundation in Florida, "Victims Refuse Silence: From Victim to Survivor." Her mission: "To change the landscape of the war on sexual abuse and human trafficking." Her strategy: "to help survivors break the silence associated with sexual abuse."

Media reports continue to suggest different reasons why Roberts started the foundation. One report claimed that Roberts' attorneys, Edwards and Cassell, funded the organization with an initial seed capital of eighty thousand dollars. In 2016, when I prompted Edwards if this was true, he did not confirm or deny the allegations.

Given the many published opinions about this particular victim and because I have not spoken to Virginia directly, I thought it best to describe this chapter in her own words. The following statement is taken directly from the website's home page.

> *Where do I even begin? My story does not start in the way a typical fairy tale starts. Hoping for a nice life and happy ending was a fallacy. I was*

forced to endure abuse as a child. After that, I was left to my own demise. I saw the streets as a way to escape, but quickly learned that it was just as bad as before. Nothing changed. I was still being victimized.

In and out of safe-homes and rehabs, they all contained a product of treachery. Survival had to become my first instinct. It felt as though no matter where I ran, nothing would change. I couldn't see any way around this. The people closest to me rejected me.

Many days followed, bringing more shame than I could have imagined. My life was tumbling down around me. And then I turned 15.

At 15 years old, very wealthy and powerful people promised me a higher education and a better life. I was a vulnerable teenager and the offer was appealing. But before I knew it, I was thrown into a world of sexual servitude and believed that I was indebted to those who used me as a sexual servant.

While traveling the world with some of the most powerful and connected world leaders in politics, science, and business, they made me believe that I was important, yet I was really there to service these individuals sexually.

In order to protect myself, I quickly appreciated that I had no choice but to comply with my master's directives. I was still only a child, and because of the extraordinary power that my abusers had, I believed that I could not report them. I did not think that anyone would listen to me.

When I turned 19, I was sent to Thailand and finally found the opportunity to break free. I met a man who gave me the courage that I needed to escape. Instead of following orders and returning to the United States and my life of sexual abuse, I went to Australia, where I hid in fear for years.

While there, in Australia, I matured. I gained perspective. I had my beautiful children and began watching them grow.

My family and I came back to the United States with my mind set on making a difference. Not for myself, but for all of the children victims of sexual abuse and sex trafficking.

The family moved to Colorado.

In trying to make a positive difference, certain people continue to take shots at me and put me down, but I am no longer the young and vulnerable girl who could be bullied. I am now a survivor and nobody can ever take that away from me.

While I cannot save every child, I know that with my voice and my story, I can save some. And if I save just one, then my mission is a success. Sexual abuse and sex trafficking is an epidemic that crosses over all socioeconomic boundaries. By spreading awareness, we can decrease the frequency of abuse. By providing support and services, we can heal those who have suffered as victims.

By giving other victims confidence to speak up, and refuse silence, we can empower them to transition from victim into survivor, and to save the lives of others. If every victim refuses silence, we can end this epidemic. I want every victim to know that there is someone who will believe in him or her and who will help him or her heal.

Today, I am a mother of three. I have a wonderful and supportive husband, and I am just lucky to be alive. We all have choices in life. Close your eyes and just imagine peace for yourself or someone you know who has been through sexual abuse. It is daunting and no one seems to want to talk about it because of the shame associated with sexual abuse. But just know, even if you have no one to turn to, you have us!"

Virginia Louise Roberts Home Page:
http://www.victimsrefusesilence.org

CHAPTER SEVEN

GHISLAINE NOELLE MAXWELL

Virginia's introduction to Epstein was thanks to Ghislaine Noelle Maxwell, born on Christmas Day 1961, in Headington, Oxford, Great Britain. Her birth came only days after her oldest brother, Michael, died in a coma after six years following a tragic car accident.

Headington Hill Hall in east Oxford was her family home from 1959, when her father leased the estate until it was placed in receivership shortly after his death, in 1991. Prior to the conversion of 'The Hall' as a family residence, Maxwell used the estate to operate his successful publishing business, Pergamon Press.

Like all great family homes Headington Hill has a storied past where C.S. Lewis came to stay in 1919 and supposedly never left. Decades earlier, another legendary English author, Oscar Wilde was invited to a May Day Ball. The story has it that Wilde came dressed in costume as Prince Rupert. The famous Hall built in 1824, was designed by architect John Thomas for the Morrell's, a family of local brewers who lived there for over one hundred years.

Unlike Epstein's public education, Maxwell was educated near her home at Headington a private school for girls. After graduation she went off to university to finish her studies at Marlborough and Balliol College, Oxford. On December 10, 1984 after her graduation, her father made Ghislaine Director of Oxford United, a British football club, where she received the Fiat Team of the Year Award. Maxwell, who is fluent in several languages, is also a helicopter pilot and a certified deep-sea diver. She recently started a non-profit, The Terra Mar project to protect the High Seas.

In the hierarchy of siblings, Ghislaine was the youngest of nine children born to the late Robert Maxwell, nee Jan Ludvik Binyamin Hoch in Czechoslovakia. She lived a charmed childhood as her father's doted daughter. In July 1991, somewhere between dusk and dawn, Maxwell disappeared off the Canary Islands. It was a warm summer evening in the Mediterranean when Robert Maxwell capsized off *The Lady Ghislaine*, the yacht he named after his favorite daughter. Perhaps, her life congealed upon his untimely death.

Some media reports insinuated that following his disappearance Ghislaine was "desolate and almost destitute." Her financial state was not much better. Her state of bereavement coupled with the financial insecurities might help explain the instant attraction to Epstein and reason she agreed to go along with his unusual lifestyle. According to various accounts, they met and fell in love although she never mentioned her feelings to me during any one of our conversations.

During their years together she introduced Epstein to many of her friends including HRH Prince Andrew. She was so enamored with Epstein that she brought him along to attend a birthday celebration for Queen Elizabeth II at Sandringham Hall in Norfolk, England, the Queen's hunting lodge. She also helped solidify the friendship between Epstein and former President Clinton.

Not too many years into their romance their relationship took an unusual turn. Maxwell apparently became a sort of 'Madame' for Epstein, and as Virginia Roberts' claimed, the woman became, "the undisputed leader of the girls in Epstein's entourage." Roberts also said Maxwell was, "funny and boisterous. I was scared of ever saying no to her. I was always compliant. I knew if I said no to anything, I would be on the street."[73]

Several sworn testimonies reveal Virginia's relationship with Maxwell. "Ghislaine was a photographer, and took many of the nude pictures that were all over Epstein's houses, including the ones of me in a hammock that Bill Clinton and Prince Andrew and all their visitors had to have seen."[74]

"One year," Roberts claimed, "I couldn't think of what to give Jeffrey for his birthday," so I asked Ghislaine. Maxwell told the girl, 'Just give him a photograph of you.' "I had a nice picture, lying against a tree, fully clothed. But when I showed it to her," she said: 'No, you can't give him that,' so she took me and laid me naked across a hammock and put a sheer piece of net across me and I posed with my legs open, a bit provocatively, and that was the picture she had me give Jeffrey."[75]

In 1995, before Maxwell's relationship with Epstein formally began, Alex Witchell, a reporter at The New York Times interviewed her mother, Elizabeth 'Betty' Maxwell. Witchell claimed the Maxwell family, or at least Mrs. Maxwell, was in "spectacular ruin," as a result of her husband's fiscal mismanagement. "Debt, dishonor and the potential destruction of two sons' careers were the only thing Maxwell bequeathed his family," wrote Witchell, "in spite of his vast holdings, which included The Daily News in New York and Macmillan Publishing."[76]

His story insinuated that Maxwell's father was, "trying to escape the consequences of accumulating a $5 billion debt," a debt that automatically catapulted her two older brothers, Ian and Kevin, into a criminal investigation, "liable for the pension funds of thousands of employees (their father) had illegally utilized as collateral against other businesses." Of all his children, Robert Maxwell employed only Ian and Kevin.[77]

If Kevin and Ian were in financial ruin as media reports claimed, then Ghislaine, her mother, and the rest of the family still dependent on their father's generosity, might also have been insolvent. To make matters worse, less than one month after Maxwell's death, the Serious Fraud Office in England began an investigation into Ian and Kevin Maxwell's participation in Maxwell's companies.

As a result of the investigation, both sons, Kevin and Ian, were arrested and charged with conspiracy to commit fraud; allegedly misusing pension funds; use of pension funds to finance the Maxwell Group of companies; and use of fraud by the Maxwell's to extend bank credits.

In 1996, after an eight months trial, Kevin and Ian Maxwell were acquitted on charges of fraud. Three financial institutions: Lehman Brothers, Goldman Sachs, and Coopers & Lybrand, interceded on their behalf in an effort to rescue them and their partner, the American financial advisor, Larry Trachtenberg.

Trachtenberg 38 years old at the time of the indictment, "Was a former compliance officer at London & Bishopsgate, the pension fund managing company at the center of the 400 million pound sterling black hole in Maxwell's Mirror Group pension assets."[78]

The Los Angeles Times also reported the story. According to the article, "Kevin Maxwell and Trachtenberg were charged with defrauding Swiss Bank Corp of $101 million by selling stock they did not own and stealing $13 million worth of stock belonging to Mirror Group Pension Trustees Ltd., one of Robert Maxwell's company pension funds."[79]

When Ian, Ghislaine's older brother, "was charged with defrauding Swiss Volks Bank of $35.5 million by misrepresenting ownership of stock in Berlitz International after his father's death, according to the fraud office documents," Trachtenberg and Kevin were also charged with same crime."[80]

Ghislaine may not have been privy to her father's business activities even if that was never proven. With the exception of the late Maxwell, no one will ever know with any certainty the professional relationship between Ghislaine and her father. One speculation sounds convincing, Maxwell's media empire was considerably overextended by the time he attempted to take over The New York Daily News and MacMillan Publishers. It was at the New York Daily News Ghislaine Maxwell was to begin her apprenticeship.

Perhaps, had the deal materialized, Ghislaine would have moved to a position of power as reports claimed. One can assume that if she was going to participate in a managerial capacity then during her father's negotiations, Ghislaine might have been privy to some of the financial details of the deal.

What is known in fact is that, "at the time of her father's death, auditors discovered that about $670 million was missing from the Maxwell companies' pension funds. All but some $50 million were recovered, mostly through settlements among the funds and Maxwell companies, their auditors and financial advisers, including Lehman Brothers, Goldman, Sachs, and Coopers & Lybrand, "the very same financial institutions that later came to the brother's rescue.[81]

During that emotionally volatile period for Ghislaine Maxwell, a number of stories surfaced about her father's financial misdeeds. A New York Times article stated Maxwell's "trial attracted intense publicity in Britain, and the Serious Fraud Office, the Government agency that prosecutes white-collar crime, who invested a reported $30 million on its investigation and legal case."[82]

Not unlike Epstein's near miss acquittal, Kevin and Ian's cases, "brought immediate criticism of the Serious Fraud Office from politicians who said the agency had a record of failure in high-profile financial fraud cases…Technically, the Serious Fraud Office could bring additional charges against the Maxwell brothers and

CHAPTER EIGHT

CONVERSATIONS WITH EPSTEIN AND MAXWELL

Not everything I learned about Maxwell and Epstein came from sources close to the couple–"insiders," court files, conversations with law enforcement officials and media reports. I met Maxwell in London at a dinner party hosted by a mutual friend. Cannot reveal the friend since a handful of mutual friends do not wish to be identified.

That evening Maxwell exuded charm, warmth and self-assurance. Bubbling over with witticisms, I sensed she was quite a character. In the course of the last two decades Maxwell and I saw each other several times. We did not become friends in the traditional sense rather friendly social acquaintances.

Maxwell was always giggly, curious and friendly. She asked me a lot of questions about my life. In the early years, there was nothing I did not like about her. I never felt uneasy around her and did not suspect anything unusual even though I was familiar with her family history. In the early nineties it was difficult not to like her. Everyone has a history and not everyone can choose his or her family, so in spite of her father's tragic ending, I chose not to listen to rumors and innuendo. On the rare occasions we met, either at a social function or a friend's dinner party, we chatted about whatever was going on at that time. Several times we met in London. A few more times in New York and perhaps a couple more at a mutual friend's home on New Year's Eve in Palm Beach, Florida.

It was in or around 2002 when I first became aware of Maxwell and Epstein's romantic relationship. I saw the couple at our friend's home during a New Year's Eve celebration in Palm Beach. Their house was only blocks away from Epstein's. The host, a friend of mine who attended Oxford with Ghislaine mentioned they were together.

The 'ringing in the year' bash was the family's annual theme party. It was held annually at their home on Via del Lago, just a few blocks north of El Brillo. It was always a magnificent and generous affair and like the family who hosted the evening, their home too was beautiful, inside and out. Built in 1934 by Sims Wyeth, the Colonial Revival style home overlooked the Florida Inter Coastal. It might have been almost visible from Epstein's side lawn. Somewhat reminiscent of a Spanish *hacienda,* the house was surrounded by three acres of beautiful manicured gardens and lush foliage.

Every year that I attended the party, Maxwell and Epstein happened to be there. Our host and I spent time chatting with them and I became better acquainted with the couple. On several occasions, Epstein and Ghislaine invited us to brunch at his home usually the following day. The invitation was for just the four of us. On one occasion, my friend could not attend at the last minute and I felt awkward going alone, so I asked Maxwell if I could invite a female friend. She said yes.

My friend and I had met years earlier while I was studying at Columbia University in New York. A lawyer by profession, she was working for a local Miami TV station at the time. Today, she is a Judge in Berks County, Pennsylvania. Punctuated by Maxwell's characteristic wit we had an interesting afternoon chatting about the latest coming and goings and "getting lost in let's remember."

That New Year's Day brunch was the only time I visited Epstein's Palm Beach house. As a matter of fact, it was the only time I visited any of his homes. On that day, nothing in the house screamed for attention. In fact, Ghislaine and Epstein gave the impression they were a happy go-lucky couple.

I never saw one nude photograph of a young girl in the living room where we spent a few minutes before we were briskly escorted out into the patio for brunch. The photographs displayed on the coffee table in question showed mostly politicians, Epstein and other luminaires. I did not walk up the grand staircase so I did not see the photographs covering the staircase walls.

When I began the investigation, I rang my friend to confirm I was not forgetting important details about that day. Her recollection was the same as mine. Nothing at Epstein's house seemed out of place during our brunch on New Year's Day.

A year or two later, again I attended my friend's New Year's Eve celebration. Epstein and Maxwell did too. Once again they invited us for lunch the following day. This time we both declined their invitation. That was the last time I saw Epstein.

Several years went by before I ran into Maxwell again. It was 2007 while attending the Clinton Global Initiative (CGI) in New York City. CGI, as it is commonly known, is a mammoth quasi-political/ public relations fund-raising conference created by former President Clinton. According to a well-known global events executive who wishes to remain anonymous, the former president modeled CGI after Professor Klaus Schwab's, World Economic Forum.

The World Economic Forum (WEF), which began in 1971, is the foremost global public policy conference in the world. It is held annually in Davos, Switzerland. A perennial high-octane platform for debate, it is committed to improving our world by catering to King's, heads of state, world leaders, and CEO's of multi billion dollar corporations who influence our planet.

The same source revealed the Clinton Global Initiative was originally funded by a generous gift from Epstein in the amount of four million dollars. I have been unable to verify or refute the amount of this claim since the organization's accounting records do not disclose the information and Clinton did not return my call. However, one media report claimed that one of Epstein's lawyer's, Gerald Lefcourt confirmed in a media report that his client was among the founders.

That same year, while attending CGI, I ran into former President Andres Pastrana of Colombia, an exceedingly charismatic and intelligent man. He is a longtime acquaintance. During our conversation, Maxwell sneaked up behind me. She physically lifted me off the ground and hugged me from behind. The whole thing was very strange. Perhaps Maxwell was attempting to add a bit of humor or simply wanted to show the former president that she and I were friends? I don't know the reason. Whatever were her intentions, her gesture was quite peculiar since we had not seen each other in several years and more importantly the former president was a former Head of State.

What I didn't realize then was that Maxwell and the former president were friends. I found out later when a source close to Maxwell and Pastrana confirmed it and mentioned his name was listed on Epstein's pilot logs.

His reaction to that incident took me aback. I will never forget the look in his eyes when my body lifted halfway off the ground. Still dangling in midair, before I could wriggle myself down to the floor again, he asked how I knew Ghislaine? I was very embarrassed. By the time my feet hit the ground I could barely speak.

Suddenly, his tone took on an air of familiarity. It reminded me of my father's—surprised and concerned all at once.

Until that moment and in spite of our narrow relationship, I believed Maxwell was charming and very engaging. Yet that one gesture gave me a different perspective of her personality. Perhaps, it also gave me an insight into her character. I did not see Maxwell again during that conference except to say hello in passing. In all the years I have known Maxwell, we have never had a discordant word. That year was the last time we had a conversation.

In 2010, the day I collected the police reports and after I read the complaints I telephoned Maxwell. She answered at once. We said hello and chatted a minute or two about the last time we met at CGI. Maxwell had given me her cell number to confirm a dinner invitation she had extended during CGI. The dinner was going to be at her New York home on 116 East 65th Street in Manhattan. I could not attend.

For a few minutes our conversation revolved about nothing in particular. As delicately as possible I approached the subject. The line was soundless. Suddenly she blurted out, "Nonsense. All lies," and dismissed the allegations. I wanted to give her the benefit of the doubt since early on in life I had learned that common values, common interests, mutual alliances, and good times spent together, count. It was also difficult to believe that Maxwell was on the wrong side of the issue. I offered to help and suggested she hire a lawyer. Little did I know what was to come?

We did not continue the conversation. I wished her well and hung up. I returned to the court files craving to make sure I under-stood her alleged participation in this case. I read the files for a third time that day. While I was reading the papers a flashback jolted me back to the moment at CGI when Maxwell lifted me off the ground. It caught me by surprise. I remembered the pres-ident's expression too. With eyes wide open I carried on with the investigation knowing I was on the right track. Maxwell and I have not spoken since.

Sometime in 2012 or 2013, after the Daily Beast reports posted, I ran into Maxwell at a neighborhood café—Amaranth--on Manhattan's Upper East Side. It is casual and intimate and unknown to tourists. A friend and I were having dinner when Maxwell walked in accompanied by a couple. We had a center table in the back of the room facing the entrance. We were midway through our dinner when they arrived. There was no escaping as I was in her direct line of vision.

The Maître d' walked directly toward me as he escorted Maxwell and her friends to the table. For a split second we locked eyes. I continued my conversation. I was a bit concerned and uncertain of her behavior. Would she come to the table and say something unpleasant in front of my friend? She did not. Instead, as she walked past the two of us she drew a blank expression, sauntered around the table and sat down. Their table was to the right of ours. They sat down. Maxwell did not ask to change tables even though her chair faced mine. Until my friend and I stood up to leave, we did not exchange a single glance. That was the last time I saw her.

To this day, the media continues to report her whereabouts. Maxwell continues to live an active social life. Photographs and many news reports show her shuttling between San Francisco, New York, London, Paris and all points in between. In early 2016, a handful of online journals revealed she was quietly selling her Sixty Fifth Street townhouse for $19 million. She considered leasing the house for $50,000 per month.[85]

I never understood how Maxwell had the money to purchase her townhouse in 2010 given her alleged and well-reported inheritance. One report claimed that one of Epstein's attorneys, Darren Indyke, acting on behalf of Epstein, purchased the townhouse in his name.

By all accounts, Maxwell's professional activities are far narrower than her social life. Publicity for her foundation, The Terra Mar Project, started in September 2012. According to one article, The Terra Mar Project was blessed if not perhaps partially funded by the Clinton's because, as a Vanity Fair report claims, Maxwell "is passionate about Bill Clinton, with whom she is close friends."[86]

The Terra Mar Project, Maxwell's latest venture, was created to raise money in order "to protect the high seas." I tried to access the foundation's website to find their mission statement but could not open the home page unless I submitted my email information. It seems the public does not have easy access to the charity's home page without disclosing personal information.[87]

As for Epstein, the last time I had a face-to-face conversation with him was approximately a year before his arrest on New Year's Day, in January 2004. We discussed politics mostly local, Cuba, common friends and laughed a bit. Six years had flown by before I heard his name mentioned again. It was July 2010. I went to visit a friend in Miami, Florida recovering from surgery.

My friend and her husband lived in Palm Beach not far from *El Brillo*. Acquainted with Epstein, albeit superficially, they would spot him from time to time on the island. Given the size of the community and the close proximity of residents it is hard not to know what your neighbors are up to. The island's two most popular newspapers, The Palm Beach Daily News and Palm Beach Post like to incite the town's wagging tongues. The daily coverage of the comings and goings of its residents most likely prevent anyone from retaining anonymity. Not surprising, the islanders, like in every small town, know what everyone else is up to.

That morning, still somewhat under the influence of anesthesia, my friend causally mentioned the latest stirrings in Palm Beach. The conversation went something like this:

My friend: Did you hear about Epstein's imminent release?

Me: Release?

My friend: Yes, he's coming out sometime this week.

Me: This week! Why did he go to jail?

My friend: Prostitution with minor girls.

Me: What!

I was stupefied! Instantly, I reached for the newspaper lying beside her. As my friend continued rambling about Epstein I found it difficult to concentrate. I simply could not believe the story. It was shocking that anyone I knew and had been somewhat friendly with could be involved in such a sordid story. I asked my friend to repeat herself hopeful I had misunderstood.

It would have been far easier to believe that Epstein had been incarcerated for tax evasion or money laundering or for that matter any other white-collar crime; Anything other than solicitation of prostitution with a minor. The first time I heard the story is sounded preposterous. In hopes of finding something new about his case, although I didn't know exactly what I was looking for, I asked to use her laptop.

My friend was still a bit groggy so I quietly sat at the edge of her bed and read everything I could find. Three stories published by The Palm Beach Daily News popped up. They were particularly alarming. Michele Dargan's article, a gifted journalist and staff reporter at the Palm Beach Daily News caught my attention first. Not only did it announce Epstein's imminent release from house arrest on July 21, 2010, the story revealed most of the alleged crimes.

Dargan's story also explained how Epstein served 13 months of an 18 months sentence at the Palm Beach County jail and 18 months of 'community control' in his Palm Beach home. She mentioned Epstein had fought back his restrictions, which in comparison to other sex offenders who where charged with the same or similar crimes were ludicrously lax.

"Epstein made several apparent missteps. His probation records show he has never been arrested for any violations. In fact, all his activities seemed to be a departure from the Florida Department of Corrections guidelines. However, they all received the blessing of the court or his probation officer. A report by a Palm Beach police captain states that, Epstein violated probation in August when he was walking along State Road A1A, but his probation officer deemed him compliant," Dargan wrote.[88]

That story reported how, "Epstein spent blocks of time in Home Depot and Sports Authority multiple times. On March 31, 2010, Epstein was at Home Depot from 6 to 10 p.m., according to his daily probation logs; and on March 27, Epstein was at both stores from 11:30 a.m. to 5 p.m."[89]

Jane Musgrave a talented reporter working at The Sun Sentinel wrote another jaw dropping account. Musgrave explained how Epstein, "complained about ongoing news coverage," and 'seemed somewhat agitated by all the last-minute press,' according to his probation officer who wrote a memo on May 19, 2010."

She went on, "No longer will the 57 year old 'be forced to get permission to fly his private jet to New York or his home in the Virgin Islands or to climb aboard his helicopter to meet with his lawyers in Miami," Musgrove added.[90] "Those who criticize the breaks he has gotten say he has little reason to complain. Since he was placed on house arrest in July 2009, he has taken several trips each month to his home in New York and to his private island in the USVI," Musgrave wrote.[91]

Attorneys Spencer Kuvin, one of several attorneys who represented three underage victims during the civil cases and Adam Horowitz, who represented seven underage female victims during the civil litigation, agreed. "I thought community control meant you stayed within your community and there was some level of control," Horowitz said. "There was very little information disclosed about where he was going and why. It was shocking to me," Kuvin agreed.[92]

The articles hit home and hard because I had just returned from a harrowing trip to Mexico where my life had been threatened during an investigation. In the capital city of Mexico, Mexico City, I was followed while walking in 'La Zona Rosa,' investigating the whereabouts of a victim. Then a few days later, my life was threatened while interviewing a Mexican agency official in a small town outside the capital. San Miguel de Tenancingo, in the district of Tlaxcala, sits approximately 80 miles southwest or two and half -hours by car from Mexico City.

While investigating a Mexican human trafficking case I decided to visit a sex trafficker's house to study the scene of the crime and find out more. In January 2007, a 64-year-old woman was arrested in Mexico and extradited to the United States. She was awaiting sentencing in a Brooklyn federal court in New York. I had spoken to the two lead female prosecutors handling the case. It was brutal. Until 2007, this was the most shocking international human trafficking case prosecuted in the United States. The woman, a mother of two sons and a grandmother, operated one of the most monstrous rings in Mexico. Her local operation was managed out of her home in San Miguel de Tenancingo.

The Mexican family of traffickers consisted of two sons, a cousin, a very young daughter-in-law and mother of the woman's grandchild, and a family friend. All were implicit and all had allegedly lured, coerced, sourced, and physically and sexually abused the underage girls. They had trafficked them from Tenancingo to the United States. The sons and their accomplices smuggled the girls into the United States, transported them across the country and forced them into prostitution in New York and possibly other cities. It was as shocking a case as anything I had ever read.

Interestingly, child sex trafficking was one of the alleged crimes perpetrated by Epstein and some of his alleged procurers. I felt sick to my stomach. As I continued to read Epstein's story, flashbacks of that harrowing trip overwhelmed me.

A security guard and driver, 'Victor,' was assigned to care for me during the investigation thanks to a Mexican government official who was concerned for my safety. The driver and bodyguard drove us to the town of San Miguel de Tenancingo. The drive lasted longer than the anticipated two hours. We left from the hotel early in the morning to avoid rush hour traffic that can be treacherous in Mexico.

Months earlier, while conducting research in New York, I had contacted the trafficker's New York attorneys. The attorney representing the mother gave me the family's home address in San Miguel. The reason for my visit to San Miguel was threefold. To find out the whereabouts of the daughter-in-law who had seemingly escaped or stayed behind in Mexico. At the time, the United States government was seeking her extradition. Two, to find out if the daughter in law had recovered her child, who according to my research was missing.

Lastly, I went to research the local and international Mexican cartels and how they operate and more precisely how operators smuggle children across the border from Mexico. This last reason was a particularly dumb idea.

What I found instead shocked me. Needless to say, it was not the trafficker's daughter in law or her child. It was something altogether different. By the time Victor found the trafficker's house it turned out to be an office for *Desarrollo Integral de la Familia*, (DIF). DIF is a Mexican organization that provides social services, transportation and assistance to the poorest families in Mexico. Usually, there is a DIF chapter in every village and town in Mexico. The agency headquarters are in Mexico City.

The president of DIF is always the First Lady of Mexico. Her tenure lasts six years the same amount of time, her husband, the President of Mexico, is in office. The term expires after the *sexenio* and cannot be renewed. In some ways, DIF is similar, albeit much smaller in scope and range, to the U.S. Department of Health and Human Services (HHS). HHS provides essential human services to help Americans, especially the most vulnerable families.

The only thing in that town worth researching is its lovely geography and interesting history. I don't know what on earth possessed me to investigate since the convicted trafficker's immediate family was already in jail. Whatever 'it' was certainly had power over me since I don't believe I would have risked my life in that way.

Perhaps I expected the house to be empty. Imagining that I could find the daughter-in-law and her child I was eager to investigate the case. Both sons, one being the father of her child, were serving long prison sentences, 50 years each, in U.S. federal penitentiaries. The other family members including their mother, cousin and friends were each serving sentences ranging from ten to fifty years under the Trafficking Victims Protection Act federal guidelines. What struck me as I read the Epstein case was that some of the crimes perpetrated by the Mexican family were similar to the alleged crimes perpetrated by Epstein and a number of his suspected principal procurers.

Knowing very little at the time of how human trafficking prosecutions play out in Mexico, it seemed peculiar the Mexican government would take the risk of operating a DIF chapter in the house of a convicted sex trafficker, given the likely association between the family and perhaps Mexican cartels.

When we arrived at the house, Victor told me to stay in the van. He suggested I hide on the floor of the van while he surveyed the neighborhood. As I slumped down I saw a couple of handguns underneath the seat. Strangely, and for the first time in my life, I felt safer knowing there was a gun at my side although I have never learned to shoot or owned one.

After Victor scouted the neighboring streets, which seemed an eternity, he returned. Swiftly, he opened the van door and pulled me up from the floor. At first, I could barely walk since I had tried to compress my body almost flat against the floor. Not a good idea when you're over a foot tall. He walked shoulder to shoulder with me all the way to the trafficker's house.

From that moment on I did not leave Victor's side. As we approached the house, I saw a van stationed right outside the front door with the letters DIF painted in a shaded green on the side. The same letters were emblazoned in lime green in the front of the house. I looked at Victor suspiciously. Together, almost holding hands, we walked upstairs.

What must have been the living room had been turned into an open space with desks filling the entire room. Several women ambled about. Not one man in sight. More women were sitting around at their desks chatting away. I approached a young woman sitting at the center desk and asked to speak to the Director.

Without allowing me to finish my sentence, a woman approached me. I assumed she was the director. She told me to sit at her desk but said nothing else. She did not acknowledge her position or any of my questions. It was odd. Several times I attempted to explain the case and the urgency of the problem. I told her it was important to understand why so many children were being trafficked from San Miguel de Tenancingo to the U.S.

I explained to her we had also come to find the missing child and daughter-in-law of the owner of the house. She said nothing while staring silently in my direction.

A few minutes into my monologue, a middle-aged man wearing cowboy boots and hat came sauntering in the room from my left. The entire room went silent. He approached me and asked who I was. I introduced myself and gave him a business card. Victor stood up and shook his hand.

He pulled a chair nearby and sat down directly across from me and listened. Throughout the one sided interview I looked around the room for clues. Nothing stuck out until I started looking down at the desk and noticed a document. At first, it looked like a simple sheet of paper with a handwritten directory: names, addresses and telephone numbers. I wondered what the list was for. I pointed to it and asked the lady. The woman did not respond. It should not have surprised me. Instead, she picked up the paper and turned it over so I could no longer read it.

Realizing I was getting nowhere fast, I asked the woman if she knew the convicted trafficker, her family, the daughter-in-law and the missing child. Again, the woman did not respond. Suddenly, as if she had had an epiphany, midway through my sentence, she stopped me. In an almost inaudible but firm voice she said to stop questioning her. The woman said that if I asked another question she would pick up the bell sitting next to her and ring it.

I had no idea what she was referring to or what to think. This ringing of the bell she quickly explained would alert the townspeople who would then come to lynch me. It took her perhaps one or two minutes to say that. It took a great deal longer for me to register all that information. I suppose because my life had never been threatened, not in that way anyway, did I remain somewhat incredulous.

For a split second I thought I misunderstood her. Until I suddenly remembered a story I had just read in the morning paper,

El Universal, a leading Mexican daily. According to that story, two local journalists while investigating a child sex trafficking case in a nearby town had been lynched by the townspeople and were found dead.

Lynch me? It was time to go!

This happened within seconds. By the time I came to it, 'Victor,' had shot up from his chair, pulled out a number of badges from his pocket and thrown them on her desk. The badges landed squarely in front of the woman. He was also pulling on my right shoulder. I suppose out of fear I had not felt his hand and the fact he was peeling me out of the chair. He clearly wanted us to go.

The woman was unfazed. Calmly, she collected the badges looked intently at Victor and without skipping a beat asked a woman standing nearby to make copies of the identification badges. The man who had walked in the room was staring at all this commotion without saying a word. It was all too bizarre.

The time it took the woman to make copies seemed interminable. Even while standing next to Victor, knowing he would protect me, I was racked with nerves. Within a few minutes the woman returned and handed Victor the badges. Victor grabbed my hand and together we speed walked downstairs and out the door.

As we stepped outside the house and onto the sidewalk a young woman, maybe in her late twenties, whistled to us from behind a van, the same DIF van that was parked outside the house when we arrived. The young woman called out my name and asked us to walk toward her. I wondered how she knew my name.

I was petrified. Victor seemed in total control. He gently pushed me behind him while I literally walked on his heels toward the van. Her name was 'Rita.' She warned us. We were in danger. The woman I had spoken with was indeed the director.

Quickly Rita explained the director could not speak to me since she too was in danger. She had no choice but to corroborate with the cartels or risk retribution or death. There was also the possibility that her family and children might be killed if she went to the police or an outsider. The walls had ears, she reminded us. The woman lived in fear. She had no choice but to obey and give them what they wanted.

Who were they? Who was pulling the strings? The cartels? The young woman would not say. Were local trafficking operators involved? Did they work with the cartels? Again, she would not say. She tried to silence me and handed Victor her telephone number. She suggested we leave at once and asked Victor to call her later that afternoon.

The last thing she told us was that the document on the desk, the one she saw me eyeing, was in fact a list of children living in the area. Apparently, the DIF director was forced to hand over the list of children in her area to the cartels when they came calling. That is how the cartels obtain the children's whereabouts and can so easily abduct them.

Once the abduction takes place the rest of the operation is easy. Since the majority of registered families are indigent, single parents, and or mostly illiterate, few have the courage to speak up and report their missing children to the authorities. Most poor Mexican families like many middle-income Mexican families do not trust the Mexican police or federal authorities.

In Mexico, it is a widely known fact that all three branches of the Mexican police: federal, state and municipal are corrupt. Corruption within the agencies is endemic because most police officers and government officials don't earn enough money to resist the power and influence of the cartels. Cartels have access to a lot of money and too many bribes are handed down at every level of government.

By turning a blind eye and allowing the cartels to traffick children, drugs and weapons, officials and service providers receive a handsome payout. They are also given the opportunity to spare their lives, their families and stay alive, unless of course, they decide to talk.

Child sex trafficking is a $67 billion dollar industry although the figures vary within a few percentage points depending on what human rights report you read. This figure is quickly surpassing drug trafficking in terms of profits. One reason for this dramatic twist might be the appalling statistics confirming the profits made from child pornography. After adult pornography, child pornography is reported to be the second largest business on the Internet in the United States.

By the time I decided to investigate this case child sex trafficking was already considered an epidemic in Mexico especially in San Miguel de Tenancingo. A friend and former Mexican Foreign Minister corroborated my information and took it one step further. When I asked for guidance, his remarks were cold and brutal nevertheless they made sense. He said that until the child of a rich Mexican family or perhaps the child of a government official is trafficked, there is only a small possibility that human trafficking will stop in Mexico. There are simply too many poor children in Mexico and most government officials do not care to focus on the issue.

Given Tenancingo's geographical size, population in 2012 was approximately 10,000, and the per capita income, which remains well below the minimum wage in the United States, most residents, that is about 60.2% of the population, continue to live in close to extreme poverty. The average number of years a child from Tenancingo usually attends school is 8 as compared to the state average, which is 9.

These factors coupled with all the other problems challenging Mexico today have made the town ripe for widespread corruption and a principal source of trafficked children. Recent human trafficking reports indicate the town has become a pipeline for children trafficked to New York, Miami, Palm Beach and other affluent cities in the United States.

The Mexican family I was investigating is still serving lengthy sentences in different U.S. federal penitentiaries. Mr. Epstein however, who allegedly committed some but not all of the same offenses, about the same time frame is free, as are all the alleged procurers who were never charged.

In fact, the Mexican family was prosecuted in a federal court under federal guidelines and was not given the option of a work release program, private cells, or the possibility of parole or serving a partial sentence under house arrest for perpetrating human trafficking crimes. As soon as their sentences are served in the federal penitentiaries they will be automatically deported back to Mexico.

Back in Florida and still somewhat in shock after reading the Epstein articles, I went home early to recuperate from the weariness of it all. The next morning I rang my friend and promised to visit her in the afternoon. Luckily, my cell phone had retained Epstein's telephone number. I rang him at once. If he agreed I would pay him a visit at home. He did not return my call that day.

I left Key Biscayne early the next morning. It was a beautiful summer day. The traffic was light driving northbound on I-95 toward Palm Beach. By the time I exited Okeechobee Boulevard I headed straight east, crossed the Okeechobee Bridge and drove straight to the Palm Beach Police Department on South County Road. I rang the bell waited for an Officer to respond and submitted my inquiry. The police officer asked me to return in half an hour to pick up the files.

I purchased every document available. The files contained every sordid detail of the case including the heinous sex crimes allegedly committed by Epstein, Kellen, Robson, Maxwell and others. Many names were redacted to protect the victim's identities.

After I collected the files, I was impat
I didn't to return home. Instead, I stoppe
on a wooden bench with the files in han
of beautiful fuchsia-colored bougainvillea
page of this unbelievable and repugnant s

It took about two hours to digest all the
document twice---affidavits, arrest reports, and incident reports. I
could not believe my eyes. Suddenly I felt myself emotionally shutting down. I had no idea who Epstein and Maxwell really were. All
along I was wrong, entirely wrong.

For the next few days I thought a great deal about the Epstein
case. Given the limited information I had back then his case
presented several challenges. Soon I realized that as ghastly as the
Mexican case was, it paled in comparison. The primary reason was
because Epstein and his alleged procurers were far more educated;
lived in comfortable surroundings compared to the squalid environment in Mexico; and allegedly were not trafficking the girls to
earn a living.

Apparently, their reasons were far different. One thing was
certain whoever opened up Pandora's Box, was not in an enviable
position.

Stumbling into Epstein's case that week also proved extremely
valuable because it provided a birds eye view to some of the legal
issues that continue to dog law enforcement officials, the Department of Justice and the abolitionist community. In only a couple
of readings, I understood the bigger picture and the many moving
parts that can prevent well-intentioned prosecutors such as R. Alex
Acosta and Ann Marie Villafana from doing their work.

I returned later that afternoon and drove straight to the hospital
to visit my friend. Together we poured through the documents.
Two heads are always better than one, especially when that second
head was hers. After reading the case once again we decided to

ance and more information from the victim's lawyers. I
down the information and made it a point to schedule a
eeting with each attorney: Brad Edwards, Spencer Kuvin, Adam
Horowitz and Robert Josefsberg.

All four attorneys representing the victims in the civil cases
against Epstein were South Florida attorneys. With the exception of Robert Josefsberg, a close friend of Alan Dershowitz who
was solicited by Epstein's legal team to represent Virginia Louise
Roberts (a.k.a. #102), the other attorneys worked independently
of Dershowitz and Epstein's legal team.

I rang the lawyers that week and scheduled a meeting. They
were all very helpful. As soon as my friend was discharged, together
we met Brad Edwards at his Fort Lauderdale office and two private
investigators working the case. A few days later we met Spencer
Kuvin at his West Palm Beach law office.

We were unable to meet Adam Horowitz and Robert Josefsberg
so I spoke to Horowitz and Josefsberg on the phone several times.
Over the course of the next two years, I spoke to all the attorneys multiple times. In spite of Josefsberg's close relationship with
Dershowitz and the Epstein legal team he was very cooperative.

My girlfriend was also an incredible source of support at the
beginning of the investigation. Her insights and information about
Epstein and his world were dazzling. I am forever grateful. Her
friendship and generosity propelled me forward every step of the
way and provided the momentum to continue the research to be
able to write this story.

Thanks to my friend, I also met several of Epstein's neighbors
and a handful of insiders who knew him well. They spoke openly
about their neighbor. I gleaned much insight and information,
especially about his day-to-day activities while on the island. Most
of the information I shared with several attorneys representing the

victims. One fact stuck out, everyone I met believed that Epstein was a very peculiar man.

As I moved further into the investigation it was difficult to understand why Maxwell continued her relationship with Epstein. Given her history and education it did not make sense unless other factors were at play. Maxwell seemed a very capable and intelligent woman. I often wondered what happened to that woman. The woman who seemed unbridled and ready to take on the world. Then I remembered my mother's favorite maxim, "Don't judge a book by its cover," and in this case I would add, its words.

Then one day that summer, in 2010, Epstein rang me. We resumed our conversations albeit on a very different level. He seemed a different person. His personality was radically different over the phone and his *joie de vivre* and sense of humor had all but vanished. He seemed mentally fatigued. We spoke several times while he was still serving time under house arrest. Based on his statements, I'm almost certain the FBI and perhaps other local law enforcement agencies have tapes of our conversations.

Epstein was distant. At times he seemed disoriented. Unlike the conversations we had years earlier, he was circumspect. His voice was gloomy and had lost some of that Brooklyn twang. The accent had been replaced by a somewhat monochromatic tone that left you wondering if he was on anti anxiety medication.

Several times he repeated himself and reminded me we where being taped. Once during a call he insinuated that his attorneys might not be giving him the most-sound advice. I could not judge of course although attorneys make their living by solving problems, criminal or otherwise. Inevitably, the issue of money came up. He was spending a fortune on attorney fees, he said. He asked if I was taping our conversations. I told him the truth that I was not taping him.

He insinuated that his attorneys might not be providing him with the most suitable solutions concerning the press and the "girls." I was never sure if he was telling me the truth or expecting me to refute what he was saying. I decided that in this case listening to him was far better than responding.

In view of the pending civil litigations and omnipresent attorneys and law enforcement agents occupying his life, I should not have expected otherwise. Epstein answered most of my questions with questions. He is very clever. Most people who know him won't argue this point. He seemed interested in my life and what I had to say although the reason why was not sincere. He asked me why I had taken an interest in his case. I told him I was investigating the issue of human trafficking, the Mexican cartels and had reason to believe that some of the girls trafficked to Palm Beach came from Mexico.

He said he had no idea about any of that, which might be true. Apparently, however, he did not make the connection. I asked him if he was familiar with the Mexican trafficking cartels. He said, "No." He had no idea about the Mexican Cartels. I believed him.

When I asked him questions most of Epstein's responses were repetitious, hardly informative and unidirectional. They were not introspective or remotely accurate, as you would expect. He did not explain why he ended up in his predicament; why he preferred underage girls to adult women; or why he was interested in receiving "massages" by inexperienced, unprofessional, and underage school girls. I believe he did not answer any of my questions honestly.

Epstein did not explain why he ended up in a county jail and paid millions of dollars in legal fees. If he were innocent then I believe the luminary attorneys he hired to defend him would have raked the plaintiffs over the coals before the case ever saw the light of the Grand Jury or the Department of Justice.

The hedge fund manager did not accept responsibility for any of the alleged crimes or explain the reason why dozens of girls filed civil suits against him. Several times he implied the girls were extorting him for money. Epstein said that some victims were driven to his house by their boyfriends to extort money from him. It was a scam, he said.

During one conversation, Epstein reminded me of his unfailing memory. Yet he could not remember when or how it was that we met. After our first introduction in the nineties he rang me a couple of times. We met socially through a mutual acquaintance. I ran into him only a few more times at dinner parties in New York. He was always friendly and somewhat smug. By the turn of the century, with the exception of our friend's New Year's Eve celebrations in Palm Beach and the one brunch I attended at his home on New Year's Day, I did not see him again.

By the time we spoke again and only via the telephone, it was 2010. He did not seem to be in need of redemption, quite the contrary. On July 20, 2010, a few days before my first story posted, I rang him again to let him know the story was going to print that next day. He hung up the phone on me. Predictable. After the story posted, at the insistence of my editor, I rang him one more time to ask a few more questions. Epstein did not return my call. We have not spoken since.

Unlike my conversations with Epstein, my chats with Maxwell highlighted several more shades of red. One thing was certain Maxwell and Epstein were the grand masters of profitable triangular relationships. In order to gain a more objective perspective about the couple, I spoke with as many people who knew them as I could find. During 2010 and 2011, I initiated hundreds of conversations with mutual friends, insiders, victims, law enforcement officials, the family members of one victim and the lawyers who represented the plaintiffs.

One of the more enlightening conversations took place with former Palm Beach Police Chief, Michael Reiter. Chief Reiter a likeable and serious man met with me twice, in Palm Beach, at my friend's home. That meeting was followed by several more conversations on the telephone, as my investigation unfolded. He seems to be a man with integrity, courage and not easily persuaded. Thanks to Chief Reiter's depositions, insight, and candid account, I gained a better understanding of the two complex personalities leading the apparent ring and the suspected associates who facilitated the cover up.

Chief Reiter, like so many law enforcement officials who spoke openly with me, held the same opinion of Epstein and Maxwell as several lawyers who represented the victims and many others involved in the case.

The more attorneys I spoke with, the more outrageous the case appeared. During my investigation, I learned how the U.S. government gave Epstein many 'passes' for his alleged crimes. Soon, I began to wonder what on earth was going on. One such 'pass' allowed Epstein to abstain from submitting a State psychological evaluation. When I approached the prosecutor about these issues he was reticent at first.

Thanks to an introduction by a mutual friend in Florida, I had the privilege of meeting the former prosecutor, R. Alex Acosta one day during a breakfast meeting. I spoke to him at length about the issue of human trafficking and what Florida was doing to curb this growing epidemic.

Eventually, I began to ask him questions about the Epstein case. At first he would not respond. Gradually as we became better acquainted and he learned more about my work in the field of human trafficking, I suppose he began to trust me and opened up about the apparent incongruities.

One day when new and important information had come to my attention, Acosta agreed to meet me at the Biltmore Hotel in Coral Gables, Florida. We agreed to exchange information. I had a copy of a memo written during the criminal investigation by a DOJ official to one of Epstein's attorney's. Sensing that I was not going away and that the information was going to be published he suggested I ask my editor, Tina Brown, to allow him to write a response letter for publication.

Tina Brown, the editor in charge of The Daily Beast at the time agreed to post his letter as part of the story. I first posted Mr. Acosta's letter in The Daily Beast in March 2011. The letter explains some of the prosecutor's frustrations:

March 20, 2011

To Whom It May Concern:

I served as U.S. Attorney for the Southern District of Florida from 2005-2009. Over the past weeks, I have read much regarding Mr. Jeffrey Epstein. Some appears true some appears distorted. I thought it appropriate to provide some background, with two caveats: (I) under Justice Department guidelines, I cannot discuss privileged internal communications among Department attorneys and (ii) I no longer have access to the original documents, and as the matter is now nearly 4 years old, the precision of memory is reduced.

The Epstein matter was originally presented to the Palm Beach County State Attorney. Palm Beach Police alleged that Epstein unlawfully hired

underage high-school females to provide him sexu-
ally lewd and erotic massages. Police sought felony
charges that would have resulted in a term of
imprisonment. According to press reports, however,
in 2006 the State Attorney, in part due to concerns
regarding the quality of the evidence, agreed to
charge Epstein only with one count of aggravated
assault with no intent to commit a felony. That
charge would have resulted in no jail time, no
requirement to register as a sexual offender and no
restitution for the underage victims.

Local police were dissatisfied with the State
Attorney's conclusions, and requested a federal
investigation. Federal authorities received the State's
evidence and engaged in additional investigation.
Prosecutors weighed the quality of the evidence and
the likelihood for success at trial. With a federal
case, there were two additional considerations.

First, a federal criminal prosecution requires that
the crime be more than local; it must have an
interstate nexus. Second, as the matter was initially
charged by the state, the federal responsibility is, to
some extent, to backstop state authorities to ensure
that there is no miscarriage of justice, and not to
also prosecute federally that which has already been
charged at the state level.

After considering the quality of the evidence
and the additional considerations, prosecutors
concluded that the state charge was insufficient. In

early summer 2007, the prosecutors and agents in this case met with Epstein's attorney, Roy Black. Mr. Black is perhaps best known for his successful defense of William Kennedy Smith. The prosecutors presented Epstein a choice: plead to a more serious state felony charge (that would result in 2 years' imprisonment, registration as a sexual offender, and restitution for the victims) or else prepare for a federal felony trial.

What followed was a yearlong assault on the prosecution and the prosecutors. I use the word assault intentionally, as the defense in this case was more aggressive than any, which I, or the prosecutors in my office, had previously encountered. Mr. Epstein hired an army of legal superstars: Harvard Professor Alan Dershowitz, former Judge and then Pepperdine Law Dean Kenneth Starr, former Deputy Assistant to the President and then Kirkland Ellis partner Jay Lefkowitz, and several others, including prosecutors who had formally worked in the U.S. Attorney's Office and in the Child Exploitation and Obscenity Section of the Justice Department. Defense attorneys next requested a meeting with me to challenge the prosecution and the terms previously presented by the prosecutors in their meeting with Mr. Black.

The prosecution team and I met with defense counsel in Fall 2007, and I reaffirmed the office's position: two years, registration and restitution, or trial.

Over the next several months, the defense team presented argument after argument claiming that felony criminal proceedings against Epstein were unsupported by the evidence and lacked a basis in law, and that the office's insistence on jail-time was motivated by zeal to overcharge a man merely because he is wealthy. They bolstered their arguments with legal opinions from well-known legal experts. One member of the defense team warned that the office's excess zeal in forcing a good man to serve time in jail might be the subject of a book if we continued to proceed with this matter. My office systematically considered and rejected each argument, and when we did, my office's decisions were appealed to Washington. As to the warning, I ignored it.

The defense strategy was not limited to legal issues. Defense counsel investigated individual prosecutors and their families, looking for personal peccadilloes that may provide a basis for disqualification. Disqualifying a prosecutor is an effective (though rarely used) strategy, as eliminating the individuals most familiar with the facts and thus most qualified to take a case to trial harms likelihood for success. Defense counsel tried to disqualify at least two prosecutors. I carefully reviewed, and then rejected, these arguments.

Despite this army of attorneys, the office held firm to the terms first presented to Mr. Black in the original meeting. On June 30, 2008, after yet another last minute appeal to Washington D.C. was rejected,

Epstein pled guilty in state court. He was to serve 18 months imprisonment, register as a sexual offender for life and provide restitution to the victims.

Some may feel that the prosecution should have been tougher. Evidence that has come to light, since 2007, may encourage that view. Many victims have since spoken out, filing detailed statements in civil cases seeking damages. Physical evidence has since been discovered. Had these additional statements and evidence been known, the outcome may have been different. But there were not known to us at the time.

A prosecution decision must be based on admissible facts known at the time. In cases of this type, those are unusually difficult because victims are frightened and often decline to testify or if they do speak, they give contradictory statements. Our judgment in this case, based on the evidence known at the time, was that it was better to have a billionaire serve time in jail, register as a sex offender and pay his victims restitution than risk a trial with a reduced likelihood of success. I supported that judgment then, and based on the state of the law as it then stood and the evidence known at that time, I would support that judgment again.

Epstein's treatment, while in state custody, likewise may encourage the view that the office should have been tougher. Epstein appears to have received highly unusual treatment while in jail. Although the terms of confinement in a state prison are a matter appropriately left to the State of Florida, and not federal authorities, without doubt, the treatment that he received while in state custody undermined the purpose of a jail sentence.

Some may also believe that the prosecution should have been tougher in retaliation for the defense's tactics. The defense, arguably, often failed to nego-tiate in good faith. They would obtain concessions as part of a negotiation and agree to proceed, only to change their minds, and appeal the office's position to Washington. The investigations into the family lives of individual prosecutors were, in my opinion, uncalled for, as were the accusations of bias and / or misconduct against individual prosecutors.

At times, some prosecutors felt that we should just go to trial, and at times I felt that frustra-tion myself. What was right in the first meeting, however, remained right irrespective of defense tactics. Individuals have a constitutional right to a defense. The aggressive exercise of that right should not be punished, nor should a defense counsel's exercise of their right to appeal a U.S. Attorney to Washington D.C. Prosecutors must be careful not to allow frustration and anger with defense counsel to influence their judgment.

After the plea, I recall receiving several phone calls. One was from the FBI Special Agent-In-Charge. He called to offer congratulations. He had been at many of the meetings regarding this case. He was aware of the tactics of the defense, and he called to praise our prosecutors for holding firm against the likes of Messrs. Black, Dershowitz, Lefkowitz and Starr. It was a proud moment. I also received calls or communications from Messrs. Dershowitz, Lefkowitz and Starr. I had known all three individuals previously, from my time in law school and at Kirkland Ellis in the mid 90s. They all sought to make peace. I agreed to talk and meet with each of them after Epstein pled guilty, as I think it important that prosecutors battle defense attorneys in a case and then move on. I have tried, yet I confess that has been difficult to do fully in this case.

The bottom line is this: Mr. Epstein, a billionaire, served time in jail and is now a registered sex offender. He has been required to pay his victims restitution, though restitution clearly cannot compensate for the crime. And we know much more today about his crimes because the victims have come forward to speak out.

Some may disagree with the prosecutorial judgments made in this case, but those individuals are not the ones who at the time reviewed the evidence available for trial and assessed the likelihood of success.

Respectfully,
R. Alexander Acosta
Former U.S. Attorney
Southern District of Florida

What made his case so gripping was to witness up close and personal the dark side of humanity and how Epstein knew exactly what he was doing every step of the way. It became crystal clear that money and influence almost never take a back seat to justice.

CHAPTER NINE

MONEY & SECRETS MAKE THE WORLD GO ROUND

*"Facts are stubborn things: and whatever may be our wishes, our
inclinations or the dictates of our passion,
they cannot alter the state of facts and evidence."*
John Adams

"I'm not a sexual predator, I'm an 'offender,' bellowed Epstein to the New York Post on February 25, 2011. "It's the difference between a murderer and a person who steals a bagel."[93]

Epstein grew up in a household of five including his father, a former New York City park ranger, his mother a homemaker and the three children: Epstein, his sister, Paula, and a younger brother, Mark, who oversees his brother's real estate properties.[94]

In the late seventies, while tutoring a young student in mathematics, Ted Greenberg, Epstein's life took a meteoric turn. But before the drastic career change and in spite of his lack of academic credentials—or any other meaningful credentials—Epstein had managed to eke out a living by teaching at one of Manhattan's elite preparatory schools and tutoring students after school.

One day, Epstein met Ted Greenberg's father. Alan Greenberg, better known as "Ace," became chairman of Bear Stearns after he hired Epstein as an "options trader," in 1976. Possibly, it was Ace who ultimately changed the course of Epstein's life. Given Greenberg's lofty position as chairman, their meeting became a defining moment for the ambitious Epstein.

Greenberg who died on July 25, 2014, never fully revealed why he hired and suddenly fired his protégé only months after he was made a partner at the firm. A Daily Beast story posted on January 6, 2015 claimed that Epstein was found guilty by Bear Stearns of a Reg D violation, in other words insider trading. It seems, however, the primary reason Greenberg employed Epstein was because his son, Ted, had advanced well beyond his expectations thanks to Epstein's tutoring abilities.[95]

Unlike CEOs of other investment houses, Greenberg had a penchant for hiring what he referred to as "PSD" candidates: poor, smart and disadvantaged. He coined the term because the young men he preferred to employ were just that: poor, smart, and determined. Many did not have M.B.A. degrees. During the early years of his career Ace, "had been rejected by a number of 'white shoe' investment firms when… first looking for work in New York."[96]

Another man, beside Greenberg, also played an instrumental role in Epstein's life. His name was James (Jimmy) Cayne, Greenberg's boss and CEO. Cayne also admired Epstein. Years later, after Epstein left the investment house, Cayne revealed, "Epstein's forte was dealing with wealthier clients, helping them with their overall portfolios."[97]

As one of Ace's longtime friends, an employee at the trading desk and later a substantial investor in one of the firm's largest real estate funds, Epstein, had the dirt that's fit to print on most everyone in the firm.

As history reveals, Greenberg's obituary in *The New York Times*, imparted how Greenberg, "played a major role as Bear Stearns experienced one of Wall Street's legendary roller-coaster rides, a climb to dizzying heights as one of the country's biggest brokerages, and a breathtaking free fall to the brink of bankruptcy. Stuck with billions in all-but-worthless mortgage securities as its clients made a run on the bank, Bear Stearns was taken over the JPMorgan Chase in a $270 million fire sale sanctioned by the Federal Reserve." As an insider, who played on both sides of the fence, Epstein clearly knew when to strike.[98]

Ironically, in 2007, while negotiating his Non Prosecution Agreement plea with the Justice Department and before the investment firm crashed and burned, it was Epstein who allegedly played a role in the demise of two subprime hedge funds at Bear Stearns known as structured funds.

The arrests came on June 19, 2008, when two Bear Stearns hedge fund directors, Ralph Cioffi and Matthew Tannin, were charged with securities fraud. The strange thing is that Epstein had never met Cioffi or Tannin. Cioffi's email sent to me on November 17, 2014 explained, "I never knew Epstein at Bear. Never met him while he was an employee or even as an investor in the fund."

The case brought by the Justice Department sought to prove that Cioffi and Tannin deceived their investors, including Epstein. According to several reports the case was weak and hinged on a couple of e-mails that were taken out of context. Nevertheless, Cioffi and Tannin were charged with securities fraud and Bank of America subsequently filed a Complaint against the two men.

After their arrests, The New York Times reported, they "were among the few executives to face a trial on criminal charges in the aftermath of the financial crisis… The bank accused the two men of lying about the health of their hedge funds, which had invested heavily in subprime mortgage-backed securities that plummeted in value when the housing market collapsed." Judge Alison J. Nathan of Federal District Court in Manhattan, "rejected Bank of America's claims of fraud and breach of fiduciary duty, ruling that bank had failed to prove damages tied to the conduct of the two men."[99]

Conceivably by professing to give the government inside information such as the internal workings of Bear Stearns and the structured funds, Epstein and his attorneys were able to negotiate a better plea deal with the Department of Justice in return for lesser charges and less jail time.

Perhaps Epstein realized during the beginning of the negotiations, that he was able to strike back against the firm who fired him at their most vulnerable. Two years after Epstein's sentencing, in 2009, Cioffi and Tannin were found not guilty and their cases were acquitted. The November 11, 2009 New York Times story claimed the jury had reasonable doubt on every count filed against them.

I spoke with Ralph Cioffi on a number of occasions about his case. Later, on November 17, 2014, Cioffi explained, "I do not know why Epstein was fired from Bear Stearns and doubt Matt would. I never knew Epstein at Bear. Never met him while he was an employee or even as an investor in the fund." By early January of the following year, 2015, Cioffi warned me, "Epstein is an evil person. Makes the 'root of all evil is money' phrase ring true. With Epstein, there were always rumors about what went on, on his jet when flying back and forth from Europe," Cioffi said.[100]

A New York Times best selling book that became a popular film, "The Big Short," written by Michael Lewis, tells a story about the questionable standards at Bear Stearns and how management at Stearns had a tendency to operate. In the book, Charlie and Jamie, two of the lead characters explained they, "wanted to move their account, (their investment pool was approximately twelve million dollars), from Charles Schwab to Bear Stearns and mentioned it to their accountant, who supposedly knew Greenberg." The story revealed that, "without ever meeting Greenberg, once they moved their assets to Bear Stearns, their brokerage statements soon came back with Greenberg's name on top. The investors were perplexed 'that Greenberg suddenly became their broker. They called him on several occasions to talk." Greenberg occasionally answered but did not respond. 'Hold on,' he would say and immediately pass the phone to his assistant. Months later, when the three finally met, 'the encounter was so brief, that they could not honestly say whether they had ever met Ace Greenberg. The men were ushered in for thirty seconds—literally thirty seconds—and then ceremoniously ushered out," said Jamie." Although Ace Greenberg was formally on paper their broker they never once spoke to him.[101]

During the meltdown, it was interesting to witness who refused to do the bidding. Unlike most employees who worked at Lehman Brothers, it was not surprising that "Greenberg did not entirely drink the Kool-Aid." Instead he, "cashed in and sold his stake for $50 million in Bear Stearns shares…In 2008, following the firm's collapse, Ace signed a lucrative contract with JPMorgan to stay on as vice chairman emeritus and take 40 percent of trading commissions he generated." If Ace were alive today, he might even thank Epstein for his role in that deal.[102]

With a financial collapse looming tall in the horizon and a global financial disaster quickly forthcoming, the Department Of Justice perhaps felt compelled to negotiate a deal that favored Epstein. Particularly because the Justice Department had no way of verifying the strength of his relationships. In fact, one of Epstein's better-known friend's, Larry Summers, who traveled with Epstein on his private jet between 1997 and 2005, according to pilot logs, was a very respected man in the United States.

Larry Summers, who I met during a dinner at my friend Ken Brody's Washington D.C. home, in Kalorama, was a former Treasury Secretary and Harvard University President. Brody had been one of his informal advisors between 2004-2006, when Summers was doing consulting work at Brody's company, Taconic Capital.

One thing I've learned about friends in high places is that they tend to gravitate close to one another and move in concentric circles. They remain, without a doubt, a closed boys network through and through. Brody, a brilliant financial advisor was a Goldman Sachs veteran with more than twenty years under his belt at the firm. He was former Chairman of the Export Import Bank during the Clinton administration and managed Bill Clinton's fund raising efforts in 1992 during the New York primary.

Summer's who had served as Harvard University President just a year prior to Epstein's indictment had been vociferously reporting the impending crisis. On September 23, 2007, just weeks before Epstein finalized the Non Prosecution Agreement, Summers reported to the Financial Times that, "Central to every policy discussion in response to a financial crisis or the prospect of a crisis is the connect of moral hazard."[103]

Given the high level conversations that took place behind closed doors in October 2007, I doubt the financial climate did not play a role during the negotiations that led to Epstein's final sweetheart Non Prosecution Agreement (NPA), signed October 27, 2007.

Given the long-term vision and goals of the Justice Department, perhaps keeping Epstein on the outside a while longer rather than locked behind a cell suited their purposes. Certainly, Epstein's ostensible connections on 'The Street' and disposition to cooperate, to bring forward alleged Wall Street scoundrels might have made it more palatable for DOJ. It certainly would have made it easier for DOJ to have Epstein, an informed insider, on the outside collecting information they might conceivable exploit in pending or future Wall Street cases.

In light of Epstein's personal investments and those of his primary better known client, Leslie Wexner, the predator's "inside information' might have aided DOJ in a number of ways most obviously by lessening their load and providing the agency with much needed backroom access.

As an informer, Epstein certainly made for a colorful figure. Given his position at the firm, both as an insider and client, the disgruntled Bear Stearns employee and angry investor could certainly teach DOJ a thing or two about the financial markets, hedge funds and what they needed to know about Wall Street's overreach.

It is feasible that by agreeing to reduce Epstein's sentence, the Justice Department avoided hundreds of hours of research and averted hour-long meetings with Wall Street's top executives that perhaps might not have been so forthcoming.

As the world learned only too late, the financial climate during Epstein's criminal investigation, in 2007, was bleak; Unlike anything ever experienced on Wall Street since the Great Depression of 1929. Between 2006 and 2007, given the billions being made in the markets, it seemed that only a few honest men were willing to risk their future earnings by sharing accurate information with the general public. By the end of 2007, when DOJ and Epstein negotiated his plea deal, the plunging markets began their descent.

An alarming report published in *The New York Times* a year prior to the stock market collapse, showed how Bear Stearns averted a meltdown even though "hedge funds and pensions funds"—several of which Epstein was an investor---"could be left holding billions of dollars in bonds and securities backed by loans that were quickly losing their value."[104] The same report held that a, "hedge fund and a related fund that suffered millions in losses and shocked investors had begun asking for their money back. The firm agreed to buy out several Wall Street banks that had lent the fund money, that managers hoped would avoid a broader sell-off without causing a meltdown in the once-booming market for mortgage securities."[105]

Conceivably, it was not just Epstein's high-level banking and political connections that prevented him from a stiff federal prosecution. Perhaps, his generous donations to several Democratic Party leaders protected him and secured a successful defense. Donations to Democratic Party leaders included: Bill and Hillary Clinton even after his indictment, Governor Bill Richardson, former New York Governor Eliot Spitzer, and several others. According to media reports The Clinton Foundation received a $25,000 donation in 2006, after Epstein was charged with solicitation of prostitution with a minor.[106]

A Forbes article reported, "Many people still attribute the financial crisis of 2008 to "greed," a lack of regulatory policies and free market capitalism." While other Wall Street insiders claim the *real cause*—which has yet to be acknowledged, let alone curbed or removed—was *government intervention* in *the markets*. There is no doubt that in this mix, Epstein played a role as an, albeit small, investor and more importantly, as Leslie Wexner's financial advisor. This lethal combination, Forbes maintained, included the Federal Reserve's disruptive manipulations of interest rates, massive subsidies and regulations in housing, banking, and mortgages." Forbes argued that, "for years government policy promoted reckless financial practices (aka "moral hazard") that made things worse by bailing out the worst miscreants."[107]

If this is true, then it is plausible the Federal Government acknowledged and allowed Epstein's recommendations and information relating to Bear Stearns to be part of the negotiations. Whatever the truth is, one fact is indisputable: The Department of Justice signed a plea deal that was far less defensible than what the U.S. Attorney's Office in Florida had originally prescribed and subsequently regretted given Acosta's Mary 20, 2011 letter.

One reason the Bear Stearns' financial shortcomings are worth mentioning is because, in early 2007, their stock was trading at $170 per share and by the end of 2008, after Epstein signed the Non Prosecution Agreement, their shares were selling under $2.00 per share. The price offered by JPMorgan Chase to purchase the company. Eventually, the offer was raised to $10 per share to ease stockholder backlash and to ensure a quick closure of the proposed transaction.

Could the loss in share price have been partially a result of Epstein's information? As Greenberg wrote in a book published in 2010, "The bank run that swallowed Bear Stearns in 2008 stemmed from a "groundless rumor" that it had a liquidity problem." Clearly, Greenberg felt that someone had started false rumors.[108] To answer Greenberg's question of course would require a much broader investigation to determine if Epstein had a degree of culpability.

As a result of the purchase, most of Bear Stearns' 14,000 employees lost their jobs and some of them lost their entire life savings. Many Wall Street reports claimed that 30 percent of the company's equity was held by employees including senior executives who were also wiped out. After the fact, it is easier to understand how the firm's unspoken rules and dubious ethics could attract murky characters such as Epstein. It is now also easier to understand Greenberg's attraction. After all, Bear Stearns was a competitive juggernaut that encouraged a "dog-eat-dog" attitude as part of its corporate culture.

Unlike other more genteel Wall Street investment firms, Bear Stearns was a rough and tumble boxing ring that allowed Epstein's character to flourish even if only for a short while. It was known on 'The Street' that, "Greenberg invested a decade nurturing a culture where sharp-elbowed candidates were cultivated for the benefit of the company."[109]

Although there is a 27-year lapse between Epstein's exiting the firm, in 1981, and the 2008 financial collapse, those in-between years, Epstein maintained a very close relationship with the leadership of the bank, including his friends, Jimmy Cayne and Greenberg in particular. He was also on top of his game and the direction the investment house was taking.

Beyond his relationships at the firm, Epstein's influence and success was in part due to his access to Wexner's vast wealth and investment portfolio, which over time allowed him to leverage his position, gain financial liquidity, and exploit the investment house's moneymaking mechanisms such as their financial instruments and products. Before the firm's demise, the shrewd manipulator served his revenge cold and by September 2008, when the markets imploded, Epstein had the last laugh at the crumbling firm.

Perhaps, the impending Wall Street fallout; failure of the world financial markets; and the firm's imminent collapse, all contributed in one way or another to the sweetening of Epstein's deal.[110] Given Epstein's considerable financial losses at Bear Stearns and the government's potential liability, the two became one and part of the formula for a sweetheart deal.

CHAPTER TEN

ALFREDO RODRIGUEZ: BURIED SECRETS

Two wrongs do not one right make.

Alfredo Rodriguez, Epstein's house manager cum butler committed a federal crime and was sentenced on June 18, 2010 to eighteen months in a federal prison for obstructing justice during a federal investigation.

In light of Epstein's suspected crimes, the criminal prosecution of Alfredo Rodriguez, Epstein's former house manager between 2004-2005, was a travesty. Born in Chile, the 56 year-old Rodriguez was an American citizen when he was indicted.

Rodriguez's imprudent behavior, withholding a copy of Epstein's 2005 "little black book" containing the names and addresses of Epstein's friends, victims and associates, did not warrant such extreme punishment within the context of the greater picture, given the evidence already in custody at the Department of Justice.

After Epstein was charged with sex crimes against minor girls, in 2005, most of the evidence against him was in possession of law enforcement officials. It was not until years later, in 2009 that

Rodriguez attempted to sell, for fifty thousand dollars, his 2005 version of the 'little black book,' or 'Holy Grail,' as he referred to it, when talking to an undercover agent.

Several media reports said the charge was in connection with Rodriguez trying to obtain $50,000 from civil attorneys pursuing several civil sexual assault cases against Epstein as payment for producing the book to the attorney's."[111]

"Rodriguez claimed he needed money because the journal or was his "property" and that he was afraid that Jeffrey Epstein would make him "disappear" unless he had an "insurance policy" i.e., the 'little black book.'"[112]

Rodriguez's story sounds as if perhaps someone was looking to strip him of all credibility or wanted him behind bars for fear of what else he might disclose to the government. As a result of his untimely death, many facts shall remain a mystery.

The Rodriguez case began in 2009. At the time, the former house manager lived in Kendall, a southwestern district in Miami, Florida, with his second wife, Bolivian-born, Patricia Dunn, a real estate agent. Rodriguez had four children from two marriages; Cristina Rodriguez, aged 15, who lived with her mother; and Christopher Dunn, his wife's son, who lived with the couple. His two elder children, Cristina's siblings, Monica and Sergio Rodriguez lived on their own.

Rodriguez's wife, Dunn, never met Epstein's victims although according to Rodriguez's deposition, she knew the stories. Before Rodriguez went to work for Epstein, during a career that spanned eight to ten years as house manager, Rodriguez worked for several families.

A handful of his employees were identified in court documents: "Ms. Hammond lived in Palm Beach, Florida; Arturo Torres lived between Fisher Island, Florida and his Texas ranch; and Leona

Helmsley lived in New York." Once referring to Ms. Helmsley, Rodriguez remarked she, 'was a very demanding lady.'

For a brief stint and prior to Epstein's employment, Rodriguez worked at the Montauk Lake Club & Marina in Long Island, New York, where, according to his deposition, former President Richard Nixon would occasionally visit.

During the early part of my investigation, whenever I attempted to speak with Rodriguez by phone or in person, his wife would almost always intervene. At the time, Epstein was serving the latter part of his sentence--18 months of house arrest (or community control) at this Palm Beach estate. We spoke twice. Rodriguez was undoubtedly terrified to discuss the case with a journalist given his ongoing investigation.

As with any person placed in a position of trust, Rodriguez was a pivotal witness. Someone who could provide a unique perspective into Epstein's psyche, character, and the crimes, Epstein allegedly committed. When on the rare occasion I spoke with his wife, our conversation did not prove valuable. She glossed over many facts and was perpetually in a hurry. I can't say I blame her given what she was going through.

Frustrated by Rodriguez's inaccessibility, I made it a point to have additional conversations with law enforcement, lawyers, victims, prosecutors and other insiders working his case. A former law enforcement agent turned private investigator explained extensively the house manager's role within the Epstein household. Thanks to detective I was able to secure copies of Rodriguez's video taped deposition.

Rodriguez was an important witness because unlike the rest of Epstein's Palm Beach house staff, he paid the victims directly, was close to Epstein, and was closer to most of Epstein's staff and alleged procurers. It appears Rodriguez, more than most staff members, understood Epstein, had plenty of inside information and was not afraid to speak with the police.

Like some of the victims, alleged procurers and staff, he also spoke Spanish, a benefit that added to his attributes. As a male employee, he also had more opportunities to become familiar with Epstein in ways that female employees could not. More importantly, as a disgruntled employee, he had an ax to grind. In Rodriguez's attempt to arbitrarily seek justice and make some extra money, the man did just the opposite. After he copied the 'little black book,' he hid it for a while until he felt the timing was right. Evidently, it was wrong.

An interesting detail revealed later in the case, after Rodriguez was sentenced, showed that DOJ had a copy of the same 2005 "little black book" in their possession. This would have made Rodriguez's copy extraneous. If the prosecutors had a copy of the same version, then why would they charge Rodriguez with 'obstruction of justice'?

In fact Rodriguez was never charged with physical or sexual assault, solicitation of prostitution, abuse or anything related to sexual crimes against children. He was also not charged with the intent to coerce, lure or deceive underage girls for sex. He did not harm or permanently destroy the lives of countless adolescent girls; and yet for a crime seemingly much less harmful and perhaps unfounded, in light of the evidence that later surfaced, the man served the same amount of time in a federal prison as Epstein did for sexual crimes committed against a minor.

According to my investigation, Rodriguez's life began to unravel around the same time he lost his job. Epstein's justification for firing his house manager seemed disingenuous. According to court records, Epstein claimed Rodriguez had stolen from him. In fact, the last person Epstein needed lurking around his house during a criminal investigation was the all-seeing houseman who knew his dirty secrets.

Rodriguez was the one person, alongside the alleged procurers, pilots and victims who knew where all the bones were buried. Given the butler's history and culture, he might have been the only staff member who outwardly showed contempt for Epstein's deviant behavior. No doubt, Rodriguez was far too dangerous a witness for the prosecution.[113]

His access to victims and Epstein's friends also posed a greater threat. According to the recorded deposition, he was asked many times to make the payments to a number of underage girls who came to give Epstein a "massage." Since most people believe that money usually banks on the side of money, it made it difficult for Rodriguez to look for he same line of work, as a houseman or butler, in Palm Beach or nearby areas. He was also very scared what gossip Epstein was spreading about him.

With a stain on his record and in fear of what Epstein's power and influence could buy, Rodriguez refused to approach potential employees after he was let go. What he did not know was that by mid 2005, around the same time he was desperately looking for employment, Epstein was under a criminal investigation.

By 2009, unable to find work, the man was in a desperate financial state unable to support his wife and family. Conceivably, from a place of wretched fear, he reached out unwittingly, to an undercover agent. I spoke with the agent right after their phone call and he confessed that he felt sorry for the man. Then at around the time Rodriguez's deposition was taken, August 7, 2009, several attorneys were involved in the case representing a number of victims. Those present in the deposition included Brad Edwards, Bob Kritten and Richard Willis. Below are valuable 'on the record,' slices of conversation.

The conversations I expose below make up four video taped interviews. Rodriguez's previous allegations, given to the police during the 2005 investigation exposing a handful of potential witnesses, victims, and procurers are reinforced in his deposition.

The recorded statements described his duties as house manager, which included but were not limited to "answering the door, mainly the kitchen door for practical reasons so the girls would not to walk through the main house," and "waiting in the kitchen with the girls until Kellen arrived." As a manager he was also, "required to carry with him $2,000 more or less, every day."[114]

Rodriguez revealed that his pocket money was partially used, "to pay the young girls after the massage was given, and that, Kellen would call him by telephone at the conclusion of each 'massage', but not every massage, in order to pay the girls." Rodriguez would "pay them in cash either in the kitchen or the driveway." He said, cash was always given to them inside an envelope.[115]

His testimony described how "Kellen kept notes and pieces of papers with names of girls who came to give 'massages' and telephone numbers." Rodriguez said, "everything we did would be recorded in the internal circuit through Citrix so it could be accessed by other employees." In other words, most of the staff's activities "everything the house staff organized was recorded on house computers that way all staff could access [that] information." He said Kellen worked mostly out of the dining room, had a laptop, but did not send emails to Rodriguez.[116]

The transcript stated that Rodriguez, not Kellen, was the person in charge of communicating with staff via email and always used the Citrix house system. He would email everyone including "Ms. Maxwell, who Rodriguez claimed kept a list of names and phone numbers and photos of young girls who came to do "massages" on her computer too…

Maxwell kept her office under the stairs next to the kitchen," he said. Rodriguez also communicated via email with Bella, Epstein's assistant in New York and Leslie, his secretary in New York and all household managers in Paris, Manhattan and the island." 'The island' as he referred to it, was Epstein's home base in Little St. James, a private and secluded island in the U.S.V.I.[117]

Rodriguez said that Kellen kept photographs on her laptop of many, ostensibly underage girls who would come to give 'Epstein massages'. Some "pictures," Rodriguez confirmed, "Of the girls were taken out of the country and some in the Palm Beach house. There were several photographic cameras in the house, small compact cameras."[118]

"Kellen used one of those cameras to take pictures of some girls," and some were nude young girls, Rodriguez claimed. One nude was "Nadia Marcinkova, alias Nadia Marcinkov, Epstein's underage girlfriend from Yugoslavia at the time, and a Brazilian girl who would stay on occasion at the El Brillo house but I can't remember her name."[119]

Rodriguez confessed that he was unaware that Epstein had surveillance video equipment installed throughout the house during his employment. It was not until after his termination notice that he found out when he read about the cameras in a court file. He remembers however, "there were always problems with the computers and so a young technician from New Albany, Ohio would come to the Epstein's house to maintain the computers and equipment.

The technician "was the only one allowed to touch the equipment in the house because it was very sophisticated equipment. The man was in charge of computers, videos and phone system. They had about 15 phones in the Palm Beach house," Rodriguez said.[120] He does not remember the technician's name, but said the man, "worked for Mr. Epstein in New Albany, Ohio." New Albany was the city Epstein and Leslie Wexner had their offices. Epstein travelled extensively to New Albany, Ohio where his friend Leslie Wexner and his family live and maintain their base of operations.

"Sometimes, David," Epstein's chef, "also interacted with the young girls who came to give Epstein 'massages.' Some young girls who came to the house brought other young girls to give 'massages,'" Rodriguez explained. "Sometimes, I would pay the girls who brought other girls to give Epstein 'massage' between $300 and $500 dollars even though they did not give Epstein a massage."

Rodriguez admitted he never had a conversation with Maxwell or Kellen concerning the photographs taken of young girls he found in their computers. Richard Willis, an attorney present at the 2009 deposition asked Rodriguez if he had spoken to anyone concerning the Epstein case in the years following his termination. Rodriguez confirmed that he spoke about the Epstein case only to his wife. He kept notes and a journal that where eventually given to Palm Beach Police Detective, Joe Recarey. He claimed to have kept the journal at home for a while and then offered it to the detective. "I had some information and put everything in the file that I gave to Detective Recarey."[121]

Some of Rodriguez's allegations taken from his first deposition initiated by the Palm Beach Police Department and witnessed by a Florida State Attorney, identified as Ms. Weiss, were later used by attorneys to question him during the 2009 deposition. During the taped deposition, Rodriguez told the attorneys that during several conversations with the Palm Beach Police Department and FBI, the agents took notes, but did not ask him to review the statements, or sign a document relating to their conversation. In fact, according to the 2009 tapes, Rodriguez never had the opportunity to review his statements.

Presumably, on three or four occasions, the houseman spoke to Detective Recarey yet, according to Rodriguez, the Detective noted only one taped statement of a single conversation. If that statement is accurate then Detective Recarey failed to follow police protocol since he should have taken notes of all their conversations and had Rodriguez sign a document each time they met. Perhaps there was a lapse in judgment by the Detective given the pressure on the Police department to perform during this particular investigation.[122]

Rodriguez also informed Epstein's attorney, Bob Kritten that, "when all these actions were taking place I was under an environment where I was…afraid of reprisal, from Mr. Epstein and Ms. Maxwell against me, because I had signed a confidentiality agreement."[123] Given the butler's premature death, the public will never know if Rodriguez was truly afraid of Epstein and Maxwell or perhaps felt pressured by the circumstances and those protecting his former boss.

At the time his original statement was given to the Palm Beach Police Department, Rodriguez believed the victims were over the age of 18. During the 2009 deposition, he admitted he miscommunicated and misinterpreted some facts. When answering questions about Ghislaine Maxwell's participation, Rodriguez claimed, "we use to have internal books for pilots, masseuses, and chefs, so Ghislaine had a copy of the black book as well and copies in the computer."[124]

It wasn't until 2009 that Rodriguez revealed he had gone into Maxwell's computer in her office without permission. He "turned it on to send some documents to the New York office since it was the only computer working at the time in the house," he told attorneys.[125]

Rodriguez sent a number of files to Epstein's New York office using the Citrix system. His computer, he claimed, "Was slower and always breaking down which is why the guy from New Albany, Ohio was always coming over."[126] He informed Kritten, that he logged on (Maxwell's computer) because "it was the only computer working in the house that day," and he felt he had the right and "could use anything in the house to accomplish my job." When asked if Maxwell also kept names of girls who came to give massages, Rodriguez, answered, "Yes."[127]

Most of the computers, he said, including Ghislaine's, contained a transcript of all incoming calls, message and telephone numbers. In fact, that was not the only time Rodriguez accessed Maxwell's personal computer, he logged on several more times without her permission. Rodriguez also admitted he used Kellen's computer but never Epstein's. Rodriguez confirmed that, "all incoming calls that came to 358 El Brillo were recorded via a transcript of sorts through several computers," so whenever, Epstein or Maxwell wanted to see the missing calls they could access the appropriate computer and retrieve the information.[128]

"The only computers that could access missed calls and messages were Maxwell's, Kellen's and El Brillo's main computer," he said. He could not remember any of the email addresses given to him or those that belonged to the staff during his employment.[129]

Later on during the deposition, Kritten questioned Rodriguez about Alan Dershowitz and his presence at Epstein's home in Palm Beach. Rodriguez confirmed, "Dershowitz was there. Epstein and Mr. Dershowitz were friends," he said. Kritten asked Rodriguez if, "Dershowitz was at Epstein's house when the woman who gave the massage was present in the home?" "I don't remember that, Sir," responded Rodriguez.[130]

Rodriguez was told to clarify the potential allegations swirling around Dershowitz and the alleged "massages" with underage girls. Rodriguez said he did not know. Kritten asked several more times in several different ways. "Is it your testimony that Mr. Dershowitz was there when any of the women came to Mr. Epstein's home to give a massage?"

"Yes," Rodriguez said.[131]

Kritten asked him, "Were any of those women ever associated with Mr. Dershowitz? Would it be a correct statement you have absolutely no knowledge?" Rodriguez answered, "I don't know, Sir. " Kritten asked again, "You don't know?"

"Where you in any way attempting in your response to imply that Mr. Dershowitz had a massage by one of these young ladies. "I don't know, Sir," Rodriguez responded. "You have no knowledge?" Kristen said. "No, Sir," Rodriguez responded. Not satisfied with his answer, Kritten asked the same question again. Rodriguez responded again, "No, Sir."

"You certainly weren't implying that that occurred, you just have no knowledge," Kritten said. "I don't know. I don't know," Rodriguez repeated.[132] Later, during the deposition, Rodriguez, confirmed he had seen pictures of Nadia, *nee* Marcinkova, now Marcinko and "Epstein's girlfriend at the time," in Ghislaine's computer. She appeared, he said, to be in her twenties. In fact, Nadia Marcinkova was allegedly 14 years old, in 2005, when Epstein brought her to the U.S. from Eastern Europe to live with him in Palm Beach. It is still a mystery how Epstein met the 14 year old and convinced her family to allow their teenage daughter to move with him to the United States.

Rodriguez made several important statements that day. He confirmed Kellen worked for Epstein starting in 2002 or 2003, two years prior to Rodriguez's arrival. He said that during a conversation with Luella, Epstein's housekeeper in Palm Beach, she shared her uneasiness about the sex toys Epstein kept in his bedroom. Rodriguez was receptive to her concerns and said he had placed them inside an armoire at the end of his bed. This prevented her from having any further contact with the objects.

A man named Balson became also his mentor and "a good friend" during his tenure at Epstein's home. Balson was Epstein's Brazilian house manager in Paris. Apparently, Epstein sent Balson to train Rodriguez in Palm Beach when he first arrived because the Brazilian house manager knew Epstein's taste and style and had been in his service awhile.

Rodriguez explained that besides owning the largest triplex in Manhattan, Epstein also had a home in Paris, in one of the finest streets at 22 Avenue Foch in the 16th *Arrondisement*. This is one of the most exclusive neighborhoods in the city where the road is lined from top to end with chestnut trees. It is an important avenue that runs from the *Arc de Triumph* to the *Port Dauphine* at the edge of *the Bois de Boulogne,* one of Paris's most coveted parks.

Rodriguez explained that Balson had initially confessed to him how Epstein, "had a lot 'massages' over there too," meaning, at his Paris home. Brad Edwards then asked him, "How did it come up whether or not Epstein had massages at the Paris home?"[133] Balson "came to Palm Beach on two occasions," Rodriguez explained, "and stayed with me for a week." Epstein required his new houseman, "to get into Balson's style of running the house. He was good enough to give me some inside information about what he liked and didn't like."[134]

In 2005, and again, in 2009, Rodriguez admitted that whenever Epstein was in Palm Beach, he usually had two "massages" per day. Based on the earlier deposition, Edwards asked him if, "Balson had described the Paris massages and the girls in a similar fashion to the ones given him in Palm Beach? "Yes, Sir," replied Rodriguez. Their conversation then picked up speed.[135]

EDWARDS: "Did he indicate how old these girls were," Edwards asked.

RODRIGUEZ: "No, Sir."

Beside Balson, Rodriguez did not befriend or speak to other house managers about the girls and alleged "massages," even though he was friendly with "JoJo" and his wife, Epstein's house manager at the New York property.[136]

EDWARDS: For the time period you have been familiar with Epstein is it fair to say that he would have roughly 2 girls a day in that same age group wherever he was?

RODRIGUEZ: Yes

EDWARDS: Do you know any of the girls who have been over to his island?

RODRIGUEZ: Yes, Nadia and the girls who use to stay at the home in El Brillo use to go over to the island too.

EDWARDS: How many girls?

RODRIGUEZ: There were so many names girls, I can't remember, Sir.

EDWARDS: Were the girls staying at the island house also the same as the girls staying at the Palm Beach house?

RODRIGUEZ: Yes. Kellen and Nadia Marcinkova would also come over to the island house.

EDWARDS: Was Epstein intimate with Sarah?

RODRIGUEZ: Yes.

EDWARDS: With Nadia as well?

RODRIGUEZ: Yes.

One evening, Rodriguez explained that he rang 911 because he was terrified. He was walking alone in the dark carrying a lot of cash in his pockets when he saw a 'clunker,' a dilapidated old car, sitting inside Epstein's driveway. Fearing he might be robbed he rang the police. "The police responded immediately and pulled in the driveway," Rodriguez said. One of Epstein's victims identified as A.H. in court files was sitting in the car. "What did you tell the police," asked Edwards, "That I was paying A.H.," Rodriguez said. The police then asked who are these people" and I told them, "They are masseuses."[137]

In the car, there was a man sitting beside A.H. "That was the only man I ever saw accompanying a masseuse at the Epstein house." Rodriguez did not know his name. Edwards asked if the man was Tony Figueroa. Rodriguez said he did not know.[138] When Epstein realized I called the police he was very upset.

I explained to him, "I saw a clunker" parked in front of his house. Since I was coming from Publix and carrying a lot of cash, I was concerned for my safety," Rodriguez told attorneys.[139]

EDWARDS: Why would you call AH a masseuse?
Is this the name you were supposed to call them?

RODRIGUEZ: Yes, Sir.

EDWARDS: And for the massages, given to Epstein, you were paying the girls $300 to $500 per hour, each time, and that was usually for an hour, up in the bedroom with Mr. Epstein?

RODRIGUEZ: More or less yes Sir.

EDWARDS: Did you tell your 15-year-old daughter that she could come over Mr. Epstein's for $500 an hour?

RODRIGUEZ: No, Sir.

EDWARDS: Why is it that you never asked your daughter that she could come over if it was just a massage?

RODRIGUEZ: My daughters are too clean for that, Sir.

EDWARDS: Too clean to give a massage?

RODRIGUEZ: Yes. They are good students they are in another type of environment, Sir. We are poor, but you know, they are good students, Sir.

EDWARDS: Is it because you knew there was more than just a massage going on in the bedroom?

RODRIGUEZ: Yes, Sir.

EDWARDS: Did you ever ask what he did in terms of making money?

RODRIGUEZ: No, Sir, I didn't inquire as to what he did. I learned that through Google.

EDWARDS: During the day when Epstein was in the cabana (pool house)…

RODRIGUEZ: I would put his coffee there and that was it. It was very private there.

A few minutes later, Edwards realized Rodriguez did not know or would not say much about his business life with the exception of Epstein's ownership of price.com, a local Palm Beach telephone company. A company, Rodriguez said, was later sold.

RODRIGUEZ: There were other offshore companies that I cannot recall. There are too many companies, Sir.

EDWARDS: What about Sarah Kellen's work?

Rodriguez: Kellen would set up appointments for the Comedy Shop, massages, make pilot arrangements and keep track of all the girls in all the houses including Paris, etc.

EDWARDS: What about the black book?

RODRIGUEZ: We had a book in every house, plane, boat, classifying all the people, masseuses,

chefs, and important people in the life of Mr.
Epstein. So there were many 'black books.' There
were tons… in the house. They were organized
and once in a while updated and we would discard
the old ones.

While working for Epstein, Rodriguez maintained that he never heard of or met Virginia Louise Roberts. He remembered seeing a number of photographs of young girls in Maxwell's computer and a naked girl stretched out on a hammock, apparently Virginia, inside a book made for Nadia however, that was it. Rodriguez said the girl's face was printed on the cover.

Rodriguez also remembered Adriana Ross-Muscinska, the alleged procurer who had gone with Haley Robson to pick up Jane Doe #1 at her home. "She was like Nadia. In the totem pole of responsibilities, she was somewhere between Sarah and me…there to help Sarah in her duties," Rodriguez said.[140]

At some point the attorneys read him a portion of the police report filed November 28, 2005. Suddenly, Rodriguez had an "Aha" moment. He finally understood the reason he was fired and the gravity of his situation.

The police report revealed that Rodriguez had overheard a conversation between the victim A.H. and Officer Munyon of the Palm Beach Police Department (PBPD).

> RODRIGUEZ: Mr. Epstein use to give lots of
> gifts to the police department so we had certain
> latitude when it came to speeding and other
> things… We were asked to place a PBPD baseball
> cap on the dashboard of our car to help police
> identify the Epstein household. The PBPD cap
> was evidently some kind of password that offered
> 'generous' Palm Beach residents certain 'perks.'

On the subject of secrecy, Epstein's black book,' referred to as Exhibit "F" in the deposition and several court documents, identified many names of females who Rodriguez confirmed were underage. The girls' names, he said, were classified under 'massages.'

Most of the girls who 'massaged' Epstein, had met Rodriguez at *El Brillo* before or immediately after their 'sessions.' Rodriguez revealed he was aware that sex toys and vibrators were also found in Epstein's bedroom after those massages. He confessed, "the message pads located in the first floor of the house" proved that Epstein's staff was frequently working to schedule multiple young girls between the ages of 12 and 16, literally every day, often two or three times per day."[141]

Rodriguez reiterated that he was terrified of Epstein's power. He needed money and believed the journal was his rightful "property." He was so afraid that Epstein would make him "disappear" that he christened the directory the "Holy Grail." It was his ultimate "insurance policy," to keep him alive.

While Epstein served out his 13 months in a private cell, in a private building, on an all day work release program for 'solicitation of prostitution with a minor,' after allegedly committing multiple sex crimes against underage girls, Rodriguez was serving 18 months in a federal prison without any of the perks Epstein was granted, for a single obstruction of justice charge. On April 6, 2010, Rodriguez was charged a second time with a different criminal offense: "Being a felon in possession of a firearm." Three other men, all friends, were also charged in the case. Rodriguez was arraigned before U.S. Magistrate Judge Stephen Brown on April 6, 2010.

According to that complaint, "the three other defendants bought hundreds of firearms at gun shops in South Florida for resale to Bolivia. Rodriguez was not one of those. Some of the arms were shipped by a common carrier to Bolivia without making known the real contents and falsely claiming the boxes contained automobile parts. None of the men or the Bolivian recipient was licensed to deal in firearms."[142]

Soon after his release from federal prison, Rodriguez was diagnosed with mesothelioma. He died December 28, 2014.

CHAPTER ELEVEN

"ABSENCE OF EVIDENCE IS EVIDENCE OF ABSENCE"

As New Year's begin, the 2015 New Year's Day began poorly for Harvard law Professor Alan M. Dershowitz. A renowned American lawyer, Harvard University law professor Emeritus, jurist and author, Dershowitz is a leading scholar on U.S. constitutional law.

In December 2014 a complaint submitted by two Victim's Rights attorneys, Brad Edwards and former federal Judge, Paul Cassell, also a University of Utah law professor, revealed, "Epstein forced Virginia Louise Roberts to have sex with former Harvard law professor, Alan Dershowitz, 'on numerous occasions while she was a minor, not only in Florida but on private planes, in New York, New Mexico and the U.S. Virgin Islands," The sworn statement accused Professor Dershowitz of having sexual intercourse with Roberts-Giuffre at least six times, in various places, including Epstein's Palm Beach residence.[143]

These humiliating and disgraceful accusations given Professor Dershowitz' lifelong accomplishments made for an anticlimactic ending to an otherwise illustrious career. Outraged, Dershowitz filed a sworn affidavit in Florida refuting the allegations and challenging Edwards and Cassell to file affidavits.

Dershowitz disputed the victim, Virginia Roberts' claims and publically dared Roberts to file a criminal complaint with the Palm Beach State Attorney and the U. S. Attorney as regards to her sexual abuse allegation. The professor also threatened Edwards and Cassell with disbarment. Shortly after the Roberts' complaint was filed, Dershowitz organized his own defense strategy. He went numerous times on air, online and on the advise of his counselors participated in more than two-dozen television interviews and numerous online reports. At all times, Dershowitz passionately rejected Roberts' allegations of sexual abuse.

Sometime in April 2015, Dershowitz claimed that he and David Boies, another superstar attorney who was representing Virginia Louis Roberts in a separate case, a defamation claim against Ghislaine Maxwell, in New York, held a private conversation. Dershowitz alleged that during their conversation Boies apparently, "told him he believed Dershowitz was innocent and (that) his accuser (i.e. his client Virginia Roberts) was mistaken or confused."[144]

Dershowitz then filed an Affidavit claiming, "Boies told him he could not ethically continue to represent the woman if she did not withdraw her claim."[145] Dershowitz' affidavit included notes written by him of his conversations with Boies. The notes said that, "over the course of several conversations in person, over the phone, and on Skype, Mr. Boies repeatedly stated that he did not believe the allegations that his (client) had made against me were factually true."[146]

Boies, who had been Chief Counsel and Staff Director of the United States Senate Antitrust Subcommittee, in 1978, and served as Chief Counsel and Staff Director of the United States Senate Judiciary Committee, in 1979, denied making those comments. "I never said to him that I concluded that my client's assertions were incorrect," Boies told the New York Times, "I didn't say anything like that."[147]

Dershowitz was surprised and responded to Boies' denial in a statement he gave to the American Bar Association (ABA) Journal. It went like this, "I doubt that my friend David Boies will be willing to state under oath that he did not make the statements that I quote in my affidavit. It's one thing to deny making them to the media. It's quite another thing to deny them under pains and penalties of perjury." I rang Boies in New York to find out the truth. He did not return my calls or emails.[148]

As a result of Virginia's claims, Dershowitz agreed to take a deposition. His deposition was set for October 15 and 16, 2015. Dershowitz was deposed in Fort Lauderdale, Florida at the law offices of Cole Scott & Kissane. Former Judge Thomas Scott was Dershowitz' principal attorney in the case. More media drama ensued. On December 12, 2015, The New York Times published, "Dershowitz on the Defense-His Own," where snippets of the private conversation held between Dershowitz and Boies appeared. Apparently, Dershowitz divulged their private conversation in public, which is a big "no, no" for any lawyer, especially while litigating a case. Soon after that incident, another volcano erupted and on December 28, 2015, The Palm Beach Daily News disclosed Dershowitz's statements concerning his conversation with Boies.

To the surprise of many the, "Judge ruled against Dershowitz, in filing an affidavit regarding conversations he had with David Boies." The supposed 'settlement discussions' were private and confidential and should not have been made public," the Judge claimed.[149] Boies who amongst his many clients represented Vice President Al Gore in 2000, following the U.S. presidential election in *Bush vs. Gore,* is also a loyal Clinton supporter. Oddly enough, given the players implicated in the case, he agreed in 2015, to represent Virginia Louise Roberts Giuffre, *pro bono.* Boies later filed a motion to protect the privacy of those conversations.

Judge Gerard E. Lynch who had been appointed to hear the case, agreed with Boies' request. The Judge ruled, "The conversations between the two attorneys were protected under settlement discussions and should not have been filed," by Dershowitz.[150] Judge Lynch, a United States Federal Judge on the United States Court of Appeals for the Second Circuit was confirmed on September 2009 after having been selected by President Bill Clinton, in 2000, to serve on the U.S. District Court for the Southern District of New York. Lynch was also the first appeals court judge nominated by President Barack Obama to win confirmation from the United States Senate.

Dershowitz' close relationship with Epstein, the bevy of influential players implicated in the case, and the scope of sexual abuse claims possibly committed by the procurers, perhaps explain the motive why Dershowitz agreed to represent Epstein in the first place. In fact, in December 2015, The New York Times published a story defending Dershowitz position when asked the question. Dershowitz said that at first he, "Hesitated when Mr. Epstein called (me), in 2006 to ask for help because he was being investigated in connection with sex crimes.... 'You know Jeffrey, we're acquaintances, maybe that's not such a great idea.' Epstein did not take no for an answer. Dershowitz revealed that Epstein responded, "No, no, no I really need you to do this." But after careful consideration, the case "was right in my wheelhouse. "[151]

Information that was later unearthed has sparked further interest into Epstein and Dershowitz's long-standing history and Dershowitz's possible role as his *consigliore*. The very nature of a consigliore is a man who can contend with 'the boss.' A real-life consigliore is usually the number three-person in the pyramid, after the boss and underboss. Arguably, Dershowitz's role provided a shocking glimpse into the power and influence that a rich predator and politically well-connected client can exert over a potentially compromised system.

Given the revelations and the length of time it took for the news media to print the story it should come as no surprise. Like with many high profile criminal cases involving rich and influential defendants such as: Bill Cosby, the American actor accused of allegedly sexually assaulting women; or OJ Simpson, the American football player accused of murdering his wife and her friend; or the infamous Claus von Bulow accused of attempting to murder his wife, money, influence, and political alliances, can at times determine the outcome without necessarily attaining justice or truth.

As far as the Epstein case is concerned, the truth might never be revealed until perhaps the documents exposing the communications and negotiations between Epstein's attorneys and the Department of Justice are unsealed and made available to the media and Court of Public Opinion.

These documents are currently unavailable to the media because perhaps they might implicate a number of high-level leaders and reveal the extent of the Epstein, Maxwell, Clinton, and Dershowitz relationship. These same documents were released to attorneys, Edwards and Cassell after Judge Marra ruled in their favor in the *Jane Doe #1 and Jane #2 vs. United States Government* case.

It might not be a coincidence that after years of media silence, the media's interest piqued again right before the kickoff of the 2016 presidential campaign. I suppose that as party politics play out and political loyalties and treason goes, reports exposing "Clinton's acceptance of a $25,000 contribution from Epstein after Epstein's conviction," monies the Clintons have so far not returned, have become more interesting to some in the opposing camps and mainstream media.[152]

As a result of the negotiations that took place during the Non Prosecution Agreement and the massive cover up that followed, it is no surprise that Edwards and Cassell felt compelled to move forward with their case: *Jane Doe #1 and Jane Doe #2 vs. United*

States Government. This case, still pending in the Florida court, will no doubt continue to attract the media's attention and become another sought after, grotesque, and colossal media circus unless it is settled early on before the convention. I would not doubt if the Epstein case and all its related cases have become the most public and humiliating human trafficking cases ever brought before the United States Department of Justice.

Against this powerful current, I have struggled for years to unearth the truth about the Epstein investigation. Thanks to many unnamed sources that have guided me throughout, I have been able to discover particles of truth beneath the obvious layers of deception and manipulation. Layers of dishonesty that covered up the rights of victims and pointed to a case where human rights were trampled upon from the very beginning of the investigation.

By the time the Daily Beast report published my first report, I had a clear understanding why I needed to write the first comprehensive book about the Epstein case. Still in spite of the many setbacks there is no doubt, the victims plight and truth kept me afloat. One thing is clear irrespective of the final outcome I had no choice but to carry on for the sake of Epstein's survivors and all future victims.

Given my work in the field of human trafficking, I was able to understand Epstein's case from a number of perspectives. His was not simply a case about an inconsequential mistake made against a minor or a misdemeanor or as he told the New York Post, "stealing a bagel." No, his case is about justice not served at any level because the prosecution was "assaulted" and unable to perform their duties.

Possibly, the Epstein case was and continues to be the greatest cover up ever manufactured in a human trafficking case in the United States. It is evident that the attorneys he hired to defend him exposed the system to a degree of corruption and secrecy never seen before in this type of case. The cover up created to protect Epstein and later the Non Prosecution Agreement brings to light the corrupted elements that also were evident in The Watergate Scandal, Lewinsky Scandal and Profumo Affair. A cover up against human rights and human decency that is so vast, that it extends from the halls of Harvard University all the way to The White House.

Epstein's alleged criminal sexual activities illustrate how a highly structured human trafficking network, with an important international cast of characters and far-reaching tentacles, can conceivably exploit and abuse defenseless underage girls and get away with it.

As Virginia Louise Roberts' tried to explain to Scarola and Edwards during the telephone deposition, the procurers, pedophiles and pimps were caught in Epstein's web from day one. A web that only the predator could ostensibly manipulate. Politicians "who owed him favors" thanks to his generous donations and who could theoretically shield him from a long-term prison sentence were implicated as well as other high-powered friends. His bevy of friends, were also invited to play in his 'den' and perhaps unwittingly facilitated and secured his defense thanks to their participation, directly and indirectly. Like his political cronies, overnight, Epstein became one of them caught in the same web of deception, donations for favors and secrets that in the end only absolved the offender.

If justice were to prevail, the current Crime Victims Right Act (CVRA) case, *Jane Doe #1 and Jane Doe #2 vs. United States Government,* will not settle for anything less than the truth, a truth that is absolute and not colored in 80 shades of grey. Given the thousands of court documents filed in relation to that case, it seems Maxwell, Robson, Kellen, Ross, Marcinkova, Jean Luc Brunel and several other procurers, were equally as responsible as Epstein for their contribution in forging a successful human trafficking operation employing underage girls.

It might well be that Epstein and Maxwell created a criminal enterprise that thwarted an ongoing investigation by brokering influence at the highest levels of government to protect each other and other predators and traffickers implicated in the case. Perhaps Epstein's legal shield came as a consequence of his generous political donations? As the popular liberal blogger Mother Jones pointed out, "Epstein has given tens of millions of dollars to political and philanthropic causes."[153] And like the latest 2016 high stakes financial scandal stealing the global headlines, The Panama Papers scandal confirms how money, power and greed can tear open the curtains behind the secretive world of high finance and the commingled relationships between money, greed and power.

In Latin the term that best describes this state is *ancilla politicae.* Roughly translated it means "the maid political," referring to the whims of those who wield money. Not unlike the Epstein case, the men behind The Panama Papers fiasco reduced themselves to puppetry, mere marionettes of the political and financial elite neglecting everything and everyone else.

Washington most certainly played its role, as clearly established in the thousands of court files made available to media. By creating a shield around the defendant, Epstein's attorneys successfully thwarted the prosecution's efforts to seek justice. R. Alex Acosta and Ann Marie Villafaña were no doubt "assaulted" as Acosta later pointed out. They were "assaulted" by the financial-political dynamic that trumps all else and has for centuries controlled the corridors of power. One can even argue that Epstein's money and his attorneys' influence gratuitously exposed a system to contemptible acts of corruption and turned his case into the longest running human trafficking case in the United States.

An example of how his generous political donations might have worked in his favor is shown below. Figures were compiled between 1990-2012. Epstein's campaign contributions to Democratic candidates in those years, excluding universities and other organizations with possible ties to a handful of politicians, exceeded hundreds of thousands of dollars. Epstein's donations expose the dangerous challenges confronting campaign finance reform in 2016.

His contributions between 1990-2012 included upwards of two hundred thousand dollar donations to: Democratic Senatorial Campaign Committee ($34,000), DCSS/Non-Fed Unincorp. Association ($25,000), Democratic National Committee ($20,000), Independence Party Federal Committee ($5,000), Liberal Party of New York ($5,000), Utah State Democratic Committee ($5,000), DNC Non-Federal Individual ($5,000), Campaign America Inc. ($4,000), Democratic Party of New Mexico ($1,000), Freedom Project ($1,000), Hillary Clinton ($21,000), Chuck Schumer ($22,000), Jeff Bingaman ($8,000), Daniel Robert Glickman ($4,000), John Kerry ($4,000), John Glenn ($3,000), Joe Lieberman ($3,000), Tom McMillan ($3,000), Daniel Patrick Moynihan ($2,000).[154]

CHAPTER TWELVE

A PROCURER OR A MADAM?

"There is no presumption of innocence
in the court of public opinion."
Alan Dershowitz

In spite of the thousands of campaign contributions donated by Epstein to key party operatives over the years and the number of victims who testified, there is only one woman who truly knows it all. All the dirty secrets that Epstein has so cleverly hidden throughout the decade long investigation.

This 'keeper of secrets' whose deposition can presumably answer all questions, if she decided to tell the truth and not plead the Fifth against self-incrimination, can perhaps reveal all the dirty secrets. The challenge of course continues to be the many ifs that exist since her deposition remains sealed and tucked away from the penetrating gaze of the media.

On the other hand, if Virginia Roberts Giuffre is telling the truth, the defamation suit filed against Ghislaine Maxwell, in New York, will become an important legal victory for the victim, perhaps other victims of human trafficking awaiting justice and at-risk-children, if she wins the case.

In the latest twist of events, U.S. District Court Judge Robert Sweet of the Southern District of New York ordered Ghislaine Maxwell to submit her deposition by March 25, 2016. Maxwell, who had been served in September 2009, was able to avoid taking an earlier deposition also in reference to the Epstein case.

A hearing that took place Thursday, March 17, 2106, at the New York City Court House although both Maxwell and Roberts-Giuffre live in different states, "and the amount in controversy was greater than seventy-five thousand dollars," awarded jurisdiction to the State of New York.[155]

The reason the Court was awarded jurisdiction over the case although Virginia lived in Colorado at the time of the filing and Maxwell resided and maintained a residence in New York City, was a win for Roberts'. According to Roberts-Giuffre, Maxwell's defamatory statements were made in New York, and she was sexually abused by Jeffrey Epstein "in the District," which gave the Court additional leverage to claim jurisdiction.

After hearing the motions, Judge Sweet ordered Maxwell to produce all documents and e-mail communications exchanged between Epstein and her from 1999 until 2016 concerning the "sex trafficking ring," they allegedly created.

Sigrid McCawley, the representing attorney for Virginia Roberts-Giuffre did not respond to my calls or most e-mail communications except to forward the transcript. Brad Edwards, representing Roberts Giuffre in another Florida case said, "This is going to be along case. A marathon, not a sprint."[156]

The New York complaint revealed that, "between 1999 and 2002, with the assistance and participation of Maxwell, Epstein sexually abused Giuffre at numerous locations including his mansions in West Palm Beach, Florida, and in this District. Between 2001 and 2007, with the assistance of numerous co-conspirators, Epstein abused more than 30 minor underage girls, a fact confirmed by state and federal law enforcement. As part of their sex trafficking efforts, Epstein and Maxwell intimidated Giuffre into remaining silent about what had happened to her."[157]

Maxwell's testimony is significant because, "in September 2007, Epstein entered into a Non-Prosecution Agreement ("NPA") that barred his prosecution for numerous federal sex crimes in the Southern District of Florida. In the NPA, the United States Attorney's Office agreed that it would not introduce any federal criminal charges against any potential co-conspirators of Epstein's." At the time of his arrest the alleged procurers included: Ghislaine Maxwell, Jean Luc Brunel, Haley Robson, Sarah Kellen, Nadia Marcinkova, Adriana Ross, and several others.[158]

This case comes on the heels of Alan Dershowitz's deposition taken October 15, 2015 where he confirmed that his legal team negotiated the NPA deal. Several media reports published that story. "As a co-conspirator of Epstein's, Maxwell was consequently granted immunity in the Southern District of Florida through the NPA."[159]

Virginia's attorneys argued that, "Maxwell's fabrications constitute libel since they exposed Giuffre to public contempt, ridicule, aversion, and disgrace, and induced an evil opinion of her in the minds of right-thinking persons." Maxwell's comments, McCawley argued, "Tended to injure Roberts Giuffre in her professional capacity as the president of a non profit corporation designed to help victims of sex trafficking, and attempted to destroy her credibility and reputation among members of the community that seeks her help and that Virginia seeks to serve."[160]

Maxwell's public statements about Virginia were offensive and implied that "Giuffre acted with fraud, dishonesty and unfitness for the task," when "speaking out against sex trafficking," the complaint explained. In other words, Maxwell insinuated that Virginia "lied about being recruited by Maxwell and sexually abused by Epstein and Maxwell." According to Virginia, "Maxwell lied directly and through agents who, distributed and published Maxwell's statements in 'reckless disregard of the truth and with the malicious intent to destroy Virginia's reputation and credibility."[161]

The Complaint closely followed Virginia's long standing narrative that, "Maxwell sexually abused Roberts-Giuffre and helped Epstein to sexually abuse Giuffre, and then, in order to avoid having the crimes discovered, Maxwell wantonly and maliciously set out to falsely accuse, defame, and discredit Roberts-Giuffre."[162] "Virginia now wants punitive and exemplary damages to deter Maxwell and others from wantonly and maliciously use a campaign of lies to discredit her and other victims of sex trafficking."[163]

Maxwell's attorneys, Laura Menninger and Jeffrey Pagliuca told reporters that Giuffre's lawyers were "overly broad," in their demands. "What the heck does communication with the Duke, HRH Prince Andrew Duke of York, in 2013, have to do with this case? Nothing!" Pagliuca cried out. McCawley contradicted his argument and responded, "Epstein's long standing practice of luring girls, some minors, with cash to have sex with him and his friends, was relevant to her client's charges."[164]

In fact Prince Andrew has a great deal to do with this case since he remains a close friend of Maxwell's and she was the person responsible for introducing Epstein and Roberts-Giuffre to the Duke. Thanks to Maxwell's public relations efforts, several photos of a young Giuffre with the Prince can be viewed online during the time she was apparently coerced and paid for having sex with the Prince. In the past five years, photographs and media reports have also corroborated the close friendship between the Prince and Epstein.

As far back as April 2007, during Virginia Roberts' telephone conversation with Edwards and Scarola, the victim described Ghislaine Maxwell's place within the Epstein organization.

Her description was quite different than Professor Dershowitz's portrayal of Maxwell in his deposition.

On October 15, 2015 during the taking of his deposition, Professor Dershowitz referred to Maxwell as Epstein's "Major Domo." Her role, Dershowitz said, was to, "arrange travel as well. She would tell you when you could meet with him, when to come over. She would call me at my office… I would say that Ghislaine was the senior person organizing his kind of academic contacts and Sarah Kellen was the junior person. They worked in overlapping roles."[165]

That was an unusual title Professor Dershowitz assigned Maxwell, especially because she's a woman who primarily relies on her social pedigree and family name to open doors build key relationships including the one with former President Clinton who apparently considers her part of his inner circle and perhaps helped fund or "funded Maxwell's The Terra Mar Project nonprofit according to the Foundation website."[166]

There was no doubt that Maxwell's relationship with Epstein and Clinton was a close relationship. One report claimed that, "even after Epstein's prosecution, Maxwell donated to Hillary Clinton's presidential campaign with a maximum personal contribution. Maxwell's contribution may be illegal given that she is not a U.S. citizen and foreign nationals are prohibited under criminal penalty from contributing to any U.S. political campaign."[167]

CHAPTER THIRTEEN

THE PROSECUTION

The back-story is usually as important if not more than the story.

> *"After an extensive investigation by the Palm Beach police and the FBI, the Justice Department immunized Epstein, for multiple alleged offenses involving underage girls in exchange for his guilty pleas, to two comparatively minor sex crimes in Florida state court.*
>
> *Epstein's lawyers persuaded the federal government to keep the terms of the agreement secret, according to the court filing by victims' attorneys Bradley Edwards and former federal Judge Paul Cassell, (District Federal Judge from 2002-2007 appointed by President George W. Bush now Special Council with Hatch James & Dodge in Salt Lake City)."*[168]

Apparently, in addition to this position, Epstein's counselors convinced the Department of Justice that his private physician's evaluation was a sufficient indication of his mental health and character. It was not difficult to predict the end result. Epstein's unusual request to have his private physician submit his evaluation was considered exceptional by the Palm Beach Police Chief, Michael Reiter.

Reiter a man of character and laser sharp intuition mentioned that during the investigation both he and Detective Joe Recarey, were under surveillance for several months, without knowing who ordered it. This extraordinary behavior on the part of the defense team was unusual. As Epstein's investigation progressed several more allowances were swept under the rug or extended to Epstein over the course of the two-year investigation. These activities exposed many layers of the infected onion; the power of his defense team; and the level of influence peddling taking place at the highest echelons of government during his prosecution.

Another example of the power of his defense team came by way of Bruce Reinhart, a distinguished former Assistant U.S. Attorney between 1996-2008. His unexpected exit from the United States Attorneys Office was surprising given the timing. According to a number of defense lawyers representing the victims, it seemed Reinhart left USAO midstream while still working on the Epstein case with prosecutors R. Alex Acosta, Villafaña and others. In fact, Reinhart apparently went to work for Epstein and his attorneys for a period of time.

Then there was the case of Cecile de Jongh, wife of United States Virgin Islands (USVI) Governor, John de Jongh, a Democrat and close Epstein friend. It is no secret the USVI is a recognized tax haven for the rich. It is also a hop, skip and a swim away from its sister island, the British Virgin Islands (BVI), a notorious tax haven for all sorts of questionable characters and assets. It seemed very expedient that Epstein hired the Governor's wife to be his 'Office Manager' at Financial Trust Company, his offshore company, while she worked simultaneously as a board member at the Antilles School on St. Thomas.

Apparently, it is strange if not unprincipled that Mrs. De Jongh did not notify the private school and parents in light of the fiduciary and ethical responsibilities. Given her close association with Epstein and the laws governing the proximity between a predator and school aged children, it might have made sense to at least notify the school board of their professional relationship. As it happens, Mrs. De Jongh was the first wife of a sitting governor in the United States to be employed by a convicted sex offender. In January 2016, Cecile de Jongh, no longer first lady, remains in her employ as Epstein's office manager.[169]

Epstein's company, domiciled in the USVI manages his investments and the 72-acre private island, Little St. James that he owns. The island has also been his primary residence since he was released from house arrest. According to several sources, Epstein received tax breaks from the Virgin Islands Economic Development Corporation apparently thanks to Cecile de Jongh's efforts and relationships.

A Daily Caller story on April 22, 2012 reported, "The benefits' allow recipients to avoid some and in a number of cases, all of their tax burden if they live in the U.S. for the majority of a year and fulfill certain financial and development obligations to the local economy."[170]

Given Mrs. De Jongh's privileged position as the Governor's wife and Epstein's employee, she was in the position to facilitate many benefits to help her boss including perhaps obtaining tax breaks. A recent report claimed that, "Governor de Jongh and his tax break programs have come under increased scrutiny. When the Daily Caller questioned the Economic Development Corporation concerning the story they declined to answer.

A source at the Justice Department also revealed, "Governor de Jongh allegedly accepted part of a $20 million cash-bribe payout from alleged financial criminals who are under sealed federal indictments, in exchange for favors from his administration."[171]

The same scandal involving The Virgin Islands Economic Development Corporation program was published by The Daily Caller, "The (USVI) Governor, his attorney general and a number of USVI legislators also accepted bribes. The former U.S. Attorney General, Eric Holder, was aware that prosecutors and the elected officials were bribed and compromised but did not hold anyone accountable."[172]

Which brings me back to the Department of Justice and why they might have been influenced by Epstein's lawyers to allow the testimony of only a few victims rather than the many more who were willing to testify. The court files made available to the public also showed how more than 100 minor girls courageously testified. Of these sworn statements no more than two-dozen or so were allowed by the prosecutor's office to come forward.

U.S. Attorney, R. Alex Acosta's email to Jay Lefkowitz, one of Epstein's principal attorney's helps explain this phenomenon. The email dated December 13, 2007 began like this:

> *"Dear Jay,*
>
> *I am writing to respond to your "policy concerns" regarding Mr. Epstein's Non Prosecution Agreement, which will be addressed by the United States Attorney, but the time has come for me to respond to the ever-increasing attacks on my role in the investigation and negotiations.*
>
> *It is an understatement to say that I am surprised by your allegations regarding my role because I*

thought that we had worked very well together in resolving this dispute. I also am surprised because I feel that I bent over backwards to keep in mind the effect that the agreement would have on Mr. Epstein and to make sure that you (and he) understood the repercussions of the agreement.

For example, I brought to your attention that one potential plea could result in no gain time for your client; I corrected one of your calculations of the Sentencing Guidelines that would have resulted in Mr. Epstein spending far more time in prison than you projected; I contacted the Bureau of Prisons to see whether Mr. Epstein would be eligible for the prison camp that you desired; and I told you my suspicions about the source of the press "leak" and suggested ways to avoid the press.

Importantly, I continued to work with you in a professional manner even after I learned that you had been proceeding in bad faith for several weeks—thinking that I had incorrectly concluded that solicitation of minors to engage in prostitution was a registrable offense and that you would "fool" our Office into letting Mr. Epstein plead to a non-registrable offense...

Another reason for my surprise about your allegations regarding misconduct related to the Section 2255 litigation in your earlier desire to have me perform the role of "facilitator" to convince the victims that the lawyer representative was selected by the Office to represent their interests alone and that the out of court settlement of their claims was in their best interests.

"You now state that doing the same things that you had asked me to do earlier is improper meddling in civil litigation... You and your co counsel also impressed upon me from the beginning the need to undertake an independent investigation. It seems inappropriate not to complain because our independent investigation uncovered facts that are unfavorable to your client...

You do not want our Office to inform the State Attorney's Office of facts that support the additional charge nor do you want any of the victims of that charge to contact Ms. Belohlavek or the Court.

Ms. Belohlavek's opinion may change if she knows the full scope of your client's actions. You and I spent several weeks trying to identify and put together a plea to federal charges that your client was willing to accept.

Yet your letter now accuses me of "manufacturing" charges of obstruction of justice, making obscene phone calls, and violating child privacy laws. When Mr. Lourie told you that those charges would "embarrass the Office," he meant that the Office was unwilling to bend the facts to satisfy Mr. Epstein's desired prison sentence—a statement with which I agree...

The indictment was postponed for more than five months to allow you and Mr. Epstein's other attorneys to make presentations to the Office to convince the Office not to prosecute. Those presentations were unsuccessful…Since the signing of the Non Prosecution Agreement, the agents and I have vetted the list of victims more than once.

In one instance, we decided to remove a name because, although Mr. Epstein touched the minor victim inappropriately, we decided that the link to a payment was insufficient to call it "prostitution." I have always remained open to a challenge to the list, so your suggestion that Mr. Epstein was forced to write a blank check is simply unfounded… None of the victims was informed of the right to sue under Section 2255 prior to the investigation of the claims. Three victims were notified shortly after the signing of the Non Prosecution Agreement of the general terms of that Agreement.

You raised objections to any victim notification, and no further notifications were done… All documents related to the grand jury investigation have been filed under seal, and the Palm Beach Police Department's probable cause affidavit has never been filed with the Court.

If, in fact, you are referring to the *Ex Parte* Declaration of Joseph Recarey (the police officer working at the Palm Beach Police Department in charge of the Epstein case), that was filed in response to the motion to quash the grand jury subpoena, it was filed both under seal and *ex parte,* so no one should have access to it except the Court and myself…

> *You also accuse me of "broadening the scope of the investigation without any foundation for doing so by adding charges of money laundering and violations of a money transmitting business to the investigation. Again, I consulted with the Justice Department's Money Laundering Section about my analysis before expanding that scope. The duty attorney agreed with my analysis."[173]*

A separate e-mail dated September 16, 2007 was sent by Ann Marie Villafaña, Assistant U.S. Attorney during the criminal investigation, to one of Epstein's lawyer, Jay Lefkowitz. Villafaña sent the note using her personal e-mail account rather than the official DOJ account.

When I realized this, it reminded me of the 2016 Clinton 'E-mail-gate,' currently under investigation. The Clinton e-mail investigation stems from the former Secretary of State, Hillary Clinton's, use of her personal blackberry for State Department business and the potential breach of national security interests. Ms. Villafaña's e-mail read:

> *"Hi Jay…I talked to Andy and he still doesn't like the factual basis. In his opinion, the plea should only address the crimes that we were addressing, and we were not investigating Mr. Epstein abusing his girlfriend (she is referring to Nadia Marcinkova)."[174]*

It was odd USAO did not investigate the Marcinkova case since the girl was apparently 14 years old when she moved in with Epstein from a foreign country. As several court documents confirmed, Marcinkova, had been a victim turned procurer since she was underage when she and Epstein first met.

Marcinkova along with Ross-Muscinka, Maxwell and a handful of alleged foreign-born victims turned procurers were implicated although never charged. Most girls who testified in the Florida case were American. Given the importance of jurisdictional authority in a criminal case such as this, it is curious that other federal agencies beside the FBI and DOJ did not participate in the investigation involving non-nationals like Marcinkova, Maxwell and others. Two that come to mind are: US Citizenship & Immigration (USCIS), and Immigration & Customs Enforcement (ICE).

Another question that troubled me concerned Marcinkova. If indeed she was more a victim than a procurer, given her age at the time she met Epstein, and Epstein's 14 year-old 'girlfriend' when the alleged crimes were committed, why was her visa status not investigated? Why did the United States Attorney's Office abstain from moving forward with an investigation into Marcinkova's case?

Villafaña's e-mail presented an interesting point:

> *"As to timing, it is my understanding that Mr. Epstein needs to be sentenced in the state after he is sentenced in the federal case, but not that he needs to plead guilty and be sentenced after serving his federal time. Andy recommended that some of the timing issues be addressed only in the state agreement, so that it isn't obvious to the judge that we are trying to create federal jurisdiction for prison purposes. My understanding is that Mr. Epstein should sign a state plea agreement, plead guilty to the federal offenses, plead guilty to the state offenses, be sentenced on the federal offenses, and*

then be sentenced on the state offenses, and then start serving the federal sentence.

Re the two paragraphs following your paragraph 8: I will mention "co conspirators," but I would prefer not to highlight for the judge all of the other crimes and all of the other persons that we could charge. Also, we do not have the power to bind Immigration and we make it a policy not to try to, however, I can tell you that, as far as I know, there is no plan to try to proceed on any immigration charges against either Mr. Ross (Adriana Ross) or Ms. Marcinkova (Nadia Marcinkova).

Also, on the grand jury subpoenas, I can prepare letters withdrawing them as of the signing of the plea agreement, but I would prefer to take out that language. In my eyes, once we have a plea agreement, the grand jury's investigation has ended and there can be no more use of the grand jury's subpoena power."

An early Plea Agreement draft dated September 14, 200 and e-mailed to attorney Jay Lefkowitz by USAO made the following stipulations:

"1. The defendant agrees to plead guilty to the Information which charges the defendant as follows: Count 1 charges that the defendant intentionally harassed another person, that is Jane Doe #1, in an attempt to delay, prevent, and dissuade Jane Doe #1 from reporting to a law enforcement officer of the

United States the commission of a federal offense; in violation of Title 18, United States Code, Sections 1512 9d) (2), and 2: and Count 2 charges that the defendant, while in an airplane over the high seas, did knowingly commit a simple assault on a person who was over the age of 16 years, that is S.K. (Sarah Kellen); in violation of Title 18, United States Code, Section 113 (a) (5)."

Yet another curious e-mail was sent by USAO to Lefkowitz instructing him to talk to his client. It read:

"...Talk to Mr. Epstein about a young woman named redacted... We have hearsay evidence that she traveled on Mr. Epstein's airplane when she was under 18, in around the 2000 or 2001 time frame. That falls outside the statute of limitations, but perhaps we could construct a 371 conspiracy around that?"

In legal parlance, a 371 conspiracy is defined as a scheme, "when one or more persons conspire to commit an offense against the United States, or any agency thereof or for any purpose, the persons shall be fined under this law and imprisoned for no more than five years or both."[175]

It seems that in most criminal cases involving similar charges and a sizeable number of victims, the allegations would have met, at the very least, the federal stipulations for a federal rather than a state prosecution.

The seemingly overwhelming evidence cannot explain why Epstein's case did not qualify for prosecution under the federal law Trafficking Victims Protection Act (TVPA). By any prosecutorial standards, a case of this magnitude should have been prosecuted under the federal bill, TVPA, enacted in Florida in 2000.

Over the years I have sought out the opinion of many criminal attorneys, law enforcement officials and immigration lawyers working on this subject. In the final analysis, by perhaps failing to protect the victims under the TVPA, most attorneys agreed the Non Prosecution Agreement did a great disservice to the victims and all future victims and at-risk girls, including those living in or nearby Epstein.

One of the greatest concern's today is whether Epstein can become a repeat offender? Although it is not an exact science the rate of recidivism for convicted pedophiles is high. Some stories indicate that sex offenders are mostly repeat offenders. If this is true, then Epstein's alleged sex crimes might continue to pose a threat to the local communities he lives in or frequents such as: Palm Beach, New York, Paris, London, Stanley, New Mexico and the USVI.

By pairing down the criminal charges and withholding prosecution to the full extent of the law, and not prosecuting the alleged procurers, many vulnerable underage girls perhaps continue to be in danger of the predator's potential inability to control his sexual urges with underage girls.

If you take this premise a step further, Epstein was never properly diagnosed for his condition and has not, to anyone's knowledge, undergone therapy on an in patient or out patient basis since his release from house arrest. Pedophilia has recently become such a widespread and disturbing concern that only a few weeks ago, a science magazine announced Swedish clinical trials are now testing a medication to control pedophilic impulses. The drug, developed by a Swiss pharmaceutical is currently on the market for a different indication.[176]

The most recent photographs of Epstein, taken by a couple of newspapers in New York City continue to show Epstein in the company of very young girls. One photograph in particular showed the predator with his hand hugging the derriere of a young girl while looking into the camera. These photos and other stories recently published are disturbing and perhaps indicate that he continues to frequent the company of very young girls and that he continues to invite some of these young girls on his travels.

After some photos were published where Epstein was photographed with very young girls, two incidents were brought to my attention in August 2012. Both incidents occurred at Inter Mix a clothing boutique and chain for young women in New York. According to a salesgirl and confirmed by the manager of the shop at the time, who prefer, to remain anonymous, Epstein visited Manhattan's Inter Mix boutique on June 11, 2012. The boutique located on 1003 Madison Avenue between 77th and 78th Streets is just seven blocks from Epstein's triplex on East 71st Street.

At the Manhattan boutique, store number 440002, Epstein purchased over one thousand two hundred dollars worth of girls clothing. The items included girl's roll-up shorts, high-rise cuffed shorts, linen Tee shirts, and an open back 'Stewart.' All the items were girl's size small. Once Epstein paid the bill and the purchases were made the salesclerk handed the young girls their items.

During that visit, the salesgirl was aware of Epstein's criminal history because of the reports that had been published earlier by the New York Post and other local dailies that year. According to the girl, Epstein came to the shop with approximately five young girls in tow.

Clearly, it is not a crime for an adult male to escort young girls to a boutique to purchase clothing. It is also not a crime for an adult male to gift adolescent girls clothing except that it becomes a questionable activity when the older man in question happens to be a level-3 registered sex offender. At the very least the activity should have raised eyebrows and perhaps an investigation by the Manhattan District Attorney's office when it was brought to their attention.

The girls in question were not relatives or seemed particularly close to Epstein according to the salesgirl. The manager confirmed how Epstein entered the boutique by himself immediately after the young girls entered the store. Except for Epstein, no other adult was present during the shopping spree. The girls and Epstein did not greet each other when he walked in according to the salesgirl. That seemed odd especially if Epstein had accidentally bumped into them at the shop. The salesgirl assumed the girls and Epstein were casual friends shopping together. Inter Mix did not have a camera inside the boutique so it did not record the incident. After Epstein paid for the clothing in cash he left the shop by himself. The young girls trailed behind.

The employees described their meeting, Epstein and the girls', as casual and friendly. While looking around for clothes, the girls and Epstein were huddled together talking. They were in the shop perhaps half an hour to forty-five minutes before the items were paid for. The salesgirl never questioned the girls or asked for identification since that would have been unusual and inappropriate. Epstein was also a regular client at the boutique according to one of the salesgirl's.

A second incident occurred at the Manhasset Inter Mix boutique, store number 440013. At that shop, on July 29, 2012, Epstein purchased two articles of clothing for $119.40. I do not have the specifics about that incident only the receipt.

Soon after I was informed of these events, I forwarded the information and receipts to attorneys Jack Scarola, Brad Edwards and the Manhattan D.A. Cyrus Vance Jr. As far as I know, there has not been a follow up investigation. On November 26, 2012, I forwarded a second e-mail to the Manhattan D.A. concerning the incident. I copied Mr. Vance's assistant, Marlene Turner. This was the response from the District Attorney's office.

Dear Ms. Sarnoff,

As noted in response to your prior inquiries, our office does not comment on hypotheticals nor provide individualized responses to general questions about NYS law.

Marlene Turner

Given the United States Attorney Office's golden record in protecting the most vulnerable, the Epstein prosecution seems like an *in flagrante delicto*. Could the USAO have been influenced by Epstein's defense team, rather than stand by the laws that to protect the most vulnerable?

Three reasons why the Department of Justice should have proceeded more prudently come to mind. One, the outrageously aggressive tactics used by Epstein and the defense team against the victims during the investigation. Two, the outrageously aggressive tactics deployed by Epstein and his defense team against the Palm Beach Police Department specifically the Chief of Police, Michael Reiter; And three, the same outrageously aggressive tactics displayed by Epstein and his defense team against the United States Attorneys Office.

The bizarre e-mail trail between the prosecutor's office and Epstein's attorneys, and the peculiar exchange negotiated in Washington D.C., after the Florida prosecutor, R. Alex Acosta handed down what should have been the final order, should have raised far more eyebrows in Washington and left everyone wondering.

As a result of the disclosure of the NPA caused such an inflammatory response by the media that in 2016, ABC News reported the following news:

"Prosecutors went to great lengths to keep secret the non-prosecution agreement reached in 2007 with Jeffrey Epstein, attorneys for the victims allege, "because of the strong objection they would have faced from victims of Epstein's abuse, and because of the public criticism that would have resulted from allowing a politically-connected billionaire who had sexually abused more than 30 minor girls to escape ... with only a county court jail sentence...

Throughout the negotiations -- and for nearly a year after the agreement was signed -- the victims were kept in the dark, their attorneys said, strung along as government lawyers promised victims they were still investigating even long after they had cut Epstein an "indulgent" deal...

And as Epstein first faced federal prosecution a few years later, one of his lawyers, Gerald B. Lefcourt, wrote to prosecutors to tout Epstein's pedigree as "part of the original group that conceived of the Clinton Global Initiative," according to a letter attached to Wednesday's court filing...

On the day the deal was signed, an attorney for Epstein sent an email to the federal prosecutor handling the case which read, "Please do whatever you can to keep this from becoming public," according to an email exchange attached to Wednesday's filing."[177]

Hundreds of pages of newly-disclosed correspondence between federal prosecutors and Epstein's defense lawyers, including Jay Lefkowitz, Kenneth Starr, Alan Dershowitz, Roy Black, and Lefcourt, provided an inside look at Epstein's efforts to forestall the federal prosecution and conceal the resulting deal, despite repeated acknowledgements by government lawyers that they were legally required to inform the victims.

> *"Neither federal agents nor anyone from your Office should contact the (alleged victims) to inform them of the resolution of the case," wrote Lefkowitz in a letter to then-U.S. Attorney R. Alexander Acosta a month after the deal was signed. "Not only would that violate the confidentiality of the agreement, but Mr. Epstein also will have no control over what is communicated to the identified individuals at this most critical stage. We believe it is essential that we participate in crafting mutually acceptable communication to the (alleged victims)."*[178]

While the relationship between Epstein's legal team and the U.S. attorneys developed into what Acosta later described as "a yearlong assault on the prosecution and the prosecutors," the early negotiations seemed to possess an accommodating tone that allowed defense lawyers and prosecutors to work together to formulate lesser criminal charges for Epstein. The question is, why?

CHAPTER FOURTEEN

THE DERSHOWITZ DEPOSITION

For the sake of transparency, and after being accused of sexually assaulting one of the victim's, many years after the Non Prosecution Agreement was signed, a former Harvard University law professor, Alan Dershowitz, agreed to take a video taped deposition on October 15 and 16, 2015 at the offices of Cole Scott & Kissane at 110 Southeast 6th Street, Fort Lauderdale, Florida.

More than any other attorney hired to defend Epstein in the 2005 criminal case, Dershowitz understood the complexities of the case. His longtime friendship with Epstein, perhaps Maxwell, and other high profile players associated with the Epstein case played a pivotal role in constructing Epstein's defense.

Unlike the other brilliant attorneys hired to defend Epstein, Dershowitz also knew who needed the most protection. During his deposition, Professor Dershowitz testified about his relationship with Epstein, Virginia Louise Roberts, Leslie Wexner, Bill Clinton and others implicated in the Epstein story.

Several lawyers were present during his deposition. Jack Scarola was there representing his clients, Brad Edwards and former federal Judge Paul Cassell also former Judge Thomas Scott Emerson Jr. and

Steven Safra, represented Professor Dershowitz. Martin Weinberg and Darren Indyke represented Jeffrey Epstein and participated via the telephone. Sigrid Stone McCawley, a partner at David Boies, Schiller & Flexner represented their client, Virginia Louise Roberts-Giuffre.

The reason for Professor Dershowitz' deposition is rooted in the January 2015 defamation case filed by Brad Edwards and Paul Cassell against Professor Dershowitz for character assassination. Cassell and Edwards sued Dershowitz who counter sued the attorneys.

The case *Bradley Edwards, Paul G Cassell vs. Alan Dershowit,* # CACE: 15-000072 was filed exposing several prominent politicians and high profile business leaders because their client, Virginia Louise Roberts, accused Dershowitz along with Prince Andrew and other high profile men of having sex with her when she was a minor. Dershowitz denied the charges and accused her two lawyers of acting improperly.

In my attempt to simplify the case and not lose the integrity of the conversation, segments of the deposition are set down exactly as they unfolded. The opening exchange between Scarola and Dershowitz went like this:

> SCAROLA: In fact, you have been making public statements of your intention to seek the disbarment of Bradley Edwards and Paul Cassell for approximately ten months, correct?

> DERSHOWITZ: That's right. That's correct.

> SCAROLA: You are aware of the ethical obligation that a lawyer has when that lawyer has direct knowledge of unethical conduct on the part of another member of the Bar-

DERSHOWITZ: That's right.

SCAROLA: To report that unethical conduct, correct?

DERSHOWITZ: Yes.

SCAROLA: Have you done that?

DERSHOWITZ: I have conferred with three leading ethics experts and I have been advised that to file a report while there is ongoing litigation is not the proper approach. But rather to gather the evidence and the information and to make sure that all of the allegations I make are well founded, unlike what your clients did, and then at the appropriate time, when the litigation is concluded, seek the disbarment of Bar Association... I fully intend to seek disbarment... of your clients because I believe they engaged in unprofessional, unethical and disbar- able conduct. And I've continued to do so until as recently as last week.

When Scarola asked Dershowitz who was representing him, the professor identified over two-dozen lawyers. The list was so extensive it covered 17 pages of the deposition, beginning on page 25 through 42 of the October 15, 2015 transcript.

Dershowitz said he was "offered legal advice by his research assistant at Harvard, Carlos Sires— also a partner in the Boise firm —who volunteered to represent me along with one of his partners, but then withdrew from the representation when he discovered that I had a conflict of interest."[179]

Given the dates when the Roberts' Defamation case was filed, September 21, 2015, and the Dershowitz counter suit against Edwards and Cassell was filed, January 4, 2015, the dates seemed at odds. Assuming that Dershowtiz approached Sires to represent him in early January 2015, after Edwards and Cassell first filed the defamation complaint, it would place Dershowitz ahead of Virginia Roberts' request to have David Boies represent her in the Maxwell defamation case.

So unless the filing dates were incorrect, why would Sires believe there was a 'conflict of interest,' when Dershowitz first approached him? The time line is important because Roberts' statement, alleging she was forced to have sex with Dershowitz, was published by politico.com on December 31, 2014. In any case, given the actual filing dates, it was David Boies and not Carlos Sires who should have raised 'the conflict of interest,' clause with their potential client.

When I asked Scarola to comment on Dershowitz's claims and dates regarding the conflict he said, "Dershowitz's conflict claim is not supported by facts or law." I called Carlos Sires. He did not return my call. During the deposition, Dershowitz identified two new players never before mentioned in the case. A woman named Rebecca and her husband Michael. The family names were 'purposefully omitted to prevent the media from chasing them.' Dershowitz claimed that Rebecca "had been told directly by her friend, Virginia Roberts, who stayed with her overnight for a period of time, that she never wanted to mention me in any of the pleadings. And that her two lawyers who filed the pleadings, Cassell and Edwards, pressured her in to including my name and details."[180]

DERSHOWITZ: Virginia Roberts never wanted to mention me, but she was pressured by her lawyer into mentioning me… And that was the truth.

Rebecca then said that I was not the object of this effort. The object of the effort was a billionaire who lives in Columbus, Ohio, (Leslie Wexner), who owns Victoria's Secret and The Limited, too.

DERSHOWITZ: Rebecca told me she did not know the name of that billionaire, but that Virginia and her lawyers hoped to get 1 billion, B-I-L-L-I-O-N, $1 billion or half of his net worth from him by alleging that he had improperly engaged in sexual misconduct with Virginia Roberts.

That money would be divided three ways: A third of it to Virginia Roberts, a third of it to a charity that she and her lawyers were setting up for battered women, and a third of it to the lawyers.

She then told me they were trying to get ABC News to interview Virginia Roberts so as to give her credibility in order to pressure the billionaire from Columbus, Ohio Leslie Wexner into paying a large sum of money. And that I was named as an effort to try to show the billionaire what could happen to somebody if they were accused of sexual misconduct. And that would encourage him to settle a lawsuit or pay money in exchange for his name not being mentioned or revealed. I had no idea about this. And I didn't -- I didn't ask about this. She just stated this. And I then corroborated the fact that she was absolutely correct in everything she had said to me.

SCAROLA: You corroborated the fact that she was absolutely correct in everything that she had said to you?

DERSHOWITZ: That's right.

SCAROLA: How?

DERSHOWITZ: Okay. Let me answer that question. I was very -- I wasn't sure, so I called Leslie Wexner. I got his wife on the phone, Abigail Wexner. Obviously I knew that the only billionaire in Columbus, Ohio who owned Limited Too and who owned Victoria's Secret was Leslie Wexner. I had met Leslie Wexner on two occasions, I think, and his wife. I called Abigail on the phone and I said, I think you ought to know that there is an extortion plot being directed against your husband by unscrupulous lawyers in Florida.

And she said, oh, we're aware of that, they've already been in contact with us, which surprised me… I then also -- I can't give you the chronology of that. I then was in touch with ABC and found out she was absolutely correct about her efforts to try to get interviewed on ABC television.

DERSHOWITZ: In fact, I learned that your client, Brad Edwards, had sent a communication to people in the area urging them to watch her interview that was scheduled to be on three Television programs.

If I'm not mistaken, it was Good Day Show, the evening news, and the show Nightline. I then was in communication with ABC and helped to persuade them that they would be putting false information on the air if they allowed Virginia Roberts to tell her false story.

So, I was able to corroborate that. Then also corroborated the fact that she had never mentioned me when her boyfriend appeared on Television and publically stated that she had never mentioned me in any of her description of people whom she had sexual contact with.

So, I was then completely satisfied that Rebecca was telling me the complete truth. And that in my view, there was an extortion plot directed against Leslie Wexner, a criminal extortion plot directed against Leslie Wexner, and that your clients were involved in that extortion plot.

SCAROLA: If we were to try to fix the time of this second phone call, one way in which we would fix the time of this second phone call, in addition to getting your telephone records, would be to find out when this ABC interview took place, correct? Since the phone call you're telling us came after the ABC interview, that you convinced ABC not to air?

DERSHOWITZ: No, I didn't state that. Let me be very clear. I found out from her that there was going to be an ABC television interview. I don't think I was aware of the fact that there was going to be a television interview at that point.

I remember then getting a -- either a phone call or e-mail from ABC informing me of that and that corroborated to my mind the fact that she, Rebecca, was telling me the truth about the ABC interview.

She also told me -- and this was corroborated, she also told me that the television interview with ABC had to be postponed because her husband-Virginia Roberts' husband, had beaten her up so badly that she was hospitalized and that she could not appear on television with the bruises because she didn't want to have to explain that her husband had beaten her up.

And I ultimately corroborated that information as well by investigating the fact that she, in fact, filed a complaint against her husband and had been hospitalized. So everything that Rebecca told me has proved to be absolutely true and absolutely corroborated. And, therefore, I believe it and believe that your clients were engaged in what I believe is an extortion plot against Leslie Wexner, conspiracy to commit extortion in which I was a victim, as well as Leslie Wexner, of being a victim.

SCAROLA: Did you speak directly to Leslie Wexner or only to his wife?

DERSHOWITZ: Only to his wife and his lawyers.

SCAROLA: And you spoke by telephone?

DERSHOWITZ: Yes.

SCAROLA: Where were you and where was she?

DERSHOWITZ: I called from, I think, New York and I spoke to her about it. I told her what I said I said. She said what I said she said. And then she said that her lawyers would be in touch with me. And her lawyer then called me and corroborated again that there had been contact and eventually there was greater contact.

SCAROLA: Contact by whom with whom?

DERSHOWITZ: Contact by Virginia Roberts' lawyer, lawyers. I wasn't – it wasn't clear at that point.

SCAROLA: Which lawyer or lawyers?

DERSHOWITZ: I wasn't clear at that point. They didn't indicate to me which lawyer or lawyers–

SCAROLA: Didn't you ask?

DERSHOWITZ: Who were the contacts?

SCAROLA: Didn't you want to know who is– making this request?

DERSHOWITZ: I asked–whether there was a letter and they wouldn't show me a letter. I asked if there were phone calls. They were a–they wanted to be discreet about how the contact had occurred. But they told me that the contact had occurred.

SCAROLA: But they wouldn't tell you who?

DERSHOWITZ: They wouldn't show me any letter.

SCAROLA: That's not my question. Did they tell you–did you ask who contacted Leslie Wexner?

DERSHOWITZ: The first answer was Virginia Roberts' lawyer. I then subsequently learned that among those who contacted Leslie Wexner's lawyers, was David Boies and Sigrid McCawley.

SCAROLA: Not Bradley Edwards, correct?

DERSHOWITZ: I was not given the name Bradley Edwards at that time. But was subsequently told by David Boies that Bradley Edwards and Paul Cassell–

SIGRID McCAWLEY: I'm going to object to the extent this reveals any conversations that happened in the context of settlement discussions.

DERSHOWITZ: That I was ultimately told by David Boies that he had done an extensive investigation of the allegations against Leslie Wexner and had concluded that they were–

McCAWLEY: Again, I'm going to object to this since that happened in the context of settlement–

DERSHOWITZ: False.

McCAWLEY: –negotiations. I'm going to move for sanctions if information is revealed that happened in the context of settlement discussions.

SCOTT: I don't know whether -- I don't believe there were settlement discussions. But even if they weren't, they would still be admissible.

DERSHOWITZ: Let me continue–

SCOTT: For discovery purposes–

DERSHOWITZ: -- that David Boies had done–

McCAWLEY: I disagree. I think we're going to have to take this to the judge, then, if we're going to reveal settlement conversations in this conversation, then we need, to go to the judge on it.

SCOTT: Whatever you need to do.

DERSHOWITZ: Let me continue the–what he told me. That David Boies had–

McCAWLEY: No, we're–

SIMPSON: No, no, no.

McCAWLEY: –going to discontinue. We will contact the judge.

SCAROLA: We'll move on to another area and address that issue with the judge as to whether or not a protective order is appropriate.

DERSHOWITZ: Would you like to establish the foundation for why it's not protected?

SWEDER: Alan–

SCOTT: Alan, just let it alone. Let it alone.

DERSHOWITZ: Okay.

SCAROLA: This second conversation you've told us was conducted while you were in New York, correct?

DERSHOWITZ: That's my best recollection.

SCAROLA: The first conversation also conducted while you were in New York?

DERSHOWITZ: That's my best recollection.

SCAROLA: Are you aware that New York is a one-party consent state for purposes of permitting the recording of communications, correct?

SCOTT: Objection. Do you know?

DERSHOWITZ: I'm–I think that's right, yeah.

SCAROLA: Okay. So you knew that these significant conversations could have been recorded by you had you chosen to record them, correct?

DERSHOWITZ: I don't think I thought about that at the time.

SCAROLA: Are you aware that years before December when the CVRA pleading was filed, that your name had come up repeatedly in connection with Jeffrey Epstein's abuse of minors, correct?

DERSHOWITZ: Let me answer that question. I am aware that never before 2014, end of December, was it ever, ever alleged that I had acted in any way inappropriately with regard to Virginia Roberts, that I ever touched her, that I ever met her, that I had ever been with her. I was completely aware of that.

There had never been any allegation. She claims under oath that she told you that secretly in 2011, but you have produced no notes of any such conversation. You, of course, are a witness to this allegation and will be deposed as a witness to this allegation. I believe it is an entirely false allegation that she told you, in 2011, that she had had any sexual contact with me. I think she's lying through her teeth when she says that.

DERSHOWITZ: And I doubt that your notes will reveal any such information. But if she did tell you that, she would be absolutely, categorically lying.

DERSHOWITZ: So I am completely aware that never, until the lies were put in a legal pleading at the end of December 2014, it was never alleged that I had any sexual contact with Virginia Roberts. I know that it was alleged that I was a witness to Jeffrey Epstein's alleged abuse and that was false. I was never a witness to any of Jeffrey Epstein's sexual abuse.

And I wrote that to you, something that you have falsely denied. And I stand on the record. The record is clear that I have categorically denied I was ever a witness to any abuse, that I ever saw Jeffrey Epstein abusing anybody.

And–and the very idea that I would stand and talk to Jeffrey Epstein while he was receiving oral sex from Virginia Roberts, which she swore to under oath, is so outrageous, so preposterous, that even David Boies said he couldn't believe it was true.

McCAWLEY: I object. I object. I'm not going to allow you to reveal any conversations that happened in the context of a settlement discussion.

DERSHOWITZ: Does she have standing?

McCAWLEY: I have a standing objection and, I'm objecting again. I'm not going to–

DERSHOWITZ: No, no, no. Does she have standing in this deposition?

DERSHOWITZ: I'm not sure she has standing.

SCAROLA: Are we finished with the speech?

SCAROLA: I'd like him to finish the speech so that we can get to my question and then we can take a break.

DERWSHOWITZ: So the question–the answer to your question is–

SIMPSON: Wait a minute. Wait a minute. Wait a minute. Please don't disclose something that she has a right to raise that objection if she wants to.

DERSHOWITZ: Okay.

SCOTT: Ask your question.

SWEDER: Maybe you want to read back the last couple of sentences.

SCAROLA: No, how about just reading back the last question and maybe we can get an answer to the question.

SCOTT: Again, I move to strike your comments, Counsel, because it's inappropriate and you're too good a lawyer to know that that's not true–

SCAROLA: Nothing inappropriate about my insisting upon an answer to   the question that I asked instead of a speech.

SCOTT: Well, you know, he's trying to answer your question to the best of his ability. Counsel objected to it. I wanted to take a break to make sure that we explained to him the position so that we didn't have a problem, and I was trying to protect everybody in this room.

SCOTT: But if you want to proceed, we can do it.

SCAROLA: Well, if we simply answer the questions that are asked, there won't be a problem.

SCOTT: Well, I guess everybody -- you can characterize it one-way, I can characterize it another, that he's doing the best he can to answer your questions.

SCAROLA: And ultimately Judge Lynch will make that determination.

SCOTT: Absolutely. So be it.

SCAROLA: So read back the last question, if you would, please. We'll get a–hopefully get an answer to that and then we can take a break.

COURT REPORTER: "Are you aware that 12 years before December of 2014, when the CVRA pleading was filed, that your name had come up repeatedly in connection with Jeffrey Epstein's abuse of minors, correct?"

SCOTT: Objection, asked and answered.

DERSHOWITZ: And then—we discussed the charity. And I think it was called VR, which is her initials, Virginia Roberts, and also it stood for something, I don't know, Victims Rights or something like that.

And she said that the lawyers had contributed $80,000 of their own money to start the charity. She didn't indicate which lawyers.

DERSHOWITZ: But the lawyers had contributed $80,000 of their own money to start the charity and that they were going to fund the charity by contributions from Leslie -- from the man from Columbus who owned Victoria's Secret and they expected a very substantial contribution. They also said that—

SCAROLA: I'm sorry, but "they" is not helpful to me.

DERSHOWITZ: She—when I say "they"—when I talk about the substance, I'm always talking about her Abigail. I never had any conversations about the substance with him Wexner. She said that they were hoping to fund the charity by substantial contribution from Leslie Wexner and that they thought that by getting on television, they would increase the chances of raising this money from Leslie Wexner.

And that she thought they had already made contact with Wexner and that they had already made–with the man from Columbus Wexner, and they had already made contact with ABC. But I don't think she knew at that point whether the actual interviews did or did not occur.

SCAROLA: So it has been ten months since you allegedly became aware of that suborning of perjury and some eight months since your allegedly having become aware of the extortion plot, but you have filed no criminal complaints against anyone, correct?

DERSHOWITZ: To answer that question requires me to disclose conversations I had with David Boies. I would love to answer that question.

SCAROLA: No, sir, it does not.

DERSHOWITZ: Yes, it does.

SCOTT: Whoa, you can't–how can you.

SCAROLA: Whether you filed a criminal complaint or not?

DERSHOWITZ: Yes, it does.

SCOTT: Please, Jack, he can't say that.

DERSHOWITZ: It does involve conversation I had with David Boies.

SCAROLA: Well, in that case, in light of the fact that that is a matter that will be addressed by the Court, we'll save that question for another time.

DERSHOWITZ: I'm anxious to answer it.

SCAROLA: And I'm anxious to get an answer.

DERSHOWTIZ: Well, I hope we can agree I should be able to answer it.

SCAROLA: Have we exhausted, You know that Virginia Roberts is not the only person who has sworn under oath that you were present at Jeffrey Epstein's Palm Beach home with young girls, right?

DERSHOWITZ: No.

SCAROLA: You don't know that?

DERSHOWITZ: No. I know that–

SCAROLA: Well, that's fine. You've answered my question. That's not something you know?

DERSHOWITZ: I was not present in Jeffrey Epstein's home with any underage young women, period. Never, ever under any circumstances. I am not aware that anyone has sworn under oath that I was there during the relevant periods of time, which is a three-year period between the summer of 1999 and the summer of 2002. Because I was never–as far as I know, I was never in Jeffrey Epstein's home during that period of time, period.

SCAROLA: I want to go back to the Ashes, if I could. Joanne Ashe is not a lawyer, is she?

DERSHOWITZ: Joanne Ashe is not a lawyer, no.

SCAROLA: And is Alexi Ashe a lawyer?

DERSHOWITZ: Yes.

SCAROLA: Has Alexi Ashe ever been your lawyer?

DERSHOWITZ: I have discussed the case with Alexi Ashe. She is a full-time sex trafficking prosecutor whose whole career has been going after sex traffickers in the Brooklyn District Attorney's office and I have discussed my case with her.

SCAROLA: Has Alexi Ashe ever been your lawyer?

DERSHOWITZ: I would say not, no.

SCAROLA: Beginning approximately January 3 or 4 2015, you began a mass media campaign battle against Bradley Edwards and Professor Paul Cassell alleging that they were sleazy, unethical lawyers who fabricated false charges against you, correct?

DERSHOWITZ: That's a false–

DERSHOWITZ: That's a false statement. I did not begin. It was your clients who began it. Your clients began it by filing false statements in a federal court, which the judge struck and sanctioned them for as being irrelevant and pertinent and he used other language.

They began it. It is my belief that they began it in order to get massive press attention to it. And my—my responses were when the press called me, the press called me immediately and asked me for my reaction.

I was totally shocked that any lawyer would make these kinds of outrageous career-destroying allegations without even calling me and asking me if I would deny it or have any evidence to provide for them. And when I was called by the media I did what you would do, Mr. Scarola, or what your clients would do, I defended myself. What any American would do under the First Amendment, I categorically denied career-destroying false statements and I told the truth, which is what the United States Constitution is all about and why we fought for liberty. Yes, I told the truth to the media.

SCAROLA: You engaged in a mass media campaign to convince the world that Bradley Edwards and Professor Paul Cassell were unethical lawyers who had fabricated false charges against you, correct?

DERSHOWITZ: No, that's not correct. I responded to press inquiries by telling the truth.

My goal was to let the world know that Virginia Roberts' allegations against me were totally false.

DERSHOWITZ: These stories appeared, as far as I can tell, in every single newspaper in the world and on every media, which was part of their plot and the plan of your clients, which is why they absurdly mentioned Prince Andrew, claiming in the most absurd way–that they mentioned him because he was trying to lobby prosecutors to get a reduced sentence for Jeffrey Epstein.

They obviously put Prince Andrew in there in order to get massive publicity around the world. And every media in the world practically called me from the BBC, to CBS, to ABC, to CNN and I responded to lies with the truth.

SCAROLA: And the truth that you attempted to convey was that Bradley Edwards and Professor Paul Cassell were unethical lawyers who fabricated false charges against you, right?

DERSHOWITZ: The truth–The truth that I intended to convey was that the charges against me were false and fabricated, that I never had any sexual contact–

SCAROLA: Fabricated by whom, sir?

DERSHOWITZ: Please don't interrupt me.

SCOTT: Objection, interrupting.

SCAROLA: Please answer the question.

DERSHOWITZ: Please don't interrupt–

SCOTT: He's answering them. You may not like the answer, but he's answering them.

DERSHOWITZ: Now you've–you've made me lose my train of thought, so–

SCOTT: Can you read the question back and the– read the question back and his answers, please.

COURT REPORTER: The question was: "And the truth that you attempted to convey was that Bradley Edwards and Professor Paul Cassell were unethical lawyers who fabricated false charges against you, right?"

COURT REPORTER: And the answer was: "The truth that I intended to convey was that the charges against me were false and fabricated, that I never had any sexual contact"–and then the question was–the answer was interrupted.

DERSHOWTIZ: Okay. Let me continue. That I never had any sexual contact with Virginia Roberts because Professor Cassell insisted on conveying to the public that he was a former judge and that he was a Professor, and that he was using, improperly in my view, the stationery and name of his university to add credibility to his claims, I felt that it was imperative for me to indicate that he was engaging in improper and unethical conduct.

It would have been improper for me to have allowed his use of his credibility as a former federal judge, as a professor who uses, misuses his University imprimatur, it was very important for me to attack the credibility of the messengers of the false information.

And it was important for me to also remind the public that Bradley Edwards was a partner of Rothstein, a man who is spending 50 years in jail for fraudulently creating a Ponzi scheme to sell Jeffrey Epstein cases that didn't exist. Yes, it was very important for me to indicate the back–

DERSHOWITZ: the real backgrounds of these lawyers and to make sure that the public didn't believe that because they were credible, their story must be credible.

In fact, one of the first questions that I was asked repeatedly by the media is: Why would a former federal judge level a false charge against you? Why would a distinguished personal injury lawyer level a false charge against you?

And it was important for me to indicate why they would, that they were trying to do it for crass financial reasons, they were trying to do it to open up a non-prosecution agreement, they were trying to do it for reasons that were improper.

So, yes, I did—you know, Mr. Edwards, your client, is shaking his head, but when he's deposed under oath, he's not going to be able to simply shake his head. He's going to have to answer specific and direct questions.

SCAROLA: Let me try my question. Did you charge Bradley Edwards and Professor Paul Cassell in your mass media appearances with fabricating false charges against you?

DERSHOWITZ My media appearances were largely in response to media requests of me. I did not conduct a media campaign. The object of my speaking to the media was to respond to their questions. Their questions were, number 1, did you ever have any sexual contact with Virginia Roberts? And I unequivocally stated no.

DERSHOWITZ: I stated that I knew there were no videos or photographs because the event didn't occur. I stated that I would submit a sworn affidavit, which in effect waived the statute of limitations. I stated unequivocally that I was innocent of those false charges. I was then asked by the media, well, why would somebody who is a former federal judge and professor at a law school make these false charges?

I responded to those questions. Why would some-body like a distinguished personal injury lawyer make those false charges? And I responded to those questions. And everything I said was the truth, as I believed it to be at the time.

SCAROLA: Do you remember the question that was asked of you?

DERSHOWTIZ: Yes, I've answered it.

SCAROLA: What was the question?

DERSHOWITZ: As part of massive media campaign, I did charge your clients with deliber-ately falsifying a charge against me, and my answer satisfies that question.

SCAROLA: No, I don't think it does. Can you tell us whether that's what you did, did you charge–

DERSHOWITZ: I just did.

SCAROLA: Them with having intentionally fabri-cated false charges against you?

DERSHOWITZ: I believe that they inten-tionally fabricated false evidence against me. I believe that they pressured their client into fabri-cating false evidence against me. I believe that they helped to draft a perjurious affidavit that was filed in Court after they knew that I said I could prove that I couldn't have been there four of the five places that the alleged acts could have occurred.

DERSHOWITZ: I believe that when they recently sought to submit an additional claim repeating these charges into the federal court, that they did it knowing full well that these charges were false. That's my belief, yes.

SCAROLA: Are you aware that your lawyers filed a pleading on your behalf in this case with the title Defendant Alan M. Dershowitz's Answer to the Complaint and Counterclaim?

DERSHOWITZ: I'm not aware of that.

SCAROLA: Pardon me?

DERSHOWITZ: I'm not aware of the title of any legal pleadings.

SCAROLA: Do you know that an answer has been filed to the defamation action that has been brought against you?

DERSHOWITZ: Of course I mean I'm sure there's been a legal answer prepared. Of course, that's what lawyers do.

SCAROLA: Are you aware that there's also a counterclaim that has been filed on your behalf?

DERSHOWITZ: Yes, I authorized the counterclaim to be filed because I believe that your clients defamed me and that Mr. Cassell wrote a letter to ABC, which not even plausibly is within the claim of privilege, which asserts that I had -- asserts falsely and in a defamatory way that I had had sexual contact with Virginia Roberts, yes.

SCAROLA: Did you read the answer to the complaint and counterclaim—

DERSHOWITZ: I'm sure I did.

SCAROLA: before it was filed?

DERSHOWITZ: I'm sure I did.

SCAROL: And I assume that you approved of it, correct?

DERSHOWITZ: I assume I did, yes.

SCAROLA: Okay.

SCOTT: I object to anything as far as using pleadings like this, but go ahead and do it.

SCAROLA: As a law professor, would it be fair for us to assume that you know the difference between simple negligence and recklessness?

DERSHOWITZ: That's something that you could spend an entire semester teaching the difference between simple negligence and recklessness.

DERSHOWITZ: That's very much a matter of degree and the courts are–are split very much on what the meaning of "recklessness" is, particularly in the context of defamation. It's a very complicated subject.

SCAROLA: Do you personally recognize that there is a difference between simple negligence and recklessness?

DERSHOWITZ: At the extremes, yes, simple negligence is failure to perform a duty and recklessness is failure to perform a duty knowing that there–knowing or should know that there is a likelihood of some harm being committed. That's just what I remember from first year torts.

SCAROLA: And you do also recognize that there is a distinction between simple negligence and recklessness on one hand and intentional wrongdoing on the other, correct?

DERSHOWITZ: Again, I've argued cases about this issue. And it's a continuum. Sometimes courts say "that should have known" is the equivalent of "knowing." So it's a continuum. There's not an absolute straight line between those two, yeah. Moving forward…

SCAROLA: Were there any other entourage members that traveled with Jeffrey Epstein when he came to your home?

DERSHOWITZ: I have no recollection of any of them ever coming to my home. I don't remember but if that's whom he traveled with. Sometimes he would travel–he almost always had a regular girlfriend.

DERSHOWITZ: And I remember a few of them. One of them was a student at the business school who's–I may be merging two of them. One of them was a student at the business school. Another, maybe the same one, was a wealthy woman whose father owned banks in Great Britain.

Another was a woman from either the Czech Republic or Slovakia who was probably between 20 and 25, he is referring to Nadia Marcinkova who was 14 years old when Epstein brought her to the United States, probably closer to 25. And he would travel with a posse, basically, an entourage of–of people. But I never met some of the people who are in the entourage. They were just there.

SCAROLA: They were there at the same time that you were there and Jeffrey Epstein was there?

DERSHOWITZ: Well, they were–

SCOTT: Wait a minute. That's vague.

DERSHOWITZ: I mean, there in the house, there in Massachusetts?

SCAROLA: There, wherever. When you were in Jeffrey Epstein's presence, Jeffrey Epstein usually had what you have described as some regular girlfriend.

DERSHOWITZ: That's right.

SCAROLA: And you have described a variety of different regular girlfriends who were with him, correct?

DERSHOWITZ: Yes.

SCAROLA: Usually in the age range, you would estimate, between 20 and 25; is that correct?

DERSHOWITZ: I would say—

SCOTT: Objection. That's not it.

DERSHOWITZ: I would say between 22 and 25 would be a closer -- closer estimate. But 23, in that range. There were none that I ever believed were in any way teenagers and they all performed tasks. They were taking notes or they were arranging, serving coffee or doing various things. And that's the way Jeffrey would travel when he went to academic meetings. And these people were seen not only by me, they were seen by Larry Summers, they were seen by Church, they were seen by Marvin Minsky, they were seen by some of the most eminent academics and scholars in the world.

There was no hint or suggestion of anything sexual or improper in the presence of these people.

SCAROLA: Describe the motor vehicle that Jeffrey Epstein used to travel from the airport to your home on those occasions when you observed–

DERSHOWITZ: I have no recollection. They were rented cars.

SCAROLA: Limousines?

DERSHOWITZ: Limousines, yeah, yeah.

SCAROLA: And did you ever travel from your home with Jeffrey Epstein in a limousine?

DERSHOWITZ: Not during the relevant time period, no, no.

SCAROLA: So, you can state with certainty, that at no time between 1999 and 2002 did you ever travel from your home in a limousine with Jeffrey Epstein?

DERSHOWITZ: I can't imagine any reason why I would have. I did not fly in his plane during that period of time, my records establish. And I would see no reason why I would have. I don't have any recollection whether I specifically drove with him during that period of time. But I think I did not because I did not have any reason. Normally if I drove with him, it would be to go to the airport to get on his plane. That was the only reason that I would have ever to go in a limousine that I know of.

SCAROLA: What records establish that you were not on Jeffrey Epstein's plane during what you have described as the relevant time period?

DERSHOWITZ: No, you've described it as the relevant time period. You said 2009 to 2000–

SCAROLA: No, sir. In the answer you just–

DERSHOWITZ: –1999–

SCAROLA: –gave, you used the phrase "relevant time frame," time period.

DERSHOWITZ: Yeah, I was picking up on your terms between 1999 and 2002. So can we agree that's the relevant time period?

SCAROLA: You can tell me what–what your response is based on that you never traveled on Jeffrey Epstein's airplane during the relevant time period, whatever you consider that to be.

DERSHOWITZ: Okay. Number 1 my own calendars, which have been provided to you. Number 2, my cell phone records. Number 3 my wife's calendars. Number 4 my teaching and other schedule. Number 5 my own recollection.

DERSHOWITZ: And number 6, as far as we know, the airplane manifests do not have me on any airplanes during that time period.

Scarola asked Dershowitz if he understood that, "More than 30 underage women have come forward to report that your friend, Jeffrey Epstein, paid them for sex and that he pled guilty to procuring underage girls for prostitution, and that he paid very large sums of money to settle their civil claims against him."

SCAROLA: Do you still insist that he had not engaged in sex or erotic massages with any minors?

Martin Weinberg, Epstein's attorney, immediately interrupted and instructed Dershowitz not to answer the question. Thomas Scott, Dershowitz's attorney, also instructed him not to answer.

In spite of their recommendations and knowing that he was Epstein's attorney, Dershowitz responded:

DERSHOWITZ: Marty, you're the lawyer for my client. Do you—do you order me to answer the question or not? I am going to follow the instruction. I have no choice. He's my client.

SCAROLA: You know that he pled guilty to sexual abuse of minors, correct?

DERSHOWITZ: Could you tell me exactly what he pleaded guilty to so I can answer that question?

SCAROLA: Well, do you know? You represented him during the period of time that he was under–that he was–that he was under criminal charges, didn't you?

SCOTT: So you're withdrawing the prior question; you're now asking this question? Okay.

SCAROLA: That's correct, I'm asking–this question

DERSHOWITZ: So I represented him–I represented him first in Palm Beach County, and at that point, he had been prepared to plead guilty to, I think, one count–

WEINBERG: Alan, I'm sorry. This is again, going right into the work that you did for him as his lawyer and I instruct you not to answer.

SCOTT: That's it, then follow his–as your attorney, I'm telling you to follow the lawyer's advice.

DERSHOWITZ: Uh-huh.

SCAROLA: Do you agree, Mr. Dershowitz that deciding the issues in this case will depend on evaluating not only Virginia Roberts' credibility but your credibility as well?

SCOTT: Objection, legal conclusion, not relevant here.

DERSHOWITZ: I think that I can prove my complete innocence and the fact that–Virginia

Roberts made up the story out of whole cloth without my credibility being at issue, but I'm perfectly happy to put my credibility at issue because I am telling the blue absolute truth about everything regarding Virginia Roberts.

SCAROLA: One way to evaluate credibility is to compare an individual's statements with available documentary evidence, correct?

DERSHOWITZ: That's too broad a question. Depending on what the documentary evidence could be. Documentary could be lies. Documents contain lies and oral statements contain truth. So, no, I don't think that's a particularly good way. It depends on the nature of the document. For example, videotape would be very good.

If you had a videotape that in some way supported Virginia Roberts' statements and it undercut what I said, that would be fine. That's why from day one I've asked to have if there is any videotape shown or any photographs because I know what happened.

DERSHOWTIZ: I know that I never had any contact, any sexual contact, any, improper contact with Virginia Roberts. And I know, therefore, that there cannot be any evidence that contradicts that because you can't simply make up facts. So I am telling you the absolute truth.

SCAROLA: You also know that all of the video-tapes that were taken through surveillance cameras throughout Jeffrey Epstein's home were destroyed don't you?

DERSHOWITZ: Of course I don't know that.

SCAROLA: You don't know?

DERSHOWITZ: Of course not.

SCAROLA: So you didn't read the police reports then?

SCOTT: Objection. Mr. Epstein, do you want him to answer that question?

SIMPSON: Mr. Weinberg.

SCOTT: Mr. Weinberg?

WEINBERG: It's the same objection.

DERSHOWITZ: Oh, so there's no question.

SCAROLA: You have stated publicly repeatedly that the airplane manifests will exonerate you, correct?

DERSHOWITZ: I have stated publicly that the airplane manifest, the one that I have seen, do not show me on any of Jeffrey Epstein's airplanes in the 7 relevant period of time, which I define as the summer of 1999 through the summer of 2002, number one. Number two, that none of the airplane manifests will show me on the same plane with Virginia Roberts. And three, that none of the manifests will show me on an airplane with Jeffrey Epstein and any underage girls that were at least visible in the passenger part of the airplane.

SCAROLA: Well, that raises an interesting point, Mr. Dershowitz. Tell us about the interior—of that plane.

DERSHOWITZ: Why is it interesting? My recollection is the plane was a 160 Gulfstream IV. That it had a cabin that seated approximately one, two, three, four—maybe ten—ten people. It had mostly seats—I used to sit in the seat facing backward, that's the way, I prefer to fly. And in the back of the plane there was a toilet, a place to serve food. And a couch that served as a seat with seat belts for maybe two or three additional people. But I never saw the plane—the only time I ever saw the plane filled to capacity was when I went down to watch a launch of a satellite—

SCAROLA: Does that have—anything to do with the configuration of the interior of the plane?

DERSHOWITZ: To outer space, yes. Yes, I'm telling you that I've mostly seen it only with four or five people. The only time I've seen the couch—

SCAROLA: Did I ask you how many people–

SCOTT: Well, you're interrupting–

SCAROLA: Were in the plane, at the time I asked you, what the configuration of the cabin was, Mr. Dershowitz?

DERSHOWITZ: I'm explaining–

SCAROLA: Is that part of the question that I asked–

DERSHOWITZ: I'm explaining the couch.

SCAROLA: or is that your effort to make speeches in an effort to consume the limited amount of time that we have?

SCOTT: I would object to that characterization.

DERSHOWITZ: I wanted to start at–I wanted to start at 12:00–at 1:30 today.

SCOTT: And the speech.

SIMPSON: Alan, Alan.

DERSHOWITZ: All the delays have been caused by you not me. And I'm ready to go to 5:30, but you're quitting at 5–or 4:30.

SCAROLA: Yes, sir, I have–a commitment–I have a commitment to chair an–Easter Seals fundraiser.

DERSHOWITZ: So don't blame any delays on me, sir. Don't we all. We all have commitments.

SCAROLA: You've known–did you see a bed in the plane?

DERSHOWITZ: I never saw a bed in the plane. As far as I know, there was no bed in the plane. And that's what I was trying to explain. That the only time I've seen that couch used is when two or three people were sitting in it when we went down to watch the launch of the satellite because that was the only time I saw the plane filled.

Other than that, it was a plain, ordinary couch that was never used by anybody during the flights. We were all sitting in our seats. I do not know for a fact that that couch becomes a bed. I never saw it as a bed. And the answer is categorically no.

SCAROLA: Well, the question was: Is there a bed on the plane? The answer to that question is not a categorical no; the answer to that question is you don't know; is that right?

DERSHOWITZ: The answer to that question is there is a couch on the plane like it is on all–as far as I know, all Gulfstream IVs. I have no idea whether or not that couch becomes a bed.

SCAROLA: You told the American lawyer on January 15, 2015 a statement that you have repeated on multiple occasions: "I've been married to the same woman for 28 years. She goes with me everywhere." Do you acknowledge making that statement?

DERSHOWITZ: Yes. My wife goes with me everywhere today. These days, now that our daughter is grown, 18 up and went to high school and college, she travels with me everywhere. It's a rare, rare occasion when my wife doesn't travel with me. In fact, I have a condition of my speaking engagements that the speaking engagements have to pay for my wife to come with me.

I hate traveling alone. I almost never do it unless there is an absolutely essential reason for Carolyn to be somewhere else, such as taking care of her 96-year-old mother. But it is true I travel with my wife.

SCAROLA: In fact, the airplane manifests that have been produced reflect your having traveled on Jeffrey Epstein's airplane on ten separate occasions and on none of those occasions–

DERSHOWITZ: Is that testimony, Sir?

SCAROLA: On none of those occasions–is your wife reflected as having been a passenger at the same time that you are were on Jeffrey Epstein's airplane, right?

SCOTT: Object to the form. There's no timeframe or anything of that nature. If you can answer–

SCAROLA: All of the manifests that have been produced in this litigation, the ones that you say corroborate your testimony and exonerate you, demonstrate that you never flew on Jeffrey Epstein's plane in the company of your wife, correct?

DERSHOWITZ: No. That's not true. I flew in the company of my wife and my daughter from Charleston, South Carolina to Guadalupe–

SCAROLA: I'm asking about what the manifests show, Sir.

DERSHOWITZ: I'm telling you what–

SCAROLA: the ones that you say exonerate you.

DERSHOWITZ: Well, I said that–

SCAROLA: Is there a manifest that shows that you and your wife were on Jeffrey Epstein's plane at the same time together?

SCOTT: Let me object to the–

DERSHOWITZ: I don't know that.

SCOTT: –argumentative nature and compound nature. He's trying to answer you questions.

DERSHOWITZ: Let me go through each of the times.

DERSHOWITZ: Okay. Okay.

SCAROLA: Is there a manifest that shows that your wife ever accompanied you on a flight on Jeffrey Epstein's private airplane?

SCOTT: Let me object again. There's no reference to the timeframe or the relevant timeframe–

SCAROLA: Any time ever.

DERSHOWITZ: My wife accompanied me on two occasions, my nephew SCAROLA: Is there a manifest–

SCOTT: You're cutting him off, Counsel.

DERSHOWITZ: Let me finish.

SCAROLA: He's not answering my question.

SCOTT: Yes, he is answering your question.

DERSHOWITZ: My nephew accompanied me on one occasion. My research assistant, Mitch Webber, accompanied me on one occasion.

My son or grandson, I'm not sure which, accompanied me on one occasion. And the occasions that I flew on Jeffrey Epstein's plane were almost always business occasions during a time when my daughter, Ella, was in elementary school, if we're talking about the relevant period of time. And during that period of time, on occasion my wife did not fly with me.

SCAROLA: Is there—

DERSHOWITZ: But let me emphasize—let me emphasize that the manifests that do exculp me, do not show me flying with Virginia Roberts, they do not show me flying with any young women.

They know that on every trip I took, there was a business reason for it, there were other people on the plane, and it is inconceivable that during any of those periods of time, the lies that Virginia Roberts told about me could have been true.

SCAROLA: So it's your contention that no manifests show you traveling outside the company of your wife is that correct? —No manifest shows you traveling outside the company of your wife?

DERSHOWITZ: I'm confused. That's a double, triple negative.

SCOTT: Do you understand the question?

DERSHOWITZ: I don't, no.

SCOTT: Rephrase it.

SCAROLA: There is not a single manifest of the ten that shows you as a passenger on Jeffrey Epstein's plane that shows your wife there at the same time, correct?

DERSHOWITZ: I am not aware that there are ten manifests. I would be happy to look at the manifests. I have explained–Unfortunately–

SCAROLA: –each of the times–we won't have time to do that this afternoon–but we will have time to do that eventually.

DERSHOWITZ: We will–I welcome that time, because I can give complete context to every single trip I took. And if you're trying to convey the impression that there was any occasion on which I had any improper conduct while I was on that airplane that is a categorical lie.

SCAROLA: What I am trying to do, Sir is to test the veracity of your public assertions that you have never traveled outside the presence of your wife.

DERSHOWITZ: That is a lie.

SCAROLA: That is what I'm trying to do.

DERSHOWITZ: That is a lie, Sir, a categorical lie. I challenge you to find any statement where I said I have never traveled outside the presence of my wife.

SCAROLA: Well, how about this—

DERSHOWITZ: Sir, find me that statement.

SCAROLA: —do you—do you remember having—stated publicly on multiple occasions that you never received a massage – from Jeffrey Epstein?

DERSHOWITZ: No.

SCOTT: Unless you can show and characterize them by date and time, you just can't say here—it's improper impeachment—that you've done this ten times. It's just improper completely.

SCAROLA: Can you answer the question—

SCOTT: And it's overly broad.

SCAROLA: do you have any recollection of saying that you never received a massage?

DERSHOWITZ: I did receive a massage.

SCAROLA: Do you have any recollection—

DERSHOWITZ: A. I have no recollection—

SCAROLA: –of making that public statement that you never received a massage?

DERSHOWITZ: I can't imagine me saying that. If I said it I was mistaken. I had one massage, to my recollection.

SCAROLA: Okay. Tell us about where that occurred.

DERSHOWITZ: That occurred in my bedroom of Jeffrey Epstein's home in Palm Beach. I was asked whether Palm Beach. I was asked whether I wanted a massage. I had been asked repeatedly whether I wanted a massage and I had said no.

DERSHOWITZ: Then I was told that they had a masseuse coming from Miami who was a specialist of some kind, she was very good, she was Russian, and she worked, I think, in the Russian baths or something like that, and I agreed to have a massage.

I regretted it. She massaged me in a very tough and rough way. And she wanted to put her knees on my shoulder and I said no.

I immediately called my wife when the massage was over and I told her about the bad experience I had. And I said to her, see, I really don't like massages. But my wife likes massages. And she has had -- she has massages frequently.

SCAROLA: This massage occurred in your bedroom in Jeffrey Epstein's house; is that correct?

DERSHOWITZ: Not in my bedroom, in the bedroom that I had been assigned, which was a guest bedroom. The door was open. The–a massage table was brought in. I kept my undergarments on. And I was massaged maybe for 20 minutes or 25 minutes. And then–and then she left and I had an unpleasant experience and I called my wife and I told her about it.

SCAROLA: Was the bedroom to which you were assigned, which you previously referred to as your bedroom–

DERSHOWITZ: No, no. I said "my bedroom" in the sense that I was in it.

SCAROLA: Was the bedroom to which you were assigned in the private section of the residence?

SCOTT: Do you understand the question?

DERSHOWITZ: Yeah, let me explain exactly. This requires a long answer.

There–when you walk into Jeffrey Epstein's house, there are two areas. If you walk up the left side of the stairway, there are guest bedrooms, three or four guest bedrooms.

Those were assigned to people like Senator George Mitchell, Ehud Barak, prominent guests who would stay in his house. Each one had its own bathroom and its own bed.

I stayed there with my wife for a period of time. But then there was another area of the house, which I have never been in, ever, and which nobody was allowed basically into, which was Jeffrey Epstein's part of the house, which contained his bedroom and whatever other rooms. I've read about them, but I've never seen them. So it was in the guest area of the house over the kitchen.

SCAROLA: Who told you no one was allowed in that area of the house?

DERSHOWITZ: I was told by the people that that was off–off limits, that that was Jeffrey's–

SCAROLA: Which people?

DERSHOWITZ: Ghislaine Maxwell, Sarah Kellen, that was Jeffrey's area of the house and the guests were limited to the public areas of the house and the–and I think that's common in many houses when you go and stay at somebody's house, you don't go into their bathrooms and their bedrooms.

SCAROLA: Jeffrey Epstein's art consisted of photographs of young naked girls all over the house, right?

DERSHOWITZ: Are you testifying? That's false. I never saw any such thing. Ever. Never saw a picture, with one exception, of a nude. The one exception was a sepia print of Rodin's model that appeared on one of his desks. But in all the times I was at Jeffrey Epstein's house in Palm Beach, the one time I was in his house in—on the island, certainly the one time in—in the ranch because there was nothing there, it was just a construction site, I never saw a picture—or in his house in New York, I never saw a picture of a naked woman, ever.

In late December 2015, I asked an attorney close to the case what he thought about the Dershowitz deposition. The attorney who asked to remain anonymous said, "the court is recognizing that many of the statements made by Dershowitz are not accurate. The courts in the course of the Defamation litigation are finally examining the exaggerations he made and the strategic silence of Virginia Louise Roberts in the face of various untruths. This is just one of several rulings in that case."

To date, the attorney explained, "Boies has not filed any case against Dershowitz. Professor Dershowitz simply lied about what he and Boies discussed in the course of settlement discussions, which are privileged. There is nothing unusual about counsel and their clients having settlement discussions."

The same source explained that, "If Dershowitz or any other defendant and counsel want to discuss a potential settlement, lawyers have a duty to find out what the other party has in mind. That is what happened in this case. Evidently, there was no settlement arising out of those discussions. Angry about that, Dershowitz, apparently violated the privilege and claimed that Boies had said various things that Boies actually did not say."

"Whatever the circumstances involving Dershowitz, whether he will be prosecuted for making false claims or not, that's up to the prosecutors," the attorney said. The attorney also pointed out that, "No prosecutor has expressed any opinion about whether Dershowitz is being investigated or will be prosecuted," he explained.

It seems Dershowitz perhaps had a premonition. In January 2015, Dershowitz told The Boston Globe, "Someone will be disbarred. Either it will be me, or the two lawyers. In the end, someone's reputation is going to be destroyed, either mine or theirs."[181]

As it happened, none of the attorneys were disbarred. The case was settled on Friday, April 8, 2016 when Edwards and Cassell issued a notice of withdrawal for partial summary judgment and agreed to a settlement agreement.

In "The Confidential Settlement Agreement, Ms. Giuffre reaffirmed her allegations, and the withdrawal of the referenced filings is not intended to be, and should not be construed as being, an acknowledgement by Edwards and Cassell that the allegations made by Roberts Giuffre were mistaken."

> *"Edwards and Cassell acknowledged that the public filing in the Crime Victims' Rights Act case against Dershowitz became a major distraction from the merits of the well-founded CVRA case by causing delay and, as a consequence, turned out to have been a tactical mistake. For that reason, Edwards and Cassell have chosen to withdraw the referenced filing as a condition of settlement."[182]*

On April 9, 2016, I e-mailed Professor Dershowitz asking for a statement. He did not respond. When I asked Edwards and Cassell, Edwards said, "We did not withdraw a complaint. We settled the defamation action and as part of the settlement certain pleadings that were filed by Jack Scarola as well as Alan's Dershowitz attorney were withdrawn."

On April 11, 2016, Vivia Chen, a reporter at The American Lawyer said, "I got what I always wanted. They withdrew everything!" Dershowitz told her. He also said, "He spent over $1 million on legal fees, insurance covered a chunk of it, he won't disclose if the settlement entails any monetary rewards, citing a confidentiality clause. But he says he's not suffering financially because of the ordeal, "I continue to be sought after; people call me every day for legal work…Part of me," he said, "Wanted to have a trial and have evidence come out."[183]

"If Dershowitz was looking for total vindication," Chen reported, "I'm not sure this cuts it. But he was satisfied with the wording in the settlement… As a legal matter, Giuffre's lawyers couldn't admit she was wrong to accuse him." Dershowitz explained, "they can't take back the claims because that could be used against her on a perjury indictment. That would mean throwing her under the bus." Ultimately, they'll have to make a claim that it was a case of mistaken identity, that it was done in good faith."[184] The settlement was reached with prejudice, which means that was the end of the case.

CHAPTER FIFTEEN

SOMETHING OTHER THAN THE TRUTH

Dershowitz's testimony was important for several reasons, not the least of which was shed light on a shocking account and tell the truth, set the record straight, and explain the details of his relationship, if any, with Virginia Louise Roberts, Jeffrey Epstein, Ghislaine Maxwell and former president Bill Clinton.

If past is prologue, given the calendar year, Dershowitz's statement about his insights into the relationship between former president Clinton and some underage girls is invaluable on two fronts. The years 2015-2016 are presidential campaign years. Epstein's case and the allegations of impropriety implicating Clinton and two underage girls, plus the donations gifted to them by Epstein prior to and after his indictment, could potentially derail his wife's presidential bid in November 2016.

Given Bill Clinton's history of sexual misconduct and his impeachment for perjury, in 1998; talks of the Lewinsky scandal and "bimbo eruptions" as the Secretary's staffers refer to the women who accused her husband of sexual misconduct; and Kathleen Wiley's 2015 open testimony concerning former president

Clinton, all point to a history of bad behavior of a President while holding public office.

As a result of the president's friendship with Epstein, even though their relationship was in the past, their history could have negative implications for the Secretary's presidential bid. Professor Dershowitz' transcript shed some light on the subject.

> SCAROLA: Did you state during the same inter-view, the CNN Don Lemon interview: "She, Virginia Louise Roberts, has said that Bill Clinton was with her at an orgy on Jeffrey's island"?

> DERSHOWITZ: I did state that, yes.

> SCAROLA: Was that statement intended as fact, opinion, or was it intended as rhetorical hyperbole?

> DERSHOWITZ: It was a statement based on what I believed were the facts at the time I said them… Various newspapers and blogs had placed Bill Clinton on, quote, "orgy island" on–in the pres-ence of Jeffrey Epstein when there were orgies… And at the time I made that statement, I had a belief that she had accused Bill Clinton of partic-ipating or being–as being a part of or an observer or–or a witness or a participant in orgies on what was called Jeffrey Epstein's orgy island. That was my state of belief, honest belief at the time I made that statement.

> SCAROLA: Yes, sir. And what I want to know is what the source of that honest belief was? Identify

any source that attributed to Virginia Roberts the statement that Bill Clinton was with her at an orgy on Jeffrey's island.

DERSHOWITZ: We can provide you about, I think, 20 newspaper articles and blogs, which certainly raise the implication that Bill Clinton had improperly participated in sexual activities on the island either as an observer or as a participant… The issue was raised on Sean Hannity's program. The headlines in various British media had suggested that…

It's my belief that Virginia Roberts intended to convey that impression when she was trying to sell her story to various media, which she successfully sold her story in Britain, that she wanted to keep that open as a possibility… And then when I firmly declared, based on my research, that Bill Clinton had almost certainly never been on that island, she then made a firm statement that she–which was a– perjurious statement, a firm, perjurious statement, saying that although Bill Clinton had been with her on the island and had had dinner with her. The perjurious statement was that Bill Clinton had been on the island with her…

The lie was that she described in great detail a dinner with Bill Clinton and two under aged Russian women who were offered to Bill Clinton for sex but that Bill Clinton turned down… So she then put in her affidavit that although–perjuriously, although she had seen Bill Clinton on that island, she then stated that she had not had sex with Bill Clinton... To my knowledge that was–to my knowledge at least, that was the first time she stated that–that she not had sex with Bill Clinton...

DERSHOWITZ: She had certainly implied, or at least some of the media had inferred from her statements that she might, very well have observed Bill Clinton in a sexually compromising position... So, when I made that statement to Don Lemon, I had a firm belief, based on reading newspaper accounts and blogs, that it was true.

SCAROLA: Can you identify a single newspaper that attributed to Virginia Roberts the statement that Bill Clinton was with her at an orgy on Jeffrey's island?

DERSHOWITZ: I think there–I don't have them in my head right now. But I do recall reading headlines that talked about things like, sex slave places, Clinton on 'Orgy Island', things of that kind. I would be happy to provide them for you. I don't have them on the top of my head.

SCAROLA: There's a big difference between saying that Bill Clinton was on Jeffrey's island and saying that Bill Clinton was at an orgy on Jeffrey's island, isn't there?

SCOTT: Objection.

SCAROLA: Do you recognize a distinction between those statements?

SCOTT: Form.

DERSHOWITZ: I don't think that distinction was clearly drawn by the media.

SCAROLA: I'm asking whether you recognize the distinction?

DERSHOWITZ: Oh, I–I certainly recognize a distinction.

SCAROLA: Oh, so–

DERSHOWITZ: Let me finish. I certainly recognize a distinction between Bill Clinton being on the island, which I believe she perjuriously put in her affidavit, and Bill Clinton participating actively in an orgy. I also think it's a continuum...And there is the possibility, which I don't personally believe to be true, that he was on the island...

There was the possibility, which I don't believe to be true, that he was on the island when orgies were taking place...

There was the possibility that he was on the island and observed an orgy, and there was the possibility that he was on the island and participated in an orgy.

Newspapers picked up those stories. I'll give you an example of a newspaper that actually said that she had placed or that I was on the island and– that I participated in an orgy along with Stephen Hawkings, the famous physicist from Cambridge University, that was a newspaper published in the Virgin Islands, which falsely claimed that I was at an orgy with Stephen Hawkings.

DERSHOWITZ: So, many newspapers were suggesting, implying, and I inferred from reading those newspapers that that's what she had said to the media…

If I was wrong about that based on subsequent information, I apologize. But I certainly, at the time I said it, believed it and made the statement in good faith in the belief that it was an honest statement.

SCAROLA: Okay. So you now are withdrawing the statement that you made that Virginia Roberts said that Bill Clinton was with her at an orgy on Jeffrey's island; that was wrong?

DERSHOWITZ: I don't know whether she ever said that…I would not repeat that statement and have not repeated that statement based on her denial. As soon as she denied it, I never again made that statement and would not again make that statement.

SCAROLA: Having reviewed the available airplane flight logs, you are aware that Bill Clinton flew on at least 15 occasions with Jeffrey Epstein on his private plane, correct?

According to my pilot logs, President Clinton traveled on Epstein's jet seventeen (17) times.

DERSHOWITZ: Yes.

SCAROLA: Have you ever attempted to get flight log information with regard to former President Clinton's other private airplane travel?

DERSHOWITZ: No.

SCAROLA: Never made a public records request–

DERSHOWITZ: Yes.

SCAROLA: Under the Freedom of Information Act with regard to those records?

DERSHOWITZ: Well, we have made a Freedom of Information request. My–my attorney in New York, Louis Freeh, the former head of the FBI, (appointed by President Bill Clinton who also worked on the Epstein criminal investigating team), has made a FOIA request for all information that would conclusively prove that Bill Clinton was never on Jeffrey Epstein's island, yes.

SCAROLA: And you were denied those records, correct?

DERSHOWITZ: No, no, no.

SCAROLA: Oh, you got them?

SCOTT: Well, wait a minute. Let's take it slow. Ask a question.

DERSHOWITZ: As any lawyer knows, FOIA requests take a long, long period of time. So they were neither denied nor were they given to us. They are very much in process.

MINUTES LATER:

SCAROLA: Mr. Dershowitz, what is rhetorical hyperbole?

DERSHOWITZ: Rhetorical means verbal and hyperbole means exaggeration.

SCAROLA: Something other than the truth, correct?

DERSHOWTIZ: Truth --Truth has many, many meanings and is a continuum. The Supreme Court has held that rhetorical hyperbole cannot be the basis, for example, of perjury prosecutions or generally of a Defamation prosecution. So it depends on the context. You might just look at the dictionary and probably get a variety of definitions for it.

SCAROLA: Well, what I'm concerned about, Mr. Dershowitz is not a dictionary definition. I want to know what your understanding of rhetorical hyperbole is. And do you agree that pursuant to your understanding of rhetorical hyperbole, it is an exaggeration beyond the facts?

SCOTT: Objection, argumentative and compound, three questions.

DERSHOWITZ: No–

SCOTT: You can answer.

DERSHOWITZ: I would not agree with that definition.

SCAROLA: Okay. Then define it for us, if you would, please.

DERSHOWITZ: I think I have already.

SCAROLA: … I didn't understand it, so I would like you to try to give us a direct response to that question if you're able to.

DERSHOWITZ: I will repeat exactly what I said. A rhetorical means verbal and hyperbole means some exaggeration of the facts for political or other reasons, but generally it is truthful in a literal sense but perhaps–it all depends on context…And if you tell me the context in which I used it, I will be happy to describe what I meant in that context. But I don't think you can really answer a question about what two words put together mean without understanding the context.

SCAROLA: Okay. Well, we're going to talk about some context. Do you recall having been interviewed on 'CNN Tonight' on January 5, 2015?

DERSHOWITZ: I have no current recollection of– Well I have no memory of what specifically I said.

SCAROLA: Do you recall having been interviewed on CNN Tonight by Don Lemon in early January of 2015, where you spoke about matters that have become the subject of this litigation?

DERSHOWITZ: Yes, I do.

SCAROLA: Did you make the following statement during the course of that interview: "As to the airplanes, there are manifests that will prove beyond any doubt that I was never on a private airplane with this woman or any other underage gir"?

DERSHOWITZ: That is a truthful statement. I would repeat it right now. I've reviewed the manifests. First, I know I was never on the airplane with any underage woman. I know that for a fact. I have absolutely no doubt in my mind about that. And the records that I have reviewed confirm that.

They have Virginia Roberts on a number of airplane flights with Jeffrey Epstein. They have me on a number of flights, none–let me emphasize, none within the relevant time period, none within the relevant time period.

That is, there are no manifests that have me on Jeffrey Epstein's airplane during the time that Virginia Roberts claims to have–falsely claims to have had sex with me. So, yes, not only do I recall making that statement, but also I repeat it here today. And it is absolutely true. And it just confirms what I know, and that is that Virginia Roberts made up the entire story.

It is a well-known fact that pilot logs and pilot manifestos have not always included names, ages and relevant information of every passenger on all their scheduled flights. This was the case in the logs identifying the passengers who were traveling on Epstein's jet. On many occasions, only the initials or gender of the passenger were included.

SCAROLA: Your statement was that you were never on a private airplane with this woman, which I assume was a reference to Virginia Roberts, correct?

DERSHOWITZ: It is, yes.

SCAROLA: Or any other underage girl?

DERSHOWITZ: That's right.

However, on April 16, 1999, Alan Dershowitz appeared on the pilot log alongside Emmy Taylor (an underage girl at the time and friend of Ghislaine Maxwell), Epstein and one unidentified male. David Rogers signed the pilot's signature line.

SCAROLA: All right. How many times–

DERSHOWITZ: Well, let me be very clear. I have no idea who was in the front cabin of the airplane with the two pilots. Obviously what I intended to say and what I say here now is I never saw an under aged person on an airplane. Now, when I -- when I flew with Jeffrey Epstein to the launch, my recollection is that there may have been a couple on the plane with their child who was going to see the launch.

Dershowitz flew several times on Epstein's jet unaccompanied by his wife, daughter, or son as he declared in an earlier statement according to the pilot logs. His family's names do not appear on the logs. The earliest log made available to me, dates back to 1997.

Dershowitz traveled on his jet beginning February 9, 1997 with one unidentified female, Emmy Taylor, Epstein, Maxwell, Joel Pashcow, C. Hazel, and Mandy (family name illegible). On October 21, 1998, he traveled alone with Epstein from Bedford, New York airport to Teterboro, New Jersey. Again on April 16, 1999 he traveled with Epstein, Emmy Taylor and one unidentified male.

On February 5, 2004, he flew with Epstein, his assistant and alleged procurer, Sarah Kellen. On November 17, 2005 Dershowitz traveled on a multi leg flight originating in Bedford, to CYUL

(Pierre Trudeau in Montreal) back to Bedford with a final stop in Teterboro (TEB), the private airport. He traveled with two unidentified females identified as A.M. and Tatiana.

> DERSHOWITZ: But that was certainly not the context in which I made the statement. I never saw any underage, young person who would be the subject or object of any improper sexual activities. Had I seen Jeffrey Epstein ever in the presence of an underage woman in a context that suggested sexuality, I would have, a, left the scene; b, reported it; and, c, never had any further contact with Jeffrey Epstein.

> SCAROLA: You have also made the statement that you were never on a private airplane with any underage women or any young women, correct?

> DERSHOWITZ: The context was underage women in a sexual context. If it was a—you know, a four-year-old child being carried by her mother, that would not be included in what I intended to say.

> SCAROLA: Your sworn testimony yesterday, according to the transcription, the official transcription of that testimony, was that, quote:

> "Let me emphasize that the manifests that do exculpate me do not show me flying with Virginia Roberts, they do not show me flying with any young women." That was the testimony you gave under oath. Do you stand by that testimony today?

DERSHOWITZ: The manifests that I saw corroborate my own memory–my own memory is as clear as could be–that I never saw any inappropriately aged, under aged women on any airplane to my knowledge that were visible to me at any time that I flew. That is my testimony, yes.

SCAROLA: Well, that's not a response to the question that I asked. Is it your testimony today that you never flew on a private airplane with, quote, "any young women"?

DERSHOWITZ: By young women, I obviously meant in that context underage women. And underage women in the context of sexuality and, yes, I–I stand by that statement.

SCAROLA: All right. So your–your clarification of your earlier testimony is that you never saw any young women in a sexual context?

DERSHOWITZ: That's not clarification. I think that's what I initially said. That's what I initially intended. And that's the way any reasonable–any reasonable person would interpret what my original testimony was. So I don't believe my original testimony required any clarification.

SCAROLA: So what you meant to convey by the statement that you made when you said you never flew with any underage girl or any young women was you never flew with any underage girl or young women in a sexual context?

DERSHOWITZ: Let me simply repeat the fact and that is, to my knowledge, I never flew on an airplane or was ever in the presence on an airplane with any underage woman who would be somebody who might be in a sexual context. I say that only to eliminate the possibility that some four-year-old was on the lap of a mother or somebody was on the airplane with family members.

But, no, I do not recall—and I'm very firm about this—being on an airplane with anybody who I believed could be the subject of Jeffrey Epstein or anyone else's improper sexual activities.

Scarola presented Dershowitz with a photograph of a young woman.

SCAROLA: Do you recognize that young woman, Mr. Dershowitz?

DERSHOWITZ: No.

SCAROLA: Never saw her?

DERSHOWITZ: Not that I know of.

SCAROLA: Never flew on a private airplane with her?

DERSHOWITZ: Not that I know of.

SCAROLA: Do you recognize the name Tatiana?

DERSHOWITZ: I do recall that Jeffrey Epstein had a friend named Tatiana.

SCAROLA: That you flew with?

DERSHOWITZ: I don't remember that I flew with her or not. I may have. But I don't recall necessarily. But I did meet -- I remember meeting a woman named Tatiana. This does not look like Tatiana, like the woman I met.

SCAROLA: Okay. So that's a--that's a different Tatiana?

DERSHOWITZ: No, I don't know. I have no idea. I do not recognize this woman. She's not familiar to me at all. I can tell you this: Without any doubt, I never met anybody dressed like this on any airplane or in the presence of Jeffrey Epstein or in any context--related to this case.

SCAROLA: Did she have--more clothes on, or less, clothes on when you met her? When you met the woman that you're referencing, did she have more clothes on or fewer clothes on than that woman?

DERSHOWITZ: Every woman that I met in the presence of Jeffrey Epstein was properly dressed, usually in suits and dresses and--and appropriately covered up. I never met any women in the context of Jeffrey Epstein who were dressed anything like this.

SCAROLA: Would you agree that that is a young woman in that photograph?

DERSHOWITZ: I have no idea what her age is.

SCAROLA: So you don't know whether she was underage, 12, or overage, or a young woman, or not a young woman?

DERSHOWITZ: I don't–know this woman, so I have no idea how old a woman in a picture is. She could be–17 she could be 30. She could be 25. I have no idea.

SCAROLA: Or she could be 15 or 16?

DERSHOWITZ: I don't think so.

SCAROLA: But you don't know?

DERSHOWITZ: This doesn't–well, I don't know how old you are. This does not strike me–

SCAROLA: Old enough to know that–

Approximately ten minutes later, after much back and forth between Scarola, Dershowitz and Scott, the attorneys decided to appoint a Special Master for the proceedings to help Scarola obtain some answers. Seconds later, Dershowitz answered the question:

SCAROLA: Is the last name on the photograph spelled exactly the same way as the last name on the flight log?

DERSHOWITZ: If you're talking about a flight log that I was not on that flight, the answer is yes.

SCAROLA: All right. Thank you very much, Sir. Now, that flight log also shows you flying repeatedly in the company of a woman named Tatiana, correct?

DERSHOWITZ: I've only seen one reference to Tatiana on November 17. If you want to show me any other references, I'd be happy to look at them.

Scarola shows Dershowitz Exhibit 5.

SCAROLA: Do you see the name of the woman in the photographs I have handed to you is Tatiana K-O-V-Y-L-I-N-A, a Victoria's Secret model? The photographs identify the woman as Tatiana Kovy-lina, correct?

DERSHOWITZ: Yes, but.

After much bantering back and forth over the spelling of the girl's name. Scarola resumed his questions.

SCAROLA: All right, would you describe for us, please, the Tatiana that you flew with Jeffrey Epstein on November 17, 2005.

DERSHOWITZ: First, I want to emphasize that that's three years later than any of the issues involved in this case. I have no recollection of flying with this woman. I saw the name Tatiana on a manifest. And my recollection of Tatiana—I have no recollection of flying with her, but my recollection of Tatiana is that she was a serious, mid 20s woman, friend of Jeffrey Epstein, who I may have met on one or two occasions when he was with her in-perhaps Harvard University where he was meeting with academics and scholars, or perhaps—I think that is probably the context where-where she might have been.

SCAROLA: But you never flew with her?

DERSHOWITZ: I have no recollection of flying with her.

SCAROLA: OK, Well let's see if this helps to refresh your recollection, Mr. Dershowitz.

Scarola presented Dershowitz with photographs of the woman in question and again Professor Dershowitz argued over the spelling of the last name. Apparently, it showed the woman's name on a return flight.

DERSHOWITZ: …I have nothing on the record that suggests that it's a return flight. And it has different people on it. So I have no reason to believe it's a return flight.

SCAROLA: Is the last –the question that I asked you, Mr. Dershowitz, is: Is the last name spelled exactly the same as the last name is spelled in the two photographs I have shown you?

DERSHOWITZ: Let me look. So, on the 20th of November

SCAROLA: Is the last name–

SCOTT: Whoa, whoa!

SCAROLA: Spelled the same way on both the flight log and the two photographs I have shown you?

DERSHOWITZ: On-you mean on a flight lot I was not on the flight? Is that right? You're talking about a flight log that I was not on the flight, right?

SCAROLA: That flight log shows you on multiple flights, does it not?

DERSHOWITZ: It shows me not on that flight. It shows me on a number of flights, but not on that flight.

SCOTT: What's the date of the flights?

DERSHOWITZ: The date of that flight is–looks like November 20, 2005. More than three years after Virginia Roberts left for—

After a great deal more bantering back and forth between the three attorneys Scarola asked the same question again.

SCAROLA: Is the last name on the photograph spelled exactly the same way as the last name on the flight log?

DERSHOWITZ: If you're talking about a flight log that I was not on that I was not on that flight, yes.

SCAROLA: All right. Thank you very much. Sir. Now, that flight log also shows you flying repeatedly in the company of a woman named Tatiana, correct?

DERSHOWITZ: I've only seen one reference to Tatiana on November 17th, if you want to show me any other references, I'd be happy to look at them.

SCAROLA: All right, Sir. Thank you.

CHAPTER SIXTEEN

VIRGINIA L. ROBERTS-GIUFFRE VS. GHISLAINE MAXWELL

A mong other things, another reason the Dershowitz depo-sition was important remained at the forefront of this case, to shed light on the relationship between Virginia Louise Roberts and Ghislaine Maxwell. A relationship so contentious, that on September 21, 2015, Virginia L. Roberts Giuffre filed a defama-tion suit against Ghislaine Maxwell in New York.

It occurred to me that given the cities where the plaintiff and defendant lived, it was an interesting twist of fate or perhaps a mere coincidence that Roberts-Giuffre who lived in Colorado is represented by a Manhattan firm, Boies, Schiller & Flexner, while Maxwell who resides in New York part-time, is represented by the Colorado firm, Haddon Morgan Foreman.

Sigrid McCawley, a partner at Boies Schiller & Flexner law firm represents Roberts Giuffre Laura Menninger and Jeffrey Pagliuca represent Maxwell. The presiding District Judge, the Honorable Robert W. Sweet, for the Southern District of New

York, a renowned jurist and senior United States Federal Judge was appointed by President Jimmy Carter.

Coincidentally, one of his law clerks was Eliot Spitzer former Governor of New York recently accused, in February 2016, of assaulting a twenty-year-old woman, allegedly his girlfriend, in a hotel room at The Plaza Hotel in New York City. The woman recently fled the country and no longer wishes to press charges against him. [185]

At the very beginning of the case, Judge Sweet ruled New York was the appropriate jurisdiction because Maxwell was a resident of New York City. The defamation case was filed under *Virginia Giuffre vs. Ghislaine Maxwell*, 1:15-cv-07433.

After several hearings and many motions including Maxwell's request to dismiss the victim's suit, Judge Sweet ruled on February 29, 2016, that Roberts-Giuffre had the right to pursue a defamation suit against Maxwell for describing her allegations as lies. Maxwell's attorneys argued their client was defending herself from Roberts.

Judge Sweet disagreed and said, "That to suggest Roberts Giuffre lied about being sexually assaulted as a minor, points to something deeply disturbing about the character of an individual willing to be publically dishonest about such a reprehensible crime." Maxwell and Roberts-Giuffre's lawyers did not respond. [186]

The Manhattan lawsuit filed against the 53-year-old Maxwell did not mention Prince Andrew by name. Instead, it described how Roberts, who assumed her married name, Giuffre, in the legal filings, was exploited by Epstein and became a victim of his sex trafficking ring after being recruited by Maxwell.

The Complaint stated that, "Between 2001 and 2007, with the assistance of numerous co-conspirators, Epstein abused more than thirty (30) minor girls, a fact confirmed by state and federal law enforcement. As part of their sex trafficking efforts, Epstein and Maxwell intimidated Roberts Giuffre into remaining silent about what had happened to her. After Epstein approved the Non Prosecution Agreement (NPA) that barred his prosecution for numerous federal sex crimes in Florida, DOJ, agreed that it would not institute any federal criminal charges against any potential co conspirators. As a co conspirator of Epstein, Maxwell was consequently granted immunity in Florida through the NPA."[187]

It also said, "With Maxwell's assistance, Epstein was able to recruit and sexually abuse Roberts- Giuffre for years until the girl turned 19 when she escaped to Thailand." Roberts said Epstein sent her to Thailand to bring back a 12-year-old girl, where Roberts Giuffre met a *Muai Thai* fighter, fell in love and in seven days they married. She rang Epstein to tell her she "was in love" and he said, "have a good life and hung up the phone." That was the last she heard of Epstein until the FBI called her during the criminal investigation.[188]

During the criminal investigation, Roberts claimed that, "As part of their sex trafficking efforts, Epstein and Maxwell, intimidated her to remain silent about what had transpired."[189]

The twelve -page filing explained how after Roberts went public Maxwell began a "concerted and malicious media campaign to discredit Roberts Giuffre...and ensure her claims would not be credible."[190]

Presumably, Maxwell influenced the "attack on Roberts Giuffre's honesty and truthfulness." In other words, Maxwell accused Roberts Giuffre of lying and "made a deliberate effort to 'maliciously discredit Giuffre and silence her efforts to expose the global sex crimes committed by her, Epstein and other powerful persons. Maxwell made the statements knowing full well they were false," wrote the Daily Mail.[191]

By January 14, 2016 attorneys for Maxwell and Roberts-Giuffre were in front of Judge Robert Sweet. Laura Menninger, an eminent trial lawyer, argued that her client had the right to refute the allegations and it was the reason why the defamation case should be dismissed. Sigrid McCawley, an equally illustrious lawyer, disagreed, "It's the 'old story' of wrongly portraying sex abused victims as liars." She said, "This may sound hard to believe, but it happened."[192]

So far, Maxwell "has refused to speak to the news media about her involvement with Epstein, the criminal and civil cases and has denied any and all involvement in Epstein's sex trafficking operation." While Roberts Giuffre argued that, "With the assistance of Maxwell, Epstein was able to sexually abuse her for years until she eventually escaped."[193]

Given the ongoing developments, other events may perhaps emerge that can one day open the doors for victim's rights attorneys in the Epstein case to introduce new cases against the perpetrators. However, in light of the barrage of media coverage, it would not surprise me if a new victim steps forward and new charges are filed. Perhaps then, law enforcement officials in New York, New Mexico, Florida, USVI, England and France, or wherever else it is that Epstein and Maxwell frequent, can conduct an investigation.

As of publication and unlike the Maxwell case that is in the beginning stages, there are two pending cases in Florida. The Maxwell case is important because it "contains the first public allegations made by Roberts Giuffre against Maxwell."[194]

If the Judge rules in favor of the victim, he will establish once and for all that, "Roberts Giuffre was a victim of sexual abuse while she was a minor child. Defendant Maxwell not only facilitated that sexual abuse but, most recently, wrongfully subjected Giuffre to public ridicule, contempt and disgrace by, among other things, calling Giuffre a liar in published statements with the malicious intent of discrediting and further damaging Giuffre worldwide."[195]

Roberts vs. Maxwell dates back to 1998 when the two women first met. Maxwell, like several other procurers, was never charged in the criminal case, which infuriated some victims, including Virginia, and their attorneys. During 2008-2009, "As the civil litigation against Epstein progressed, and on behalf of Giuffre and many other victims, Maxwell's testimony was sought concerning her personal knowledge and role in Epstein's abuse of Giuffre and others."[196]

Possibly to avoid taking the 2010 deposition, Maxwell claimed that her mother was deathly ill and left the United States for London. This occurred the day prior to the scheduled deposition, with no plans of ever returning. According to several sources, the elder Mrs. Maxwell, was not ill at the time of her daughter's deposition.

The 2007 telephone conversation, between Roberts, Scarola and Edwards,' became the springboard for Roberts' 2015 defamation case against Maxwell because it allowed Virginia to explain her relationship with Maxwell, establish in great detail Maxwell and Epstein's pattern of behavior, and reiterate the alleged crimes committed by Maxwell and Epstein.

The most recent depositions recognized that as far back as 2011, "Two FBI agents who found Roberts Giuffre in Australia—where she had been hiding from Epstein for several years—arranged to meet with her at the U.S. Consulate in Sidney. Since that meeting, Roberts Giuffre continues to provide information to the FBI about Epstein and Maxwell's apparent abusive behavior."[197]

It seems that all evidence to the contrary, Maxwell claimed Roberts was a liar. That story, wrote John Riley in Newsday, "became the latest in a long running legal battle involving the convicted pedophile and his alleged procurer, Maxwell."[198]

According to the New York complaint, Roberts Guiffre was allegedly recruited by Maxwell when she was 14-years-old, in June of 1998 at Mar-A-Lago in Palm Beach, Florida. Roberts Giuffre, born August 9, 1983, was just shy of her fifteenth birthday when she met them. A year or two later, while 'working' for Epstein, the girl was introduced to HRH Prince Andrew to perform sexual activities on three occasions. According to the filing Roberts also took part in an orgy on the financier's private Caribbean island where the Prince attended.

In a hearing transcript sent to me by Ms. McCawley and dated March 17, 2016, a couple of unresolved issues stood out during the hearing. Among them was Maxwell's delayed tactics to avoid taking the deposition. It seemed this was the second time Maxwell challenged attorneys in an attempt to avoid service. Like Edwards before her, McCawley, was having a difficult time obtaining Maxwell's statement.

Based on the transcript, Boies Schiller requested Maxwell's deposition in October 2015. At publication, the deposition has not been taken.

The notes published in the reports also confirmed that, "Jeffrey would send me out, just like in the U.S. to go talk to pretty girls, the younger the better. I would offer them money to come meet my gentleman friend and tell them I'd show them how to massage."[199]

According to Roberts, Maxwell and Epstein, allegedly "fooled her parents into believing she was training with them to become a professional masseuse." Instead, they, "Helped their underage play-thing get a passport for a vacation." On her first overseas trip to Europe, Roberts' first stop was Paris, France. Once there, Roberts' claims that her daily list of chores included, "Massages, sex and even dressing Epstein."[200]

After she left Paris, Roberts was taken to Spain, Morocco and England. The first night in London, Roberts stayed with Maxwell who Virginia identified as, "Madame Maxwell." "The next morning," Roberts' said, "Ghislaine (was) chirpy (and) came into my room. She sat down next to me, as I was just starting to uncover the sheets and told me excitedly we were going shopping because

I needed a new dress I could wear to dance with a prince. 'Wow, what?' were the first words that popped into my head, not knowing that meant using my body as entertainment for another rich pedophile, or worst, being convinced it was exciting."[201]

Roberts' claims that Maxwell, "didn't seem to care about anything except pleasing Epstein and Prince Andrew. She accompanied Roberts to buy everything from expensive dresses and embroidered jeans to makeup and perfume."[202]

The tragedy of this case is how Roberts' perceived her situation. During a Radar Online interview she confessed, "The way these men adored me, and many others like me, kind of made us feel like we weren't so awkward after all. That was the nice side to these predators, the other side was learning to accept money to degrade ourselves morally and end up another lost girl down a chain of…victims."[203]

Several more issues presented at the March 2016 hearing included Menninger's refusal to abide by the extensive time period of emails requested by McCawley. The second issue was the "over breath" of emails requested by McCawley.

As McCawley explained the long-standing history of this case uncovered that Epstein's, "flight logs show Maxwell traveling 360 times with Jeffrey Epstein, twenty (20) of which were with her client when she was underage." In addition, "We have the Palm Beach police report, which shows over 30 minors who reported that during that time period, up until 2006, they being abused in that circumstance in Palm Beach. Then we have the arrest that happens of Jeffrey Epstein in 2006."[204]

"In 2008, Virginia received a victim notification letter from the United States government. In 2009, Maxwell's deposition was sought in underlying civil cases. She fled the country, did not take the deposition and said her mother was ill in England, and could not be deposed. She showed up in New York weeks later and, (on

July 31, 2010), attended Chelsea Clinton's wedding. So clearly, she was around, she was able to do something, but she avoided that deposition. Her testimony was never taken in that case," McCawley said.[205]

In 2011 McCawley stated, "Maxwell started issuing different statements to the press. She issued a statement, in 2015, which is the statement that we are here about in this case. So I contend, your Honor, that all of those years have relevant information in them with respect to my client."[206]

A separate issue along with obtaining the e-mails communication, was the desire by both attorneys to issue a protective order so that Maxwell's transcript i.e. deposition could be kept confidential and not made available to the press as most transcripts usually are.

According to the court file, Laura Menninger wanted McCawley to hand over her client's diary or journal between 1996-2002, published by Radar Online. Earlier, on January 13, 2015, Radar Online published a handwritten note by Virginia given to them for publication. Maxwell's attorney, Menninger, argued the note constituted a 'journal, or diary.'

McCawley disagreed and said that her client did not keep a journal and that Radar Online's reporting was based on Virginia's hand written notes not on a diary per se. McCawley also pointed out that her client "was sent to Thailand by Mr. Epstein and Ms. Maxwell for training and to pick up another."[207]

McCawley seemed annoyed that she had forwarded three thousand documents of Virginia's testimony to Maxwell's attorneys, while Haddon had sent her only two emails and two emails in response. She was very concerned because July 2016 would mark the last month that Maxwell's deposition could be filed since the discovery phase would close that month.

McCawley explained to the Judge, "the underlying issue in this case is whether or not Ms. Maxwell lied when she said my client was not subject to the abuse that she said she was subject to. In order to prove that," the lawyer said, "for defamation with malice, we have to prove that my client was abused by these individuals, that these individuals did take advantage of her in the way that she expressed…That is why one of the requests are the documents relating to communications of Jeffrey Epstein."[208]

"What is relevant to that is the sexual trafficking ring," McCawley said. "If after my client left they are also trafficking other under aged girls repetitively, that is relevant to prove the truth of my client's allegations as well. We are entitled to that discovery, Your Honor."[209]

At the outset, Menninger objected to McCawley's request because she believed they were requesting, "All documents relating to communications with Jeffrey Epstein from 1990 to present… Not specifically concerning trafficking, or under aged girls, which makes it all documents relating to… which could be anything in the universe."[210]

Seemingly upset, Menninger asked why were, "all documents relating to communications with Andrew Albert Christian Edward, Duke of York, from 1990 to present (necessary). You know, what the heck does a communication with the Duke in 2013, any old communication, have to do with anything in this case? Nothing, if you ask me."[211]

The other side of that argument was what McCawley was trying to prove. That by restricting the time period of the relevant emails and giving them a "very short window," Menninger narrowed the possibility of a successful discovery. At play was an e-mail sent by Maxwell where she was, "e-mailing Jeffrey Epstein about the girls she's going to send over to him in 2004, before he is arrested," and that was "relevant to her client's claim…So we shouldn't be told that we're not entitled to these documents or that we're only entitled to 2 emails out of all of our requests," McCawley responded.[212]

McCawley explained that Boies Schiller asked two "people" involved in the case for documents and communications with Sarah Kellen and Nadia Marcinkova. In their depositions pertaining to Maxwell's charges involving sexually trafficking underage girls, "both individuals took the Fifth." Beside those documents, Boies Schiller wanted all e-mail communication between Maxwell and Kellen that included those issues at any time period from 1990 to present. "And while they say that day-to-day communications with Epstein wouldn't be relevant, they would. If they're communicating on a daily basis, that's relevant."[213]

In spite of her current claims, in 2015 in another Epstein related case, Roberts, now 32, was instructed by Judge Kenneth Marra, in Florida that she could not join the legal action brought by two other victims, Jane Doe #1 and Jane Doe #2 who were also under age when they Epstein allegedly abused them. So it seems, the only two cases that might help vindicate Roberts-Giuffre's and perhaps other victims' are the defamation case filed against her alleged procurer, Ghislaine Maxwell, in New York and the Crime Victims' Rights Act (CVRA) case filed in Florida on behalf of Jane Doe #1 and Jane Doe #2.

As it stands, Maxwell, 54, must comply with Judge Sweet's order instructing her to disclose "documents and records of conversations (e-mails) she had with Epstein and others related to the sex trafficking operation between 1999 and 2016," if Roberts-Giuffre is specific in her pretrial discovery questions and identifies the individuals who communicated with Maxwell about the alleged sex trafficking of girls.[214]

As of April 11, 2016 the case is pending and Maxwell has yet to be deposed.

CHAPTER SEVENTEEN

THE VALLEY OF KIDRON

Going back to March 2011 when The Daily Beast posted the first of six Epstein stories, it is now clear the media did not want to pay attention to this case, perhaps for fear of libel by Epstein, Maxwell and others implicated in the case. After A few more stories posted on the Huffington Post the media went 'dark.' Back then I did not understand what happened and why until I found out who was pulling the strings. The whole sordid story and my experience investigating the case reminded me of the famous passage about the Valley of Kidron where in the Hebrew Bible points to a, "Valley were Yahweh shall come to judge."

Given the restrictive media environment at the time, I decided to complete this book although much more information was required to fully grasp the factual challenges besieging abolitionists and law enforcement officials when investigating similar cases. For about two years, I worked hard trying to convince my editor at Random House Mexico to publish the book. A million reasons not to and the book was never published.

During the early years of my investigation, the Court of Public Opinion remained blissfully unaware about human trafficking since the information published back then was mostly obsolete and scarce. It was time to change direction and build a platform in which to educate, raise awareness and help rescue victims of trafficking. The Alliance To Rescue Victims of Trafficking was born in mid October 2013.

The years between 2011 and 2015 were somewhat troubling. Unable to publish my book for reasons beyond my control, I focused on building the platform, Alliance to Rescue Victims of Trafficking. Then on January 1, 2015 a blitzkrieg started again and all eyes were back on Epstein and several of his associates. The media was a buzz with new and scandalous developments in the Epstein case.

Wasn't everyone on holiday or at least resting, apparently not? My cell phone began to ring very early that morning and did not stop all day. At first I did not answer. There were too many calls. I listened to the messages. The media had finally caught on.

The first message I received was from a reporter at The Guardian, an English daily. The calls came in from quite a number of journals from different countries. I received a call from MSNBC in New York, ABC, NBC, the BBC in London, another from a reporter in Toronto working with the Canadian Broadcast Corporation (CBC) and yet another from an Australian television station that rang several times. Requests from other networks followed.

Again, the press was in an uproar and wanted the backstory. Specifically they wanted to know what I knew about Epstein and his special relationship with Professor Dershowitz. They wanted to know more about Virginia Louise Roberts. Was she really forced to have sex with the Harvard University professor and if so, did they?

The question everyone expected an answer to was: how could a renowned Harvard law professor allow himself to be implicated in a child sex trafficking scandal of this magnitude and involving a registered level-3 sex offender? Were the predator and professor truly friends? Most reporters requested radio and on-air interviews.

Others asked for information to help them expand their stories. The phone calls and emails continued for several days round the clock.

As you might remember, the incident that propelled the frenzy began late in the afternoon of December 31, 2014, when Josh Gerstein, an astute and courageous reporter at Politico.com, blogged about a Complaint filed by Brad Edwards and Paul Cassell on behalf of their client, Virginia Louise Roberts.

New Year's Eve usually has usually been a quiet day for the media, which made the decision to publish on that day thought provoking. The politico.com strategy evidently worked. By mid afternoon on January 1, 2015, the story had caused such an international sensation and frenzy that there was no doubt Professor Dershowitz's legacy was at stake.

In view of the public outcry, I declined to give interviews for two specific reasons. I could not reach Professor Dershowitz for comment, he did not return my call, and my book had not been published. It was not the right time to share my opinions and I knew there was a lot more to come. Evidently, what politico.com had published was simply the tip of the iceberg.

Instead, I published one more story. The report was an on-camera interview of the first victim who came forward to expose Epstein and his sex trafficking operation. The victim was Jane Doe #1 a.k.a. Rosemary. I had met Rosemary, in 2010, and was the only reporter who interviewed her beside law enforcement officials. I asked her permission to print her interview. On January 25, 2015, the Daily Beast posted the story.[215]

The year 2015 must have been an *annus horribilis* for Epstein, Maxwell and Alan Dershowitz. After Gerstein's story broke, Epstein's case commanded front-page coverage during the first quarter of the year. Dershowitz went on a media guerrilla blitz defending his virtue, innocence, and legacy. Maxwell remained silent and Epstein was unable to escape the media's radar. Dershowitz and Maxwell were again caught in Epstein's crossfire.

The history behind the 2014 Politico.com report explained a gripping case. In 2008, Brad Edwards and Paul Cassell had filed a complaint on behalf of two victims, Jane Doe #1 (not the same Rosemary as above who first came forward and I interviewed) and Jane Doe #2. The case: *Jane Doe #1 and Jane Doe #2 vs. United States Government.*[216]

Unlike Virginia Louise Roberts and Rosemary a.k.a. Jane Doe #1, this other Jane Doe #1 currently suing the Government coupled with Jane Doe #2, is living in a court-mandated rehabilitation center in Tampa, Florida without the ability to leave the facility. This has prevented her from appearing at Court during her case unless a judge granted her permission. I have also been unable to interview the girl given her situation. Sadly, Jane Doe #1 has not been one of the lucky few to make that U turn, perhaps as a result of her history with sexual abuse.

According to a telephone conference call dated March 1, 2016, between Florida Judge Kenneth Marra, U.S. Attorneys Ann Marie Villafaña and Dexter Lee (representing the Government), Brad Edwards and Paul Cassell representing the victims, the attorneys agreed they would try to settle the case and send the matter to mediation.

Before the case could go to mediation however, Villafaña and Edwards required Jane Doe #1 to participate in the mediation. Given Jane Doe's confinement, the attorneys asked Judge Marra to issue an order requesting the Tampa Court to release the girl for one day from the facility and seek out a magistrate judge in the Middle District in Tampa. Ann Marie Villafaña and Edwards agreed that Judge Marra's order in combination with the Court that confined her, could allow Jane Doe's release and the opportunity to attend the mediation. Judge Marra "agreed to make some inquiries since two of my law school classmates are district judges in Tampa."[217]

The real story however, began back in June 2007, when the FBI mailed Jane Doe #1, "a victim-notification letter explaining that Epstein's case was still 'under investigation.' " The FBI, "Notified Jane Doe #1 of her rights under the Crime Victims' Rights Act "CVRA" and in August 2007, Jane Doe #2 received a similar letter."[218]

Three months later, on September 2007, Epstein and the U.S. Attorney's Office (USAO) began to negotiate a deal. Those negotiations led to an agreement under which Epstein "would plead guilty to two state felony offenses for solicitation of prostitution and procurement of minors for prostitution if the U.S. Attorney's Office would agree not to prosecute him for federal offenses. On September 24, 2007, a Non Prosecution Agreement was signed under those terms."[219]

On January 10, 2008, "The FBI sent letters to the victims advising them their, "case was under investigation," but did not disclose the existence of the Non Prosecution Agreement. Later in January 2008, Jane Doe #1 met with FBI agents and the attorneys from the U.S. Attorney's Office to discuss her case. Again the government did not reveal the existence of the NPA."[220]

The attorneys for the victims argued that the U.S. Attorney's Office did not consult with them regarding the plea discussions and deliberately kept secret the negotiations and the Non Prosecution Agreement (NPA). In fact, the victims believed that beginning on September 24, 2007 through June 2008, USAO hid the existence of the NPA even though the attorneys representing the victims had spoken to the U.S. Attorney's Office and the FBI on multiple occasions throughout that period.[221]

Sometime in mid-June 2008, Brad Edwards "contacted the Assistant United States Attorney ("AUSA") to discuss the status of Epstein's investigation. The Assistant U.S. Attorney again did not reveal the NPA." Finally, "On June 27, 2008, AUSA notified Edwards that Epstein was scheduled to plead guilty in state court on June 30, 2008."[222]

The reason Edwards and Cassell believed their clients had a valid case was presented in emails exchanged between Epstein's attorneys and DOJ during the NPA negotiations. Florida Judge Kenneth Marra confirmed this years later when he awarded the victims the right to see all correspondence and communication between Epstein's attorneys and the U.S. Attorney's Office. Within those exchanges, the U.S. Attorney's Office did not disclose the existence of the NPA or the relationship between Epstein's state plea and the U.S. Attorney's Office's agreement to waive federal charges.

The following month, on July 3, 2008, Brad Edwards sent another letter to the U.S. Attorney's Office confirming Jane Doe #1's intentions to bring federal charges against Epstein; and on July 7, 2008, Jane Doe #1 filed a complaint in court to enforce her rights under the Crime Victims Rights Act."[223]

Like most victims of sex crimes, Jane Doe #1 and her attorney, Edwards, trusted that, "discussions between the Government and Epstein were under way. They also expected to be notified of all developments during the investigation. By failing to notify the victim, Jane Doe #1 claimed that USAO, 'violated her rights under CVRA."[224]

The United States Government responded on July 9, 2008. "The Government argued that a federal indictment had never been issued against Epstein and therefore the CVRA did not apply." The Government insisted, "They had used their best efforts to comply with the CVRA."[225]

During a court hearing on July 11, 2008, Jane Doe #2 was added on as a petitioner to the case. By August of the same year, the Court ordered USAO to turn over the NPA to all identified victims, including Jane Doe #1 and Jane Doe #2, and work out the terms of a protective order governing the NPA's disclosure."[226]

For about a year and a half, the opposing sides attempted to negotiate settlement agreements and resolve the CVRA dispute. Three years later, on March 18, 2011, "after settlement efforts failed, the victims filed a series of motions along with Epstein's attorney and former USAO officer, Bruce Reinhart's, Motion to intervene." Reinhart's Motion was denied.[227]

The Crime Victims Rights Act, CVRA was intended to, "Protect victims' rights and ensure their involvement in the criminal justice process. It was created to give the victims the right to be reasonably protected from the accused, the right to reasonable, accurate and timely notice of any public court proceeding, or any parole proceeding, involving the crime, or of any release or escape of the accused; And the right not to be excluded from any public court proceeding, unless the Court determines that testimony by the victim would be materially altered if the victim heard other testimony at the proceeding."[228]

In relation to Epstein's case, the attorneys for Jane Doe #1 and Jane Doe #2 claimed that CVRA gave the victims the right to "be reasonably heard at any public proceeding in the district court involving release, plea, sentencing, or any parole proceeding; and the right to fully and timely restitution and the right to hold proceedings free from unreasonable delay. Most significantly, it gives victims the right to be treated with fairness and with respect for their dignity and privacy."[229]

Looking back at the December 2014 politico story given what was going on politically in relation to the case it made sense that Politico.com took an interest in publishing the case. Add to that Judge Kenneth Marra's rejection of Jane Doe #3's and Jane Doe #4's petition to join Jane Doe #1 and Jane Doe #2 in their CVRA case against the government and you have at least one reason why the Epstein human trafficking case is a precedent setting case.[230]

In effect, rejection of Edwards' and Cassell's Motion to include Jane Doe #3 a.k.a. Virginia Louise Roberts Giuffre and Jane Doe #4, in the original petition, the 2008 CVRA case with Jane Doe #1 and Jane Doe #2, might set another dangerous precedent for future human trafficking cases.

Perhaps, Judge Marra rejected the intervention because Jane Doe #3 (Roberts Giuffre), described how for sexual purposes she was sold "to many other powerful men, including numerous prominent American politicians, powerful business executives, foreign presidents, a well known prime minister and other world leaders." Perhaps, the Judge has other reasons. I called Judge Marra's Chambers on April 7, 2016 to ask for comment. His assistant, Irene said, "The Judge could not comment on the case."[231]

One thing is certain, in the end the truth shall be revealed and possibly just like in the Biblical passage about The Valley of Kidron "Yahweh shall come to judge." When all is said and done, the Jeffrey Epstein case might go down in legal history and become the model for what The Department of Justice ought not to do when prosecuting a human trafficking case involving so many victims, high profile personalities, a very rich sex offender, and so many extraordinary attorneys working both sides of the aisle.

CHAPTER EIGHTEEN

WHAT LIES BENEATH

As I mentioned in the last chapter, on Thursday, April 7, 2016, I rang the Honorable Judge Marra. His assistant, Irene, said he could not comment since several cases remained open. Recently however, the Judge spoke to *The Sun Sentinel*, a Fort Lauderdale, Florida daily and said, "He hoped the case will finally be decided within the next few months, possibly after a non-jury trial in federal court in West Palm Beach." He was referring to *Jane Doe #1 and Jane Doe #2 vs. United States Government.*[232]

There are two ways the judge can rule in the case of *Jane Doe #1 and Jane Doe #2 vs. United States Government.* Judge Marra can rule in favor of the Department of Justice and the U.S. Attorney's Office and agree with their assertion: That the victims were consulted to the extent required by law and therefore not entitled to a greater level of consultation, or, he could rule in favor of the victims and agree the federal prosecutors did not adequately consult with them.

Whatever decision the Judge makes, it is unlikely the victims will receive further monetary compensation from the government and that Epstein's sentence will be changed since he already served time, however insufficient that time might seem. It is also unlikely that Epstein will be indicted on other criminal charges related to the same case.

Jack Goldberger, Virginia's primary attorney back in 2005, and a member of Epstein's defense team recently spoke to the Sun Sentinel. Mr. Goldberger and I had spoken several times between 2009 and 2010 but have not since. Goldberger told the press that, "If Judge Marra rules the U.S. government violated the Crime Victims' Rights Act, his decision will have no effect on prosecuting Jeffrey Epstein. Due process and double jeopardy would require the agreement, that was reached by the state and federal government, be honored."[233] Goldberger also explained that, "victims have no right to dictate how the case is resolved." In other words, the same victims cannot prosecute Epstein in the future for the same crimes. "No, it simply can't happen," Goldberger, explained.[234]

Since 2008, when the case was originally filed it has turned into a legal tsunami. In light of the December 2014 stipulation, filed by Edwards and Casell, where the lawyers claimed that Professor Dershowitz sexually abused Jane Doe #3, i.e. Virginia Louise Roberts Giuffre, on six occasions and that Epstein arranged for her to do so including in his U.S.V.I. island home, there has been no stopping non traditional media in their requests to unearth the truth. The same does not hold true for mainstream media. Unlike their younger more renegade brethren, they have preferred to watch through the sidelines and not get personally involved after Professor Dershowitz vehemently denied the claims made by Virginia Louise Roberts and hired former FBI Director, Louis Freeh, to conduct an investigation. Former FBI Director, Louis Freeh was appointed by former President Bill Clinton.

To prove just how much mainstream media has backed away from the Epstein, Dershowitz, Maxwell case, on Friday, April 8, 2016, the day after I rang Judge Marra's Chambers, Edwards, Cassell and Dershowitz filed another stipulation, that afternoon. It made the eight o'clock online news hour and Josh Gerstein; the courageous staff reporter at politico.com once again drove the headlines.[235]

The politico.com report said that Edwards and Cassell had withdrawn their allegation, which they called a "tactical mistake" according to the statement issued Friday. The reason politico claimed was, "they now have access to evidence that refutes Roberts' claims, which they suggested could involve a case of mistaken identity. However, Edwards and Cassell maintain they performed the required due diligence on her allegations before they were filed in court."[236]

The Politico story said, "The scope of the concession appeared limited by a court filing…in which the attorneys Edwards and Cassell maintained their client Roberts Giuffre stands by her claim." What that basically means is that although Virginia agreed to allow the attorneys to withdraw their claims, Virginia did not agree to retract the sexual abuse accusations against Dershowitz.[237]

After Politico broke the story, Professor Dershowitz once again called his friends in the mainstream media and together they heralded the good news. Most people I spoke to, who have been following the Epstein case since his arrest in 2005, were relieved to learn of Dershowitz' claimed innocence. Bluntly, it was too much to bear had the claims been confirmed.

The following Saturday, April 9, 2016, I wrote Edwards and Cassell an e-mail asking for comments. Edwards responded, "We did not withdraw a complaint. We settled the defamation action and as part of the settlement certain pleadings that were filed by Jack (Scarola) as well as Alan's (Dershowitz) attorney were withdrawn." I also sent an email to Professor Dershowitz for comment. He did not respond.

I asked Edwards about their compensation? Cassell and Edwards did not respond. By the way, the legal settlement was settled "with prejudice," which means the case was over and done with. I also learned that as part of the agreement, Dershowitz consented to withdraw his claims blaming, "Edwards and former Federal Judge Cassell of acting unethically back in December 2014," Edwards said.

Knowing that I was writing a book and not an article for publication on mainstream media it was curious to see how Edwards would not grant me access to speak with his client, Virginia Louise Roberts, during the course of the investigation. When I asked why, his response was, "everything is fine and it's going to turn out well. There is no need to fear or worry." 'Fear' or 'worry' were not exactly what was on my mind. His response was sent via a text message around noontime on Saturday April 9, 2016. As a result of all this a fresh new media cycle began. On Tuesday, April 11, 2016, Vivia Chen, an incredibly witty reporter for The American Lawyer wrote, "It's not over!"

Part two of her report was even more fascinating because it gave context to this all too bizarre agreement. It was so alarming that Chen's words describes it best.

> "If you thought the settlement that Alan Dershowitz reached on Friday with the lawyers representing Virginia Roberts Giuffre puts the controversy to bed, you're naive. Possibly delusional… Giuffre alleged that she was coerced into having sex with Dershowitz and others when she was a minor.
>
> The latest bombshell: Jack Scarola, counsel for Giuffre's lawyers Paul Cassell and Bradley Edwards, emailed me this: "If Mr. Dershowitz were to request a waiver of the confidentiality provisions, we would agree to the request."
>
> Talk about throwing down the gauntlet! That would mean spilling the terms of the settlement—about who had to shell out what to make this messy lawsuit go away. I assumed Cassell and Edwards

paid Dershowitz and wanted confidentiality, since they admitted in the settlement to making "mistakes" in alleging that Dershowitz had sex with Giuffre.

But David Boies, who represents Giuffre in a related matter, tells me I'm off target. In a phone conversation on Sunday, Boies dangled this tidbit of information before me: "I don't know the terms of the settlement, but I know that it was proposed that (Edwards and Cassell) be paid hundreds of thousands of dollars (by Alan Dershowitz) to drop the case."

My eyes widened. Go on, Mr. Boies, I said. He continued: "Ask Alan Dershowitz who paid whom. I know Dershowitz asked for confidentiality, and Edwards and Cassell will waive it . . . And if Dershowitz won't waive confidentiality, that should tell you if there's something incriminating."

So I rushed to ask Cassell and Edwards about waiving confidentiality, and got the response from Scarola that they'd essentially do it in a New York minute. Scarola also emailed me a post settlement statement that says this:

What is true is that Mr. Edwards and Professor Cassell entered into a monetary settlement that resolved the defamation claims they filed against Mr. Dershowitz, but they are precluded from revealing the economic terms of the settlement, as the agreement requires the monetary specifics to remain confidential.

Though Dershowitz, citing the confidentiality agreement, wouldn't comment about compensation when I asked him about the settlement, Edwards and Cassell's statement makes it clear that money exchanged hands. But how much? And what about the implication that Dershowitz was the one who paid big bucks for the settlement that supposedly establishes his innocence?

I went back to Dershowitz to get some clarity. Clearly miffed, he took umbrage at Boies' comment: "David Boies doesn't know terms of the agreement because it's subject by confidentiality agreement. My lawyer has advised me that my discussion of the terms would breach the agreement, but I assure you there's nothing incriminating."

So how about waiving the confidentiality agreement to make everything transparent? Dershowitz's answer: No. "I'm sticking with the agreement . . . My lawyers tell me I can't change the settlement, which is multi-faceted and complex."

Later, he adds, however: 'I'd be prepared to enter negotiations to unseal confidential information and other matters if (Edwards, Cassell and Boies) are prepared to enter negotiations to unseal Virginia Giuffre's deposition and my affidavit regarding Boies, which Boies Schiller has demanded be sealed.' The point is, he says, is that 'it has to be mutual.'[238]

A source close to the case that does not wish to be identified said, "So much of this revolves around the integrity of Virginia Louise Roberts. What will be missing though is who she is and what she is all about. To that, we will never know who has given her what advice and if she has always taken it. I hope at some point she can talk about things from her personal experience."

The same source explained, "For a young woman she has had a very complicated life and she might be able to help others but way down the road. It would probably be in her best interest to come forward unconstrained and unveil the truth about her history with Epstein, Dershowitz, Clinton *et al.*, otherwise, no one will really ever know whether she is being manipulated or if she is the manipulator."

"It seems improbable", the source added, "that a young teenager can "mistake" identifying someone who sexually molested her more than once," in Virginia's case, allegedly it was six times. "So who is Virginia Roberts? It's an ugly story that the players seem to be trying very hard to wrap up."[239]

CHAPTER NINETEEN

LOOSE ENDS

Then God said, "Let there be light," and there was light.
Genesis 1:3

As if Chen's reporting was not outrageous enough to light the entire legal community on fire, more was published about the ongoing Jane Doe #1 and Jane Doe #2 case. An unusual development, stranger perhaps than the settlement agreement, took place during a routine status check. The government eventually made known that two victims who filed the lawsuit, Jane Doe #1 and Jane Doe #2, were not victims after all because they procured other girls for Epstein and received monetary compensation from him.[240]

Edwards was outraged, "Today, is the first we've heard that the victims were complicit and this disqualifies them. This is an additional issue, which will lead to other issues. It is an outrage not to mention to have waited eight years to create another contemptible alibi," Edwards said.[241]

Representing the government was Assistant U.S. Attorney Dexter Lee who told the court, "If someone is complicit in the offenses, they can't be considered victims under the federal Crime Victims' Rights Act... A Crime Victims' Rights Act action is part of a criminal proceeding normally, but there's nothing normal about this case," Lee said. In effect, Lee's statement disqualified the victims from moving forward with their lawsuit.[242]

Edwards' expects to have other victims, he had represented earlier, come forward and testify. If the NPA agreement is overturned Epstein might face jail time again, although for now that seems highly unlikely. Perhaps if it gets to that point, he will decide to talk his way out of the conviction and agree to bring down the 'bigger fish,' or whoever gave the green light for his NPA. Although I doubt it, stranger things have happened. Knowing how important money and politics are to Epstein, the 2016 elections are also too close for comfort. That fact alone might dissuade everyone involved from allowing this case to go to trial. My guess is that once again they will settle or someone will suggest that they do so quickly.

One of the key players during the NPA negotiations, Ken Starr explained in the *Justice, Integrity Project Report*, "The Epstein saga raises serious questions about favoritism if not corruption in the courts even if plaintiffs' allegations are overblown. The immunity agreement for alleged co conspirators is so irregular that it reeks of a cover-up."[243]

Given the pending cases and various loose ends could be another the reason some politicians are nervous. In retrospect, it would have been wiser for the defense attorneys and the United States Attorneys Office to allow justice to run its course.

One thing is certain, The Trafficking Victims Protection Act (TVPA: H.R. 972 and later H.R. 7311) first passed into law in 2000 by President Bill Clinton, reauthorized under President George W. Bush in 2003, and again, reauthorized by President Barack Obama, in 2008, is a federal law created to prosecute traffickers and protect victims. It was enacted in Florida, in 2000, five years prior to Epstein's arrest.

The minimum mandatory under TVPA is twenty years for a convicted sex trafficker. The law also gives law enforcement the ability to prosecute traffickers domestically and worldwide. Had justice prevailed, perhaps the victims would have felt some sort of vindication; and the defense attorneys, prosecutors, political leaders and others who have been dragged through the mud for the past eleven years would have saved themselves a great deal of public humiliation. More importantly, the young girls who have been recently photographed in Epstein's company might have saved themselves from potential danger. All in all, the case has exposed what nobody wants to believe.

Trying to find some spiritual solace while investigating this case, I read a great many passages in the Old and New Testaments. I also read spiritual passages written in different books. One in particular struck the right cord, as it seemed to apply to the main protagonist. "The value of giving lies not simply in the amount given but in the sacrifice it requires and the love that prompts it. To a large extent, living well entails giving well—a giving of some portion of your time, or talent, or money, or all three."[244]

This phrase says to me that being rich does not necessarily mean that one lives a full life if one is bereft of the other elements that complete it. The Epstein story is not your typical billionaire's story about how his generous contributions enriched society and helped to educate young vulnerable kids. If you read the thousands public court filings available and in the future if the public is lucky to be allowed to read the many more that have been sealed, you will at once understand how tragic this case really is. A billionaire who through his alleged crimes attempted or perhaps managed to destroy the very essence of humanity by violating the rights of minors and human rights in general. Perhaps part two will have a different ending.

Addendum

On April 26, 2016 at approximately eleven in the morning, at the United States Central District Court of California, in Riverside, Katie Johnson, a 35 year-old California woman, filed a Complaint for Relief against Jeffrey Epstein and Donald Trump, the Republican 2016 presidential nominee. Johnson claimed Epstein and Trump, "sexually abused her, (in 1994), under threat of harm and conspired to deprive her of her civil rights when she was 13 years old."[245]

The Complaint, filed only days after my book was published, was self-filed by Johnson. The alleged victim asked for relief in the amount of $100 million dollars according to case # 5:16-cv-00797 DMG-KS. Then on Thursday, May 5, 2016, the public learned that Johnson had been unable to hire an attorney to represent her although she had contacted several lawyers including Brad Edwards.

Edwards, according to the latest media reports, did not agree to take on her case. I asked Edwards why. He did not respond. In the April Complaint, Johnson stated that both Epstein and Trump purportedly abused her over a four months period, from June 1994 to September 1994, when she was thirteen years old. The incidents, she claimed, took place at Epstein's Manhattan townhouse on East 71st Street the same house where several other incidents with minor girls occurred according to two survivors, Sjoberg and Roberts. Johnson also claimed that Epstein and Trump applied "extreme sexual and physical abuse," while at Epstein's house.[246]

Breitbart.com, an online news journal reported Johnson, "has been offering her alleged story to a series of news outlets, and photographs of her have been offered for sale for up to $25,000."[247]

After years of closely following the Epstein case the information stated in the Johnson court document appears to be politically motivated against the Republican 2016 presidential frontrunner. More importantly, the immediate focus surrounding this case is purely political and the ongoing spin seems fictional at best.

If this case is authentic and not politically motivated then several questions need answers. To begin with, why did Katie Johnson wait 22 years to file a sexual abuse Complaint against Epstein who was arrested in 2005 and sentenced in 2007? Why is Johnson asking for $100 million dollars in compensation twenty- two years after the fact and not when the incident occurred, that is during the filing of the civil cases in 2008-2009?

In fact many important questions have not been answered. Did Johnson contact the media directly? If not, who helped place her story? Given the heinous allegations and timing of the case, I wonder if Johnson was remunerated in any way and if so, how much and who paid her?

Could it have been Trump's Republican opponents, perhaps a former presidential candidate or any one of the legions of Republican Party loyalists who dislike Trump and don't wish to see the frontrunner become the 2016 Republican nominee?

Perhaps this particular case was encouraged by one of the Democratic Party nominees since the California primaries were just around the corner? Although this action seems unlike anything Senator Bernie Sanders would undertake, it might also have been counterproductive for Secretary Clinton to have anything to do with it given the negative repercussions it could have brought to her campaign.

The bigger question is why did Johnson allow herself to be influenced to file the claim? From a political perspective, Johnson's sexual abuse complaint filed against Mr. Trump and Mr. Epstein in California only a month short of the June 7th California Primary seems suspicious at best. Given the timing, it is fair to assume that someone involved in the business of politics might be to blame. Conceivably, it could also be more than one person who influenced the woman to file. In light of the seriousness of the allegations against a presidential frontrunner, the individual or individuals who planted this story should be exposed.

Since 2005, the Epstein case and all the related cases have been replete with dirty politics and backroom negotiations between Democrats and Republicans. The same influence peddling that secured Epstein's Non Prosecution Agreement in 2007, might conceivably be at play in 2016. The difference is that the politics at play today are riskier because it is a presidential election year and the Epstein case has received enough exposure where the Court of Public Opinion is watching and can weigh in.

On May 5, 2016 I emailed and telephoned Hope Hicks, Trump's Press Secretary and Corey Lewondowsky his Chief of Staff. They did not respond. For about a month, the Republican presidential frontrunner continued to be the center of attraction in the Johnson case whereas Epstein's participation, even though he too was accused and remains a registered level-3 sex offender, was downplayed.

Donald Trump recently spoke to DailyMail.com. His attorney, Alan Garten, also gave a statement where the nominee 'categorically' denied the claims. "Garten's statement signaled that Trump's staff is eager to stop the allegations before they gain any more traction."[248]

According to Garten, "the allegations are not only categorically false, but disgusting at the highest level and clearly framed to solicit media attention or, more likely, are politically motivated." He went further, "To be clear, there is absolutely no merit to these claims and, based on our investigation, no evidence that the person who has made these allegations actually exists."[249]

In the meantime, on the Upper East Side of Manhattan, Ghislaine Maxwell apparently sold her townhouse at 116 East 65th Street for $15 million dollars. It could well be that Maxwell was in a hurry to sell her home and escape from New York given the ongoing case with Virginia Louise Roberts. The latest New York Post report said, "A lawyer with links to Epstein reportedly bought the townhouse for Maxwell, who allegedly never earned enough or inherited enough to make the purchase on her own." I rang Shari Scharfer Rollins to confirm the sale. Ms. Rollins, the Douglas Elliman broker representing Maxwell's property, did not return my call.[250]

On May 6th, the sale was announced in "The Real Deal," a New York real estate magazine. The story revealed that Frederick Rudd, president of Rudd Realty Management Corp. in New York and his wife, Kim Rudd, purchased Maxwell's New York townhouse. I rang Mr. Rudd to confirm the transaction. He did not return my call.

Although Maxwell lived in the home since it was purchased she did not purchase it directly. Apparently, at Epstein's behest, the townhouse was sold to Darren Indyke one of Epstein's attorney's.

Shortly after the news broke about the sale of her house, I called an attorney to ask if Maxwell's nationality coupled with her upcoming non-residence status could impact the defamation case? The attorney said, "No exemptions. She is subject to the court's jurisdiction regardless of her new home base." By selling her only property in the United States, Maxwell can now claim non-residence status and return to London taking advantage of her new status.

Whether the real estate transaction is a straightforward sale or perhaps another back door negotiation between Maxwell, Epstein, Indyke and Rudd, to protect Maxwell from the ongoing media scrutiny and Court of Public Opinion, remains unknown.

As this and other related Epstein cases unfold, more stories will continue to make headlines. In the meantime, Maxwell, unencumbered by property and residency and perhaps with a good amount of cash in hand, will be able to move about more freely.

More news followed when an attorney associated with the case explained that Maxwell's deposition, which she finally carried out, was sealed. The trial, if any, will be held in October 2016. Like all other Epstein related cases, a settlement will most likely have been reached before the October date given the proximity of the 2016 presidential elections.

And so by the end of May it was evident that a momentum to settle all Epstein related cases was in full swing. After an eight-year impasse, on May 23, 2016, a hearing was held in the Palm Beach County Court to discuss the settlement agreement in the CVRA case, *Jane Doe #1 and Jane Doe #2 vs. United States Government.* I sent Edwards a message to find out more about the settlement discussions.

According to Edwards' response on May 23, 2016, "The case did not settle." After spending hours behind closed doors, Cassell and Edwards were directed by U.S. Magistrate Judge Dave Lee Brennan to move forward quickly with the negotiations so that on June 28, 2016, the lawyers could reconvene.

At stake is Epstein's freedom and final vindication for all victims especially, Jane Doe #1, Jane Doe #2, Jane Doe #3 and Jane Doe #4, and their rights to reopen a Non Prosecution Agreement that set precedent in the State of Florida for other human traffickers and will continue to do so if something is not done to stop the bleeding. Will justice prevail? Will the Department of Justice nullify the 2007 Non Prosecution Agreement?

By settling the case in June two things will happen: the Government will prevent a public trial in October, a very inopportune time politically and the United States Attorneys Office would avoid any further embarrassments. Secondly, the Court of Public Opinion will also be kept forever in the dark about the negotiations that took place behind closed doors when hammering out Epstein's Non Prosecution Agreement in October 2007. Most importantly, agreeing on an early settlement in June 2016 will protect the relationships that facilitated a favorable deal by allowing Epstein, his attorneys and the Department of Justice to negotiate a very lenient agreement.

The Epstein case became even stranger when late in May, on a Friday afternoon, at the commencement of Memorial Day Weekend Epstein was hit by yet another civil lawsuit that made the headlines from London to New York.

On May 27, 2016 The Daily Mail published another shocking story about Epstein's financial dealings in the 1980s. Financial transactions that might perhaps help explain how Epstein began to amass his fortune. Steven Hoffenberg a New York City business and Epstein's alleged former boss in the seventies filed a complaint claiming Epstein was a consultant to his company Towers Financial Corporation and worked directly under Hoffenberg.

Epstein was allegedly a full-time associate with expertise in the financial markets as business consultant. His salary was approximately $25,000 per month. Apparently, the May 27, 2016 complaint accused Epstein of assisting Hoffenberg in a 1980's financial scam that defrauded hundreds of investors by running the "classic pyramid scheme through Hoffenberg's Towers Financial Corporation."[251]

Mr. Hoffenberg, who served eighteen years of a twenty-year sentence in a federal prison for committing financial crimes between the 1970s until 1993 by the time he was caught, explained that both partners, he and Epstein, "used money from the sale of bonds and securities and promissory notes from early investors to cover losses they incurred on behalf of newer investors and affiliated businesses." They also used investor money to maintain their lifestyle.[252]

Hoffenberg's lawsuit claimed their business partnership suffered substantial financial losses in their attempt to purchase the now defunct Pan American airlines and Emery freight air carrier. Mr. Hoffenberg who is no longer on parole and served almost two decades in a federal prison also became a born again Christian.

The former New York Post owner also "paid $1 million in fines and was ordered to reimburse investors about $475 million." Hoffenberg recently formed a PAC for Donald Trump the Republican nominee in the 2016 presidential elections.[253]

Coincidentally, Judge Robert Sweet who is currently presiding over the *Virginia Louise Roberts vs. Ghislaine Max*well defamation case in New York is overseeing in Hoffenberg's ongoing restitution. Mr. Hoffenberg who according to his attorney, Alan P. Fraade, "got out October 2013, is serving a 3 year supervised probation." Specific restrictions prevent Mr. Hoffenberg from trading in the market and holding office in a public company or participate in a private offering (IPO).

Hoffenberg's Manhattan lawyer, also explained, "that on Friday afternoon, May 27, 2016 papers were sent to Epstein by a process server to his Manhattan townhouse at 71st Street. The complaint was filed online. Mr. Epstein has 20 days from that day to respond. If Hoffenberg's complaint is accurate and he wins the case, he is looking for a substantial amount of restitution. Money, Hoffenberg claims, Epstein stole from Towers Financial and their investors to fund Epstein's business.

Mr. Fraade said that his client is, "looking to take over Mr. Epstein's fund in order to help pay for restitution to the Financial Towers victims that suffered heavy financial losses twenty years ago." He also suggested that while Epstein continues to 'enjoy the spoils of the scam,' Hoffenberg refused to cooperate with the Feds during the criminal investigation and exchange information about his business partner and Epstein's "role in the scam."

This case, like the other three pending cases shall also have an ending, hopefully sometime this year. In the meantime, the Court of Public Opinion must continue to weigh the evidence and hope that at some point the Judges agree to allow the public to view all the sealed documents in the Epstein and Epstein related cases.

Epilogue

THIS IS NOT A LEGAL STORY THIS IS A MORAL STORY

What matters is usually invisible.

Has our political elite become so corrupt they can ignore moral boundaries and human rights? Why has some of the media establishment turned a blind eye? These two questions propelled me to write this book.

Between 2001 and 2005, Jeffrey E. Epstein, apparently sexually abused more than one hundred underage girls from relatively disadvantaged backgrounds in Palm Beach, Florida. Dozens of victims submitted sworn testimonies to the Palm Beach Police Department.

Police reports stated a number of alleged assaults occurred in Palm Beach, Florida. Other reports claim the assaults occurred on Epstein's private island, Little St. James, in the United States Virgin Islands. Some reports revealed the incidents took place in New York City and in London, England. Most cases were precluded from the final indictment.

As I reported in the Daily Beast, "State Attorney Barry Krischer, who also ran Florida's Crimes Against Children Unit, proved reluctant to mount a vigorous prosecution of Epstein, saying the local victims were not credible witnesses. Chief Michael Reiter wrote a letter to the State Attorney's Office complaining of the state's 'highly unusual' conduct and asked him to remove himself from the case. Krischer did not."[254]

The evidence later presented to a state grand jury produced only a single count of soliciting prostitution. Krischer had retired and would not comment for the Daily Beast article. The day after that indictment was returned, Chief Reiter found the FBI had stepped in and taken over the investigation.[255]

The case finally went to the Grand Jury. On October 27, 2007, two years after an extensive criminal investigation began that included the Palm Beach Police, FBI, county, city, state and federal law enforcement agencies, Jeffrey E. Epstein was handed a Non Prosecution Agreement (NPA) by the U.S. Attorney's Office in the 15th Judicial Circuit in Palm Beach County. Epstein did not sign the NPA until December 7, 2007.

Although Epstein pled guilty (not *nolo contendere*) to the Indictment, which means he agreed not to contest the charges in the future: one (1) count of solicitation of prostitution, and one (1) count to an Information filed by the State's Attorney's Office in the solicitation of minors to engage in prostitution, he was not satisfied with the agreement. Why did the Department of Justice identify underage victims as prostitutes and not as victims?

"Of the two offenses that he pled guilty, the second offense required Epstein to register as a sex offender. Both charges were contingent upon a Judge of the 15th Judicial Circuit accepting and executing the sentence agreed upon between the State Attorney's Office and Epstein."[256]

"The recommendation by the US Attorney's Office was to have Epstein sentenced to consecutive terms of twelve (12) months and six (6) months in county jail for all charges, without any opportunity for withholding adjudication i.e. settlement or sentencing, and without probation or community control in lieu of imprisonment, the NPA stated. Epstein was also sentenced to twelve (12) months of community control (house arrest) consecutive to his two terms in county jail."[257]

In the end, Epstein served only 13 months in the Palm Beach county jail and was allowed to leave his private cell on an all day work release program. Following his release from the Palm Beach county jail he served 18 months of house arrest in his Palm Beach estate. During that period Epstein allegedly committed 11 parole violations according to Brad Edwards, a South Florida Victims Rights attorney representing several victims in the Epstein cases.

After Epstein's release from house arrest his criminal case was closed however, the civil cases continued. Unlike other human trafficker offenders prosecuted for far less egregious crimes, Epstein was not prosecuted under the Trafficking Victims Protection Act (TVPA) enacted in Florida, in 2000. TVPA aims to protect victims and prosecute human traffickers by imposing a minimum mandatory sentence of 20 years in a federal prison.

The year 2016 marks the eleventh year (2005-2016) since several related civil cases have been snaking their way through the courts. As of May 2016, two cases are pending in Florida. One case, a Crime Victims' Rights Act case known as *Jane Doe #1 and Jane Doe #2 vs. The United States Government* is winding its way to the Florida Supreme Court.

A third case is pending in New York: *Virginia L. Roberts' Giuffre vs. Ghislaine Maxwell.* The victim and plaintiff, Virginia Roberts-Giuffre accused Maxwell of defamation. In one of the Florida cases, closely related to the Epstein case, Alan Dershowitz, former Harvard University law professor and renowned jurist, was sued for defamation by attorneys Brad Edwards and Paul Cassell. This case was the result of the professor's association with Epstein.

On New Year's Eve, December 31, 2014, politico.com posted a blog that rocked the legal world. It also stunned the law professor

I'm assuming his colleagues, Harvard Law School students, friends and detractors.

Professor Dershowitz was accused of "having sexual relations" at six different times with Jane Doe #3 a.k.a. Virginia Louise Roberts, who at the time was underage." The New Year's Eve story revealed that, "One such powerful individual that Epstein forced then minor Jane Doe #3 to have sexual relations with was former Harvard Law Professor, Alan Dershowitz, a close friend of Epstein's and well known criminal defense attorney."[258]

The report illustrated a legal pleading that said "Jane Doe #3 had sexual relations with Dershowitz on numerous occasions while she was a minor, not only in Florida but also on private planes, in New York, New Mexico, and the U.S. Virgin Islands."[259]

In January 2015, after the Dershowitz story went viral, I was invited to speak on dozens of domestic and international media outlets given my extensive research and long-standing history with the case. I declined the invitations. To protect his legacy and reputation, Professor Dershowitz went on an international media blitz defending his position and perhaps protecting his marriage. He spoke on almost every television network and news outlet in the U.S. and published multiple editorials in leading mainstream publications.

During his media campaign, the Harvard Law professor accused Florida attorney Brad Edwards, and former Federal Judge, Paul Cassell, of "character assassination." The two lawyers they sued Dershowitz for defamation. Dershowitz counter sued. Virginia Louise Roberts Giuffre, one of the alleged victim's was a possible witness in that case.[260]

The dictionary definition for a defamation lawsuit is, "As a civil wrong or 'Tort,' not a criminal offense. It is a catchall phrase made by one person that hurts someone's reputation. A spoken defamation is called 'slander,' and a written defamation is termed 'libel.'"

The case was settled Friday, April 8, 2016. All three lawyers agreed to settle the defamation action. As part of the settlement certain pleadings filed by Jack Scarola, (Edwards and Cassell's attorney), and Dershowitz's attorneys, the accusations were withdrawn. According to one report it was at Professor Dershowitz' recommendation they settle the case. Why?

In September 2015, Virginia Louise Roberts, the same victim and potential witness in the *Edwards & Cassell vs. Dershowitz* case, sued Ghislaine Maxwell for defamation. Super star attorney, David Boies, co-founder and partner at Boies, Schiller & Flexner, agreed to represent Roberts Giuffre, *pro bono*. Sigrid McCawley is her representing counselor.

The defamation case *Virginia L. Giuffre vs. Ghislaine Maxwell,* is ongoing in New York. Roberts-Giuffre (her married name), now in her thirties, is married with three children. Roberts Giuffre is the same woman implicated in the Florida criminal case who sued Jeffrey Epstein, in 2005. Her most recent case, filed in the Southern District of New York, is related to the 2005 Epstein criminal case.

It is fascinating that David Boies, in light of his political associations, the lack of financial remuneration by Roberts' and his aversion to publicity, would accept the Virginia Roberts Giuffre case. Sometime after Boies filed the Complaint on behalf of his client, I rang him to confirm the merits of the case. He did not return my calls. His assistant, Linda Carlsen suggested I e-mail the questions. Mr. Boies did not respond to my e-mail. On November 6, 2015, someone familiar with the Maxwell case responded on his behalf.

> Q: Are you personally representing Virginia
> Louise Roberts Giuffre or is someone at your
> Florida firm representing the woman in the

Ghislaine Maxwell Defamation suit filed on 9.21.2015?

A: The lawyers of record are listed on the complaint and are involved to one extent or another. But any attorney in the firm who works on the case can be said to represent the client.

Q: Why did your firm agree to take on the VLRG case pro bono?

A: I don't know the financial terms of BSF's representation, and they are not typically disclosed for publication by law firms.

Q: Is the jurisdiction of this defamation case Florida or New York?

A: The case has been filed in the Federal District Court in the Southern District of New York.

Q: What are the merits of the Defamation case against Ghislaine Maxwell?

A: The best way to understand the case is to read the complaint. You'll find that it speaks clearly and forcefully to the merits.

Q. If Roberts Giuffre wins the suit, is she looking for remuneration and/or punitive damages or both?

A: The complaint addresses the relief the plaintiff
seeks. As a practical matter, it's too early to try to
guess what specific relief might be granted.

A couple of insiders suggested that David Boies, being a well-
known Clinton supporter, might have taken the case to help string
it out past the 2016 election. Perhaps this is one reason. It is also
public knowledge that Ghislaine Maxwell, the alleged procurer, has
long since been a suspect in the Epstein case. Her role in Epstein's
household was established throughout the case in various court files.

In spite of the volumes of depositions identifying her alleged
involvement in the Epstein case, Maxwell remains a close friend
of former president Bill Clinton. She was one of the chosen guests
to attend Ms. Chelsea Clinton's wedding. In 2013, at the Clinton
Global Initiative, Maxwell pledged support to CGI through her
foundation, The Terra Mar Project.

With stakes this high and former Secretary Clinton practically
a shoe-in for the presidential nomination, one could presume that
Boies' representation of Roberts-Giuffre might have been a strategic
decision. Perhaps, to help cloak the 'behind the scene' negotiations
that took place during the Non Prosecution Agreement Negotiations, now under investigation until after the new President of the
United States is elected?

One thing is certain David Boies has a longstanding association with the Democratic Party and the Clinton family. Not long
ago, Mr. Boies was a Gore fundraiser and delivered the famous oral
argument in 2000 for Al Gore in the *Bush vs. Gore* case. Recently,
Boies and his partner, Jonathan Schiller, hired a new partner, the
notable Karen Dunn who worked for then Senator Hillary Clinton
as communications director and senior advisor. Dunn was also
Deputy to Chief Strategist, David Axelrod, on the 2008 President
Obama presidential campaign. When he took on the Virginia

Roberts Giuffre case, Boies assigned two other luminary female attorneys to the case: Ellen Brockman in New York and Sigrid S. McCawley in Florida. Ms. McCawley represented their client in a hearing as recently as March 2016.

On October 15, 2015, at Alan Dershowitz's deposition, Jack Scarola who represented Brad Edwards and former federal judge, Paul Cassell, reminded Professor Dershowitz of one of his many philosophies.

> SCAROLA: There's an old saying if you have the law on your side, bang on the law. If you have the facts on your side, bang on the facts. If you have neither bang on the table.

> DERSHOWITZ: I have never believed that, but I do believe in a variation of that theme. If you don't have the law or legal facts on your side, argue your case in the Court of public opinion.[261]

I agree with Professor Dershowitz and so as a defender of human rights, specifically children's rights fighting to help stop child sex trafficking, I have set out to shed light on the Epstein case in the Court of Public Opinion. In an attempt to reveal all the relevant facts I have uncovered, the content of this book can be mostly attributed to thousands of court documents over the course of the eleven-year long case.

As a witness to certain events and a beneficiary to hundreds of private conversations including many "off the record" conversations with prosecutors, Ghislaine Maxwell, Jeffrey Epstein before, during and after his imprisonment, victims, lawyers, the Palm Beach Chief of Police, private investigators and law enforcement officials, the facts are ready to be exposed. Having invested years researching the characters and cases related to the Epstein criminal case, it was time to write a comprehensive report about the case. This book is the first to record the Epstein case in its entirety.

Since the Epstein case was first reported in 2006, consciousness around human trafficking has exploded. A decade later media reports claim there are over 22 million children trafficked worldwide. It is time to pay attention to our most vulnerable population.

As parents, guardians, community and religious leaders we have an obligation to protect our children. They are our future. As custodians of this young population it is our duty to work closely with elementary school teachers, educators, administrators, academia, media, IT companies, government leaders, religious leaders and abolitionists to put an end to human trafficking and child sex slavery.

There is no doubt that human trafficking is a form of slavery. The distinction between the two, if any, is that in 2016 slavery includes the buying and selling of children for sex. These children are held captive mostly against their will and traded on the open market like cattle. They are sold dozens of times for a number of reasons. Primarily the children are bought and sold for: labor, sexual pleasure, pornography and organs.

Beginning in 1998 or perhaps earlier, Jeffrey E. Epstein, allegedly trafficked dozens of underage girls for sex to his Palm Beach, Florida home. Epstein and his supposed procurers apparently coerced, lured and conspired to sexually abuse impressionable and vulnerable victims.

With promises of cash and modeling jobs if the girls provided him and supposedly in some instances, Ghislaine Maxwell, with sexually charged "massages," some girls agreed to perform sexually illicit activities with the adults. The girls averaged in ages ranging between 12-16 years old, according to Complaint #09-80656, filed

May 1, 2009, in the United States District Court For The Southern District Of Florida.

The facts and merits of the cases speak for themselves. The truth might offend some very influential opinion leaders. I trust that irrespective of their personal feelings the core message is understood. This is not a political story. It is an unfiltered story about the Epstein case and how his money, friendships, and influence attempted to corrupt the legal system.

His case is also a powerful reminder of the obligations we have as American citizens to raise awareness of the blight of human trafficking, the rights of children and human rights in general. Moreover, the United States and the Department of Justice should feel duty bound in cases such as Epstein's to enforce the Trafficking Victims Protection Act (TVPA).

The Epstein case is stranger than fiction and far more contemptible than the Lewinsky case, Watergate scandal, and Profumo affair combined. Given the slow grinding wheels of justice and the politics operating behind the scenes, it is up to the reader to determine the truth.

I don't know if the victims who did not come forward will ever achieve some measure of justice. Perhaps the victims who stood up for their rights will one day attain emotional restitution. It is my desire that "TrafficKing" might somehow facilitate that process. Since Mr. Epstein's arrest it has become more evident that this case is far greater than just a story about the crimes allegedly committed by one man.

The story behind the story seems to point to the conceivable break down of the system. A respected abolitionist and author who prefers to remain anonymous said, "It seems that America is keeping "a big dirty secret." That dirty secret, he said, "points in the direction of the federal government and how a group of government officials are considering decriminalizing sex trafficking." Why?

Because, "The United States profits upwards of $100 billion dollars taxing sexual service ads per year...that's bigger than TV, film, music, radio, arms and drugs combined," he said. "While no one talks about the increasing percentages of trafficked and prostituted women who are involuntary, an entire generation of young girls are disappearing although many non-governmental organizations (NGO's) continue to make substantial amounts of money from the plight of trafficked victims.

Many decades ago, a former British Prime Minister and one of the greatest Statesmen of the Twentieth Century wrote an inspiring statement in *The Unrelenting Struggle*, "When great causes are on the move in the world...we learn that we are spirits, not animals, and that something is going on in space and time, which, whether we like it or not, spells duty."

Winston S. Churchill

The Prosecutor's Letter

R. Alex Acosta wrote this letter on March 20, 2011. Acosta was the U.S. Attorney for the Southern District of Florida (USAO) and prosecutor during the Epstein criminal investigation. Acosta hand delivered the letter to me at the Biltmore Hotel, Coral Gables, Florida. It was originally published in its entirety in The Daily Beast on March 25, 2011.

March 20, 2011

To Whom It May Concern:

I served as U.S. Attorney for the Southern District of Florida from 2005-2009. Over the past weeks, I have read much regarding Mr. Jeffrey Epstein. Some appears true some appears distorted. I thought it appropriate to provide some background, with two caveats: (I) under Justice Department guidelines, I cannot discuss privileged internal communications among Department attorneys and (ii) I no longer have access to the original documents, and as the matter is now nearly 4 years old, the precision of memory is reduced.

The Epstein matter was originally presented to the Palm Beach County State Attorney. Palm

Beach Police alleged that Epstein unlawfully hired underage high-school females to provide him sexually lewd and erotic massages. Police sought felony charges that would have resulted in a term of imprisonment. According to press reports, however, in 2006 the State Attorney, in part due to concerns regarding the quality of the evidence, agreed to charge Epstein only with one count of aggravated assault with no intent to commit a felony. That charge would have resulted in no jail time, no requirement to register as a sexual offender and no restitution for the underage victims.

Local police were dissatisfied with the State Attorney's conclusions, and requested a federal investigation. Federal authorities received the State's evidence and engaged in additional investigation. Prosecutors weighed the quality of the evidence and the likelihood for success at trial. With a federal case, there were two additional considerations. First, a federal criminal prosecution requires that the crime be more than local; it must have an interstate nexus. Second, as the matter was initially charged by the state, the federal responsibility is, to some extent, to backstop state authorities to ensure that there is no miscarriage of justice, and not to also prosecute federally that which has already been charged at the state level.

After considering the quality of the evidence and the additional considerations, prosecutors concluded that the state charge was insufficient. In early summer 2007, the prosecutors and agents in this case met with Epstein's attorney, Roy Black. Mr. Black is perhaps best known for his successful defense of William Kennedy Smith. The prosecutors presented Epstein a choice: plead to a more serious state felony charge (that would result in 2 years' imprisonment, registration as a sexual offender, and restitution for the victims) or else prepare for a federal felony trial.

What followed was a yearlong assault on the prosecution and the prosecutors. I use the word assault intentionally, as the defense in this case was more aggressive than any, which I, or the prosecutors in my office, had previously encountered. Mr. Epstein hired an army of legal superstars: Harvard Professor Alan Dershowitz, former Judge and then Pepperdine Law Dean Kenneth Starr, former Deputy Assistant to the President and then Kirkland Ellis partner Jay Lefkowitz, and several others, including prosecutors who had formally worked in the U.S. Attorney's Office and in the Child Exploitation and Obscenity Section of the Justice Department. Defense attorneys next requested a meeting with me to challenge the prosecution and the terms previously presented by the prosecutors in their meeting with Mr. Black.

The prosecution team and I met with defense counsel in Fall 2007, and I reaffirmed the office's position: two years, registration and restitution, or trial.

Over the next several months, the defense team presented argument after argument claiming that felony criminal proceedings against Epstein were unsupported by the evidence and lacked a basis in law, and that the office's insistence on jail-time was motivated by zeal to overcharge a man merely because he is wealthy. They bolstered their arguments with legal opinions from well-known legal experts. One member of the defense team warned that the office's excess zeal in forcing a good man to serve time in jail might be the subject of a book if we continued to proceed with this matter. My office systematically considered and rejected each argument, and when we did, my office's decisions were appealed to Washington. As to the warning, I ignored it.

The defense strategy was not limited to legal issues. Defense counsel investigated individual prosecutors and their families, looking for personal peccadilloes that may provide a basis for disqualification. Disqualifying a prosecutor is an effective (though rarely used) strategy, as eliminating the individuals most familiar with the facts and thus most qualified to take a case to trial harms likelihood for success. Defense counsel tried to disqualify at least two prosecutors. I carefully reviewed, and then rejected, these arguments.

Despite this army of attorneys, the office held firm to the terms first presented to Mr. Black in the original meeting. On June 30, 2008, after yet another last minute appeal to Washington D.C. was rejected,

Epstein pled guilty in state court. He was to serve 18 months imprisonment, register as a sexual offender for life and provide restitution to the victims.

Some may feel that the prosecution should have been tougher. Evidence that has come to light, since 2007, may encourage that view. Many victims have since spoken out, filing detailed statements in civil cases seeking damages. Physical evidence has since been discovered. Had these additional statements and evidence been known, the outcome may have been different. But there were not known to us at the time.

A prosecution decision must be based on admissible facts known at the time. In cases of this type, those are unusually difficult because victims are frightened and often decline to testify or if they do speak, they give contradictory statements. Our judgment in this case, based on the evidence known at the time, was that it was better to have a billionaire serve time in jail, register as a sex offender and pay his victims restitution than risk a trial with a reduced likelihood of success. I supported that judgment then, and based on the state of the law as it then stood and the evidence known at that time, I would support that judgment again.

Epstein's treatment, while in state custody, likewise may encourage the view that the office should have been tougher. Epstein appears to have received highly unusual treatment while in jail. Although *the terms of confinement in a state prison are a matter appropriately left to the State of Florida, and not federal authorities, without doubt, the treatment that he received while in state custody undermined the purpose of a jail sentence.*

Some may also believe that the prosecution should have been tougher in retaliation for the defense's tactics. The defense, arguably, often failed to negotiate in good faith. They would obtain concessions as part of a negotiation and agree to proceed, only to change their minds, and appeal the office's position to Washington. The investigations into the family lives of individual prosecutors were, in my opinion, uncalled for, as were the accusations of bias and / or misconduct against individual prosecutors.

At times, some prosecutors felt that we should just go to trial, and at times I felt that frustration myself. What was right in the first meeting, however, remained right irrespective of defense tactics. Individuals have a constitutional right to a defense. The aggressive exercise of that right should not be punished, nor should a defense counsel's exercise of their right to appeal a U.S. Attorney to Washington D.C. Prosecutors must be careful not to allow frustration and anger with defense counsel to influence their judgment.

After the plea, I recall receiving several phone calls. One was from the FBI Special Agent-In-Charge. He called to offer congratulations. He had been at many of the meetings regarding this case. He was aware of the tactics of the defense, and he called to praise our prosecutors for holding firm against the likes of Messrs. Black, Dershowitz, Lefkowitz and Starr.

It was a proud moment. I also received calls or communications from Messrs. Dershowitz, Lefkowitz and Starr. I had known all three individuals previously, from my time in law school and at Kirkland Ellis in the mid 90s. They all sought to make peace. I agreed to talk and meet with each of them after Epstein pled guilty, as I think it important that prosecutors battle defense attorneys in a case and then move on. I have tried, yet I confess that has been difficult to do fully in this case.

The bottom line is this: Mr. Epstein, a billionaire, served time in jail and is now a registered sex offender. He has been required to pay his victims restitution, though restitution clearly cannot compensate for the crime. And we know much more today about his crimes because the victims have come forward to speak out. Some may disagree with the prosecutorial judgments made in this case, but those individuals are not the ones who at the time reviewed the evidence available for trial and assessed the likelihood of success.

Respectfully,
R. Alexander Acosta
Former U.S. Attorney
Southern District of Florida

After graduating from Harvard University Law School, Mr. Acosta worked at Kirkland Ellis in Washington D.C. at the same time that Kenneth Starr was working at the law firm. Their professional association perhaps helps explain why in October 2007, Epstein's defense team recruited Starr's services to help negotiate Epstein's Non Prosecution Agreement at the Department of Justice in Washington D.C. Starr was the 39th Solicitor General beginning May 26, 1989 through January 20, 1993. Starr, a Republican also served as Solicitor General during former President Clinton's Monica Lewinsky investigation.

On December 27, 2015, politico.com posted a story claiming the Government had listed six witnesses who possessed information relevant to the case. Two USAO officials, Mr. Acosta and Ms. Villafaña, and four FBI agents who worked on the Epstein criminal case were served. All six government officials including: FBI Special Agent E. Nesbitt Kuyrkendall; FBI Special Agent Jason Richards; former First AUSA Jeff Sloman (currently employed at a Miami law firm); former Chief of the Criminal Division Matt Menchel (currently employed at a Miami law firm); AUSA Marie Villafaña; former U.S. Attorney R. Alexander Acosta (currently employed at Florida International University) are awaiting deposition. "The victims asked the Government to make the witnesses available for deposition. The Government objected and said the victims should file a motion. The Government would oppose the motion."[262]

Endnotes

1   Arrest Notice To Appear. Palm Beach Police Department Incident Report. Case #05-368 (2). Probable Cause Affidavit. Filed May 1, 2006. Arresting Officer Det. Joe Recare

2   Arrest Notice to Appear. Palm Beach Police Department Incident Report Case #05-368. (3) May 1, 2006.

3   http://www.reuters.com/article/dershowitz-lawsuit-boies-idUSL1 N0XK1VL20150423#pRtAhxiOIhyv6gxi.97

4   Case 1:15-cv-07433 Document 1 Filed 09/21/15

5   http://abovethelaw.com/2015/04/the-latest-legal-superstar-to-collide-with-alan-dershowitz-david-boies/

6   http://www.dailymail.co.uk/news/article-3245036/Virginia-Roberts-claimed-sex-Prince-Andrew-sues-British-socialite-Ghislaine-Maxwell-denying-claims-recruited-sex-slave.html

7   Arrest Notice to Appear. Jeffrey Epstein Probable Cause Affidavit. Police Case #05-368. Palm Beach Police Department. March 15, 2005. (1)

8   Probable Cause Affidavit, Palm Beach Police Department Agency ORI # FLO 500600. Police Case # 05-368 (3). Defendant Haley Robson. May 1, 2006.

9   Probable Cause Affidavit, Palm Beach Police Department Agency ORI # FLO 500600. Police Case # 05-368 (3). Defendant Haley Robson. May 1, 2006.

10 Probable Cause Affidavit, Palm Beach Police Department Agency ORI # FLO 500600. Police Case # 05-368 (2). Defendant Haley Robson. May 1, 2006

11 Arrest Notice to Appear. Palm Beach Police Department Police Case #05-368 (2) Defendant Haley Robson. May 1, 2006.

12 http://docplayer.net/4070674-Exhibit-c-epstein-vs-edwards-undisputed-statement-of-facts.html

13   http://docplayer.net/4070674-Exhibit-c-epstein-vs-edwards-undisputed-statement-of-facts.html

14   http://docplayer.net/4070674-Exhibit-c-epstein-vs-edwards-undisputed-statement-of-facts.html

15   http://docplayer.net/4070674-Exhibit-c-epstein-vs-edwards-undisputed-statement-of-facts.html

16   http://docplayer.net/4070674-Exhibit-c-epstein-vs-edwards-undisputed-statement-of-facts.html

17   http://docplayer.net/4070674-Exhibit-c-epstein-vs-edwards-undisputed-statement-of-facts.html

18   Civil Action Case #09-80656: Clerk U.S. District Court Southern District of Fla. Miami, Florida.

19   Statement of Facts, Case # 09-80656, filed May 1, 2009 in the Southern District Court of Florida

20   http://cases.bms11.com/Documents/FL76/09-34791/ECF_DOC_1603_10567451.pdf

21   Probable Cause Affidavit, Palm Beach Police Department Agency ORI # FLO 500600. Police Case # 05-368 (3). Defendant Haley Robson. May 1, 2006.

22   Probable Cause Affidavit, Palm Beach Police Department Agency ORI # FLO 500600. Police Case # 05-368 (3). Defendant Haley Robson. May 1, 2006.

23   Probable Cause Affidavit, Palm Beach Police Department Agency ORI # FLO 500600. Police Case # 05-368 (3). Defendant Haley Robson. May 1, 2006.

24   Probable Cause Affidavit, Palm Beach Police Department Agency ORI # FLO 500600. Police Case # 05-368 (3). Defendant Haley Robson. May 1, 2006.

25   Probable Cause Affidavit, Palm Beach Police Department Agency ORI # FLO 500600. Police Case # 05-368 (3). Defendant Haley Robson. May 1, 2006.

26   Probable Cause Affidavit, Palm Beach Police Department Agency ORI # FLO 500600. Police Case # 05-368 (3). Defendant Haley Robson. May 1, 2006.

27   http://www.thedailybeast.com/articles/2015/01/25/epstein-s-first-accuser-tells-her-story.html; http://www.thedailybeast.com/articles/2015/01/25/epstein-s-first-accuser-tells-her-story.html

28 Complaint and Demand for Jury Trial filed on May 1, 2009 in Jane Doe #102 vs. Jeffrey Epstein

29 http://www.thedailybeast.com/articles/2015/01/25/epstein-s-first-accuser-tells-her-story.html

30 http://www.thedailybeast.com/articles/2015/01/25/epstein-s-first-accuser-tells-her-story.html

31 http://www.thesundaytimes.co.uk/sto/news/uk_news/People/article576480.ece

32 Probable Cause Affidavit, Palm Beach Police Department Agency ORI # FLO 500600. Police Case # 05-368 (3). Defendant Haley Robson. May 1, 2006, p.5

33 Probable Cause Affidavit, Palm Beach Police Department Agency ORI # FLO 500600. Police Case # 05-368 (3). Defendant Haley Robson. May 1, 2006, p.5

34 Probable Cause Affidavit, Palm Beach Police Department Agency ORI # FLO 500600. Police Case # 05-368 (3). Defendant Haley Robson. May 1, 2006, p.1

35 Probable Cause Affidavit, Palm Beach Police Department Agency ORI # FLO 500600. Police Case # 05-368 (3). Defendant Haley Robson. May 1, 2006, p.1

36 Probable Cause Affidavit, Palm Beach Police Department Agency ORI # FLO 500600. Police Case # 05-368 (3). Defendant Haley Robson. May 1, 2006, p.1

37 Probable Cause Affidavit, Palm Beach Police Department Agency ORI # FLO 500600. Police Case # 05-368 (3). Defendant Haley Robson. May 1, 2006, p.1

38 Probable Cause Affidavit, Palm Beach Police Department Agency ORI # FLO 500600. Police Case # 05-368 (3). Defendant Haley Robson. May 1, 2006, p. 18

39 Probable Cause Affidavit, Palm Beach Police Department Agency ORI # FLO 500600. Police Case # 05-368 (3). Defendant Haley Robson. May 1, 2006, p.

40 http://www.dailymail.co.uk/news/article-3405407/The-busy-life-Jeffrey-Epstein-Group-gorgeous-Manhattan-girls-billionaire-pedophile-s-mansion-flies-private-jet-attractive-brunette.html

41 http://www.reuters.com/article/us-epstein-lawsuit-brunel-idUSKBN0MM2H420150326

42   http://www.thedailybeast.com/articles/2015//03/26/model-king-sues-billionaire-perv-jeffrey-epstein.html

43   http://www.dailymail.co.uk/news/article-3405407/The-busy-life-Jeffrey-Epstein-Group-gorgeous-Manhattan-girls-billionaire-pedophile-s-mansion-flies-private-jet.attractive-brunette.html

44   http://pagesix.com/2016/03/08 Jeffrey-Epstein's-east-side-mansion-houses-russian-playmates/

45   http://www.thedailybeast.com/articles/2010/07/20/jeffrey-epstein-billionaire-pedophile-goes-free.html

46   http://www.thedailybeast.com/articles/2010/07/20/jeffrey-epstein-billionaire-pedophile-goes-free.html

47   http://www.thedailybeast.com/articles/2015/03/26/model-king-sues-billionaire-perv-jeffrey-epstein.html

48   http://www.palmbeachdailynews.com/news/news/lawsuit-documents-link-jeffrey-epstein-to-modeling/nMGzH/

49   http://www.palmbeachdailynews.com/news/news/lawsuit-documents-link-jeffrey-epstein-to-modeling/nMGzH/

50   http://jezebel.com/5603638/meet-the-modeling-agent-who-trafficked-underage-girls-for-sex

51   http://radaronline.com/wp-content/uploads/2015/04/Epstein-Docs-4-7-15.pdf

52   http://cases.bms11.com/Documents/FL76/0934791/ECF_DOC_1603_10567451.pdf

53   http://cases.bms11.com/Documents/FL76/0934791/ECF_DOC_1603_10567451.pdf

54   http://cases.bms11.com/Documents/FL76/0934791/ECF_DOC_1603_10567451.pdf

55   http://cases.bms11.com/Documents/FL76/0934791/ECF_DOC_1603_10567451.pdf P22

56   http://cases.bms11.com/Documents/FL76/0934791/ECF_DOC_1603_10567451.pdf

57   http://cases.bms11.com/Documents/FL76/0934791/ECF_DOC_1603_10567451.pdf

58   http://cases.bms11.com/Documents/FL76/0934791/ECF_DOC_1603_10567451.pdf

59   http://cases.bms11.com/Documents/FL76/0934791/ECF_
      DOC_1603_10567451.pdf

60   http://cases.bms11.com/Documents/FL76/0934791/ECF_
      DOC_1603_10567451.pdf

61   http://cases.bms11.com/Documents/FL76/0934791/ECF_
      DOC_1603_10567451.pdf

62   http://cases.bms11.com/Documents/FL76/0934791/
      ECF_DOC_1603_1056745

63   http://cases.bms11.com/Documents/FL76/0934791/ECF_
      DOC_1603_10567451.pdf

64   http://cases.bms11.com/Documents/FL76/0934791/ECF_
      DOC_1603_10567451.pdf

65   http://cases.bms11.com/Documents/FL76/0934791/ECF_
      DOC_1603_10567451.pdf

66   http://cases.bms11.com/Documents/FL76/0934791/ECF_
      DOC_1603_10567451.pdf

67   http://cases.bms11.com/Documents/FL76/0934791/ECF_
      DOC_1603_10567451.pdf

68   http://www.nytimes.com/2008/07/01/business/01epstein.
      html?pagewanted=2&_r=2

69   http://cases.bms11.com/Documents/FL76/0934791/ECF_
      DOC_1603_10567451.pdf

70   http://cases.bms11.com/Documents/FL76/0934791/ECF_
      DOC_1603_10567451.pdf

71   http://cases.bms11.com/Documents/FL76/0934791/ECF_
      DOC_1603_10567451.pdf

72   Virginia Louise Roberts Telephone Transcript filed April 7,
      2011. Telecom Participants: Jack Scarola, Brad Edwards and
      Virginia Roberts. Taken via telephone. Privileged Pursuant to FS
      766.205(4) and /or Work Product.

73   http://www.dailymail.co.uk/news/article-1361039/Prince-
      Andrew-girl-17-sex-offender-friend-flew-Britain-meet-him.
      html#ixzz1c0ttCLPi; March 28, 2011: Mail On Sunday.

74   http://cases.bms11.com/Documents/FL76/09-34791/ECF_
      DOC_1603_10567451.pdf

75   http://cases.bms11.com/Documents/FL76/09-34791/ECF_
      DOC_1603_10567451.pdf

76   http://cases.bms11.com/Documents/FL76/09-34791/ECF_
      DOC_1603_10567451.pdf

77   http://www.nytimes.com/1995/02/15/garden/at-lunch-
      with-elisabeth-maxwell-questions-without-answers.
      html?pagewanted=all

78   http://articles.latimes.com/1992-06-19/business/
      fi-530_1_kevin-maxwell

79   http://articles.latimes.com/1992-06-19/business/
      fi-530_1_kevin-maxwell

80   http://articles.latimes.com/1992-06-19/business/
      fi-530_1_kevin-maxwell

81   http://www.nytimes.com/1996/01/20/business/international-
      business-british-jury-acquits-robert-maxwell-s-sons.html

82   http://www.nytimes.com/1996/01/20/business/international-
      business-british-jury-acquits-robert-maxwell-s-sons.html

83   http://www.nytimes.com/1996/01/20/business/international-
      business-british-jury-acquits-robert-maxwell-s-sons.html

84   http://www.nytimes.com/1996/01/20/business/international-
      business-british-jury-acquits-robert-maxwell-s-sons.html

85   http://www.nydailynews.com/life-style/real-estate/jeffrey-epstein-
      alleged-madam-lists-mansion-18m-article-1.2183607

86   http://www.vanityfair.com/online/daily/2011/03/notes-on-new-
      yorks-oddest-couple-jeffrey-epstein-and-ghislaine-maxwell

87   http://theterramarproject.org/#&panel1-1

88   http://www.palmbeachdailynews.com/news/news/
      jeffrey-epstein-house-arrest-missteps-not-deemed-u/nMGbT/

89   http://www.palmbeachdailynews.com/news/news/
      jeffrey-epstein-house-arrest-missteps-not-deemed-u/nMGbT/

90   http://articles.sun-sentinel.com/2010-07-11/news/
      fl-palm-epstein-free-20100711_1_probation-officer-jeffrey-
      epstein-virgin-islands

91   http://articles.sun-sentinel.com/2010-07-11/news/
      fl-palm-epstein-free-20100711_1_probation-officer-jeffrey-
      epstein-virgin-islands

92   http://articles.sun-sentinel.com/2010-07-11/news/
      fl-palm-epstein-free-20100711_1_probation-officer-jeffrey-
      epstein-virgin-islands

93 http://nypost.com/2011/02/25/
billionaire-jeffrey-epstein-im-a-sex-offender-not-a-predator/

94 http://www.politico.com/blogs/under-the-radar/2015/12/
victims-in-underage-sex-case-want-prosecutors-to-testify-217139

95 http://online.wsj.com/public/resources/documents/2015_0105_
epstein2011order.pdf

96 http://www.nytimes.com/2014/07/26/business/alan-c-greenberg-
is-dead-at-86-led-bear-stearns-through-its-rise-and-fall.html?_r=0

97 http://online.wsj.com/public/resources/documents/2015_0105_
epstein2011order.pdf

98 http://www.nytimes.com/2014/07/26/business/alan-c-greenberg-
is-dead-at-86-led-bear-stearns-through-its-rise-and-fall.html?_r=0

99 http://www.nytimes.com/2014/07/26/business/alan-c-greenberg-
is-dead-at-86-led-bear-stearns-through-its-rise-and-fall.html?_r=0

100 Conversation with Ralph Cioffi. November 17, 2014

101 The Big Short: Michael Lewis. P. 117, Norton Publishing House
2011

102 Conversation with Ralph Cioffi. November 17, 2014

103 Michael Lewis, "The Big Short," page 117. Norton Publishing
House, 2011

104 http://online.wsj.com/public/resources/documents/2015_0105_
epstein2011order.pdf

105 http://www.ft.com/intl/cms/s/0/5ffd2606-69e8-11dc-
a5710000779fd2ac.html#axzz40ZfqAJer

106 http://dealbook.nytimes.com/2013/09/04/judge-dismisses-bank-
of-america-suit-against-2-bear-stearns-executives/?_r=0

107 http://dealbook.nytimes.com/2013/09/04/judge-dismisses-bank-
of-america-suit-against-2-bear-stearns-executives/?_r=0

108 http://www.americarisingpac.org/
clinton-foundation-accepted-25000-bills-pedophile-party-pal/

109 http://www.forbes.com/sites/richardsalsman/2013/09/19/
the-financial-crisis-was-a-failure-of-government-not-free-
markets/#6467dc10449e

110 http://www.nytimes.com/2014/07/26/business/alan-c-greenberg-
is-dead-at-86-led-bear-stearns-through-its-rise-and-fall.html?_r=0

111 U.S. v. Rodriguez, No. 9:10-CR-80015-KAM (S.D. Fla. 2010)
(Exhibit "G")

112 http://www.palmbeachdailynews.com/news/news/
former-epstein-house-manager-alfredo-rodriguez-sen/nMGXk/

113 http://www.palmbeachdailynews.com/news/news/
former-epstein-house-manager-alfredo-rodriguez-sen/nMGXk/

114 http://www.nydailynews.com/entertainment/gossip/
billionaire-jeffrey-epstein-shells-money-latest-sex-abuse-lawsuit-
article-1.436147

115 http://www.thedailybeast.com/articles/2010/07/22/jeffrey-
epstein-pedophile-billionaire-and-his-sex-den.html

116 http://www.thedailybeast.com/articles/2010/07/20/jeffrey-
epstein-billionaire-pedophile-goes-free.html

117 https://ecf.flsd.uscourts.gov/cgibin/show_multidocs.
pl?caseid=317867&arr_de_seq_nums=931&magic_num=&pdf_
header=2&hdr=&pdf_toggle_possible=&

118 Deposition DVD #3: 15:57-16:45

119 Deposition DVD #3: 15:25-16:37

120 Deposition DVD #3: 52:07

121 Deposition DVD #3: 52:30

122 Deposition DVD #4: 4:15-4:47

123 http://www.dailymail.co.uk/news/article-2896591/Silence-
Epstein-women-Former-model-female-employees-billionaire-
refuse-answer-questions-Prince-Andrew-sex-slave-allegations.html

124 Case 09-34791-RBR Doc 1603-3 Filed 04/08/11 Page 9 of 39

125 http://www.dailymail.co.uk/news/article-2897939/
Houseman-cleaned-pedophile-Jeffrey-Epstein-s-sex-toys-feared-
billionaire-make-disappear-takes-secrets-grav

126 Deposition DVD #4:

127 Deposition DVD #4:

128 Deposition DVD #4:

129 Deposition DVD #4:

130 Deposition DVD #4:

131 Deposition DVD #4:

132 Deposition DVD #4:

133 Deposition DVD #4:

134 Deposition DVD #4:

135 Deposition DVD #4:

136 Deposition DVD #4:

137   Deposition DVD #4:

138   Deposition DVD #4:

139   Deposition DVD #4:

140   Deposition DVD #4:

141   Deposition DVD #4:

142   http://online.wsj.com/public/resources/documents/2015_0109_
rodriguez_sentencing.pdf

143   http://www.palmbeachdailynews.com/news/news/local/
victims-ask-to-join-epstein-lawsuit/njfZM/

144   http://www.nytimes.com/2015/12/13/business/alan-dershowitz-
on-the-defense-his-own.html?hp&action=click&pgtype=Hom
epage&clickSource=story-heading&module=second-column-
region&region=top-news&WT.nav=top-news

145   http://www.nytimes.com/2015/12/13/business/
alan-dershowitz-on-the-defense-his-own.
html?smid=pl-share&_r=0&mtrref=www.abajournal.
com&gwh=E16379C04F8DF815A2F3A2E1856E77C0&gwt=
pay

146   http://www.abajournal.com/files/DershowitzAffidavit.pdf

147   http://www.nytimes.com/2015/12/13/business/alan-dershowitz-
on-the-defense-his-own.html?hp&action=click&pgtype=Hom
epage&clickSource=story-heading&module=second-column-
region&region=top-news&WT.nav=top-news

148   http://www.abajournal.com/news/article/dershowitz_and_boies_
spar_in_an_increasingly_virulent_war_over_rape_accusat

149   http://www.abajournal.com/news/article/dershowitz_and_boies_
spar_in_an_increasingly_virulent_war_over_rape_accusat

150   http://www.abajournal.com/news/article/dershowitz_and_boies_
spar_in_an_increasingly_virulent_war_over_rape_accusat

151   http://www.nytimes.com/2015/12/13/business/alan-dershowitz-
on-the-defense-his-own.html?hp&action=click&pgtype=Hom
epage&clickSource=story-heading&module=second-column-
region&region=top-news&WT.nav=top-news

152   http://www.motherjones.com/politics/2015/01/
bill-clinton-jeffrey-epstein-conservative-media

153   http://www.theguardian.com/us-news/2015/
feb/10hillary-cinton-foundation-donors-hsbc-swiss-bank

154 http://littlesis.org/person/36043/Jeffrey_Epstein/political
155 https://ecf.nysd.uscourts.gov/doc1/127116800606
156 Text message send from Brad Edwards to Conchita Sarnoff on March 18, 2016.
157 https://ecf.nysd.uscourts.gov/doc1/127116800606
158 https://ecf.nysd.uscourts.gov/doc1/127116800606
159 https://ecf.nysd.uscourts.gov/doc1/127116800606
160 https://ecf.nysd.uscourts.gov/doc1/127116800606
161 https://ecf.nysd.uscourts.gov/doc1/127116800606
162 https://ecf.nysd.uscourts.gov/doc1/127116800606
163 Case 1:15-cv-07433-RWS Document 1 Filed 09/21/15 Page 10 of 12
164 http://www.nydailynews.com/new-york/court-hear-jeffrey-epstein-alleged-sex-trafficking-article-1.2568619
165 Case: CACE 15-000072 Seventeenth Judicial Circuit for Broward County, Florida. Bradley Edwards & Paul G. Cassell vs. Alan M. Dershowitz. P.180-333, Friday, October 16, 2015.
166 http://dailycaller.com/2015/03/12/clinton-ties-to-teen-sex-ring-are-still-troubling/#ixzz43q3jFjkc
167 http://dailycaller.com/2015/03/12/clinton-ties-to-teen-sex-ring-are-still-troubling/#ixzz43q9n4skh
168 http://abcnews.go.com/US/victims-feds-hid-sweetheart-deal-sex-offender-deep/story?id=36843144
169 http://dailycaller.com/2012/04/22/virgin-islands-governors-wife-employed-by-convicted-sex-offender-billionaire/
170 http://dailycaller.com/2012/04/22/virgin-islands-governors-wife-employed-by-convicted-sex-offender-billionaire/
171 http://dailycaller.com/2012/04/22/virgin-islands-governors-wife-employed-by-convicted-sex-offender-billionaire/
172 http://dailycaller.com/2012/02/01/bribery-compromised-officials-leave-indicted-financial-crime-suspects-free-from-prosecution-under-holders-doj/
173 Exhibit H. Epstein vs. Edwards, et al. Case No 50. 2009 CA 040800XXXXMBAG U.S. Attorney, R. Alex Acosta's Email correspondence to Jay Lefkowitz, dated December 13, 2007.

174 Exhibit H. Epstein vs. Edwards, et al. Case No 50. 2009 CA 040800XXXXMBAG U.S. Attorney, R. Alex Acosta's Email correspondence to Jay Lefkowitz, dated December 13, 2007.

175 Exhibit H. Epstein vs. Edwards, et al. Case No 50. 2009 CA 040800XXXXMBAG U.S. Attorney, R. Alex Acosta's Email correspondence to Jay Lefkowitz, dated December 13, 2007.

176 http://www.sciencemag.org/news/2016/04/ swedish-trial-examine-drug-men-pedophilic-impulses

177 http://abcnews.go.com/US/victims-feds-hid-sweetheart-deal-sex-offender-deep/ story?id=36843144

178 http://abcnews.go.com/US/victims-feds-hid-sweetheart-deal-sex-offender-deep/ story?id=36843144

179 Alan Dershowitz Deposition: October 15, 2015, Transcript #1 pages, 1-178

180 Alan Dershowitz Deposition: October 16, 2015, Transcript #2 pages 179

181 https://www.bostonglobe.com/metro/2015/01/06/sued-for-defamation-dershowitz-thrilled-chance-question-lawyers-sex-crime-accuser/21QibSrwNC343eKMadWNeL/story.html

182 http://m.americanlawyer.com/#/article/1202754581393/2/ Dershowitz%20Settles%20Sex%20Case,%20But%20Is%20 He%20Vindicated

183 http://m.americanlawyer.com/#/article/1202754581393/2/ Dershowitz%20Settles%20Sex%20Case,%20But%20Is%20 He%20Vindicated

184 http://m.americanlawyer.com/#/article/1202754581393/2/ Dershowitz%20Settles%20Sex%20Case,%20But%20Is%20 He%20Vindicated

185 http://www.usatoday.com/story/news/nation/2016/02/15/ new-york-ex-gov-eliot-spitzer-accused-assault/80396398/

186 http://www.reuters.com/article/ us-maxwell-defamation-lawsuit-idUSKCN0W34ZN

187 http://www.nydailynews.com/life-style/real-estate/ alleged-madam-50k-month-ues-townhouse-article-1.2316572

188 Case 1:15-cv-07433-RWS Filed 09/21/15 P. 5

189   https://ecf.nysd.uscourts.gov/doc1/127116800606
190   http://images.politico.com/global/2014/12/31/
       epsteinjanedoe102complaint.pdf
191   http://www.dailymail.co.uk/news/article-3245036/
       Virginia-Roberts-claimed-sex-Prince-Andrew-sues-British-socialite-
       Ghislaine-Maxwell-denying-claims-recruited-sex-slave.html
192   http://www.newsday.com/news/new-york/
       virginia-giuffre-files-defamation-suit-against-british-publishing-
       magnate-ghislaine-maxwell-1.10874152
193   http://www.dailymail.co.uk/news/article-3245036/
       Virginia-Roberts-claimed-sex-Prince-Andrew-sues-British-socialite-
       Ghislaine-Maxwell-denying-claims-recruited-sex-slave.html
194   Email communication on April 7, 2016. Conchita Sarnoff and
       Brad Edwards.
195   Case 1:15-cv-07433-RWS
196   Case 1:15-cv-07433-RWS Filed 9/21/15
197   Case 1:15-cv-07433-RWS Filed 9/21/15
198   http://radaronline.com/exclusives/2015/01/
       jeffrey-epstein-sex-slave-virginia-roberts-writes-sex-prince-andrew/
199   http://radaronline.com/exclusives/2015/01/
       jeffrey-epstein-sex-slave-virginia-roberts-writes-sex-prince-andrew/
200   http://radaronline.com/exclusives/2015/01/
       jeffrey-epstein-sex-slave-virginia-roberts-writes-sex-prince-andrew/
201   http://radaronline.com/exclusives/2015/01/
       jeffrey-epstein-sex-slave-virginia-roberts-writes-sex-prince-andrew/
202   http://radaronline.com/exclusives/2015/01/
       jeffrey-epstein-sex-slave-virginia-roberts-writes-sex-prince-andrew/
203   http://www.nydailynews.com/news/world/
       socialite-defamation-lawsuit-sex-slave-tossed-article-1.2497773
204   Transcript Giuffre vs. Maxwell, 15cv7433, United States District
       Court, Southern District of New York, March 17, 2016. 2:18 PM
205   Transcript Giuffre vs. Maxwell, 15cv7433, United States
       District Court, Southern District of New York, March 17,
       2016. 2:18 PM
206   Transcript Giuffre vs. Maxwell, 15cv7433, United States
       District Court, Southern District of New York, March 17,
       2016. 2:18 PM

207   Transcript Giuffre vs. Maxwell, 15cv7433, United States District Court, Southern District of New York, March 17, 2016. 2:18 PM

208   Transcript Giuffre vs. Maxwell, 15cv7433, United States District Court, Southern District of New York, March 17, 2016. 2:18 PM

209   Transcript Giuffre vs. Maxwell, 15cv7433, United States District Court, Southern District of New York, March 17, 2016. 2:18 PM

210   Transcript Giuffre vs. Maxwell, 15cv7433, United States District Court, Southern District of New York, March 17, 2016. 2:18 PM

211   Transcript Giuffre vs. Maxwell, 15cv7433, United States District Court, Southern District of New York, March 17, 2016. 2:18 PM

212   Transcript Giuffre vs. Maxwell, 15cv7433, United States District Court, Southern District of New York, March 17, 2016. 2:18 PM

213   Transcript Giuffre vs. Maxwell, 15cv7433, United States District Court, Southern District of New York, March 17, 2016. 2:18 PM

214   Transcript Giuffre vs. Maxwell, 15cv7433, United States District Court, Southern District of New York, March 17, 2016. 2:18 PM

215   http://www.thedailybeast.com/articles/2015/01/25/epstein-s-first-accuser-tells-her-story.html

216   http://online.wsj.com/public/resources/documents/2015_0105_epstein2011order.pdf

217   Doe vs. USA -08-80736 CIV-KAM March 1, 2016, p. 3

218   http://online.wsj.com/public/resources/documents/2015_0105_epstein2011order.pdf

219   http://online.wsj.com/public/resources/documents/2015_0105_epstein2011order.pdf

220   http://online.wsj.com/public/resources/documents/2015_0105_epstein2011order.pdf

221   http://online.wsj.com/public/resources/documents/2015_0105_epstein2011order.pdf

222   http://online.wsj.com/public/resources/documents/2015_0105_epstein2011order.pdf

223   http://online.wsj.com/public/resources/documents/2015_0105_epstein2011order.pdf

224 http://online.wsj.com/public/resources/documents/2015_0105_
epstein2011order.pdf

225 http://online.wsj.com/public/resources/documents/2015_0105_
epstein2011order.pdf

226 http://online.wsj.com/public/resources/documents/2015_0105_
epstein2011order.pdf

227 http://online.wsj.com/public/resources/documents/2015_0105_
epstein2011order.pdf

228 http://online.wsj.com/public/resources/documents/2015_0105_
epstein2011order.pdf

229 http://online.wsj.com/public/resources/documents/2015_0105_
epstein2011order.pdf

230 http://www.plainsite.org/dockets/ijlyjpqc/
florida-southern-district-court/doe-v-united-states-of-america/

231 http://www.palmbeachdailynews.com/news/news/local/
victims-ask-to-join-epstein-lawsuit/njfZM/

232 http://www.sun-sentinel.com/news/fl-jeffrey-epstein-victims-
civil-20151230-story.html

233 http://www.sun-sentinel.com/news/fl-jeffrey-epstein-victims-
civil-20151230-story.html

234 http://www.sun-sentinel.com/news/fl-jeffrey-epstein-victims-
civil-20151230-story.html

235 http://www.politico.com/blogs/under-the-radar/2016/04/lawyers-
underage-sex-claims-against-dershowitz-a-mistake-221751

236 http://www.politico.com/blogs/under-the-radar/2016/04/lawyers-
underage-sex-claims-against-dershowitz-a-mistake-221751

237 http://www.politico.com/blogs/under-the-radar/2016/04/
lawyers-underage-sex-claims-against-dershowitz-a-mistake-
221751#ixzz45TIa7Itb

238 http://www.americanlawyer.com/the-careerist/
id=1202754666961/Did-Dershowitz-Pay-Big-Bucks-to-Settle-
Sex-Case-?mcode=1202616610377&curindex=4

239 http://www.americanlawyer.com/the-careerist/
id=1202755043865/Whats-Everyone-Hiding-in-
the-Dershowitz-Case?mcode=1202616610377&curi
ndex=3

240 http://www.palmbeachdailynews.com/news/news/local/
epstein-victims-complicit-so-not-truly-victims-gov/npTXT/

241 http://www.palmbeachdailynews.com/news/news/local/
epstein-victims-complicit-so-not-truly-victims-gov/npTXT/

242 http://www.palmbeachdailynews.com/news/news/local/
epstein-victims-complicit-so-not-truly-victims-gov/npTXT/

243 http://www.justice-integrity.org/about-jip2

244 The Moral Compass, William J. Bennett. Simon & Schuster.
New York, 1995. Page 716

245 https://www.snopes.com/tachyon/2016/06/Donald_Trump_
Lawsuit_.jpg

246 https://www.snopes.com/tachyon/2016/06/Donald_Trump_
Lawsuit_.jpg

247 https://www.breitbart.com/politics/2016/04/29/
donald-trump-rape-lawsuit-jeffrey-epstein-sex-parties/

248 https://www.dailymail.co.uk/news/article-3564767/
Donald-Trump-furiously-denies-woman-s-claims-raped-tycoon-
billionaire-pedophile-Jeffrey-Epstein-s-sex-parties.html

249 https://www.dailymail.co.uk/news/article-3564767/
Donald-Trump-furiously-denies-woman-s-claims-raped-tycoon-
billionaire-pedophile-Jeffrey-Epstein-s-sex-parties.html

250 New York Post

251 https://www.dailymail.co.uk/news/article-3615274/
Disgraced-financier-sex-offender-Jeffrey-Epstein-accused-
swindling-1-billion-investors-former-business-partner-s-lawsuit.
html

252 https://www.dailymail.co.uk/news/article-3615274/
Disgraced-financier-sex-offender-Jeffrey-Epstein-accused-
swindling-1-billion-investors-former-business-partner-s-lawsuit.
html

253 https://www.dailymail.co.uk/news/article-3615274/
Disgraced-financier-sex-offender-Jeffrey-Epstein-accused-
swindling-1-billion-investors-former-business-partner-s-lawsuit.
html

254 http://www.politico.com/blogs/under-the-radar/2014/12/
woman-who-sued-convicted-billionaire-over-sex-abuse-levels-
claims-at-his-friends-200495#ixzz3v7mNdTTy

255 http://online.wsj.com/public/resources/documents/2015_0105_
     dershowitz.pdf

256 http://www.politico.com/blogs/under-the-radar/2014/12/
     woman-who-sued-convicted-billionaire-over-sex-abuse-levels-
     claims-at-his-friends-200495#ixzz3v7mNdTTy

257 http://online.wsj.com/public/resources/documents/2015_0105_
     dershowitz.pdf

258 http://abovethelaw.com/2015/04/the-latest-legal-superstar-to-
     collide-with-alan-dershowitz-david-boies/

259 Case 1:15-cv-07433 Document 1 Filed 09/21/15

260 http://www.dailymail.co.uk/news/article-2904115/
     Ghislaine-Maxwell-s-link-sex-scandal-court-papers-involving-
     Prince-Andrew-Jeffery-Epstein-don-t-stop-having-amazing-social-
     connections.html

261 Alan Dershowitz deposition files, October 15 & 16, 2015,
     Miami, Florida.

262 https://www.politico.com/blogs/under-the-radar/2015/12/
     victims-in-underage-sex-case-want-prosecutors-to-testify-217139

About the Author

Conchita Sarnoff is the executive director of Alliance to Rescue Victims of Trafficking, a Washington D.C. foundation that helps raise awareness of human trafficking. ATRVT's mission is to open the first safe house in D.C. to rescue and rehabilitate trafficked children and stop child sex trafficking.